Spartan Women

SPARTAN
WOMEN

SARAH B. POMEROY

OXFORD
UNIVERSITY PRESS

2002

OXFORD

UNIVERSITY PRESS

Oxford   New York
Auckland   Bangkok   Buenos Aires   Cape Town   Chennai
Dar es Salaam   Delhi   Hong Kong   Istanbul   Karachi   Kolkata
Kuala Lumpur   Madrid   Melbourne   Mexico City   Mumbai   Nairobi
São Paulo   Shanghai   Singapore   Taipei   Tokyo   Toronto

and an associated company in Berlin

Copyright © 2002 by Sarah B. Pomeroy

Published by Oxford University Press Inc.
198 Madison Avenue, New York, New York 10016

www.oup.com

Oxford is a registered trade mark of Oxford University Press

Library of Congress Cataloging-in-Publication Data
Pomeroy, Sarah B.
    Spartan women / Sarah B. Pomeroy.
        p.   cm.
    Includes bibliographical references and index.
    ISBN 978-0-19-513066-9; 978-0-19-513067-6 (pbk.)
        1. Women—Greece—Sparta (Extinct city)
            2. Sparta (Extinct city)—Social conditions.
        I. Title

    HQ1134.P66 2002
    305.4'09389—dc21   2001055961

Excerpt from Aristotle, *Politics Books I and II*, translated by Trevor Saunders.
Reprinted by permission of Oxford University Press.

Printed in the United States of America
on acid-free paper

TO JACOB, DINA, AND TALIA

PREFACE

This book is the first full-length historical study of Spartan women to be published.[1] I have not written in detail about Spartan women since the publication of *Goddesses, Whores, Wives, and Slaves,*[2] although more recently I contributed to the scholarship on this subject in two jointly authored books.[3] It was when I was writing a brief survey of the Spartan family[4] and one of the anonymous referees remarked "but there were no female Spartiates"[5] that I first realized that there was much work to be done.

My recent work on Xenophon[6] and Plutarch,[7] two of the major sources on Spartan women, made me appreciate how little had been written about the ways in which the perspectives of these two authors, more than any others, have shaped our views of Spartan women. Because of my training as a papyrologist, I have often written about women in the Hellenistic period;[8] writing about Plutarch convinced me to extend this study to Roman Greece. Thus this book covers some thousand years of history, but despite the timespan, it is short. Extant sources are few, although I have tried to exploit every ancient text and artifact that appeared relevant. The sources on various aspects of Spartan women's lives are unevenly distributed. There is far more information on education,

1. See L. Zuckerman, "Spartan Women, Liberated," *New York Times,* Jan. 1, 2000, sec. F, pp. 1, 3.

2. New York, 1975, republished with a new Preface 1995.

3. Elaine Fantham, Helene Peet Foley, Natalie Boymel Kampen, Sarah B. Pomeroy, and H. Alan Shapiro, *Women in the Classical World* (New York, 1994), and Sarah B. Pomeroy, Stanely M. Burstein, Walter Donlan, and Jennifer Tolbert Roberts, *Ancient Greece* (New York, 1998).

4. *Families in Classical and Hellenistic Greece* (Oxford, 1997).

5. A Spartiate was a Spartan with citizen rights (see chap. 5). The feminine form of *Spartiates* is *Spartiatis:* see *LSJ* s.v. Sparte. Lippold, *RE* 3A (Stuttgart, 1929), s.v. Sparta (die Ethnika), 1280–92, esp. 1283, 1291–92, notes that the feminine *Lakedaimonia* is very rare, *Spartiates* is rare, and *Spartiatis* is poetic.

6. *Xenophon. Oeconomicus: A Social and Historical Commentary* (Oxford, 1994).

7. *Plutarch's Advice to the Bride and Groom and A Consolation to His Wife* (New York, 1999).

8. E.g., *Women in Hellenistic Egypt* (New York, 1984; pbk. Detroit, 1990).

reproduction, and religion than on other subjects. These emphases are reflected in the lengths of the various chapters. The longstanding lack of serious scholarship on the history of Spartan women has meant that there has been less impetus than is usual for a scholar working in classics and ancient history to take into account previous studies. Nevertheless, this book has been the most difficult one I have ever written. It must be confessed that we know little about Spartan women, but it is not so readily conceded that we do not actually know much about Spartan men either. Compared to what is known about Athens, there is little direct evidence about life in Sparta. It is difficult to construct a realistic picture of how women and men actually lived in such a place; there is, however, a great deal of evidence for what other Greeks thought about their lives. Much current scholarship on Sparta is devoted to the latter subject. It must be emphasized that often the primary sources do not distinguish between prescriptive and descriptive writing; and pictorial representations may also be idealistic or fantastic rather than realistic. Contemporary scholars, as well, differ in their assessment of what constitutes historical reality, and what was part of the "Spartan mirage."[9] Having stated these caveats here, I will not repeat them throughout the book. I must, however, confess that my tendency is to grant more credence to the primary sources than some contemporary hypercritical Spartanologists are wont to do, and to understand that they generally reflect an actual historical situation rather than a utopian fiction. Sophocles described the versatility and ingenuity of the human race. The Greek text permits a literal and gender-free translation. The chorus reflects:

> Many the wonders, but nothing more wonderful than a human being . . .
> Having a clever inventive skill beyond hope
> A person proceeds sometimes to evil, sometimes to good.
>
> (*Antigone* 332–33, 365–68)

A survey of the sources may be found in an Appendix at the end of this book. The nineteenth century paintings that are reproduced in this book may serve to remind us that history is a conversation between the present and many pasts.

Chronological Conundrums

The traditional chronological framework for Greek history, which labels blocks of time "archaic" (ca. 750–490), "classical" (490–323), and "Hellenistic" (323–30), is based on political changes that are reflected in the visual arts. While this

---

9. See further F. Ollier, *Le mirage spartiate*, vol. 1, *Étude sur l'idéalisation de Sparte dans l'antiquité grecque de l'origine jusqu'aux cyniques*; vol. 2, *Étude sur l'idéalisation de Sparte dans l'antiquité grecque du début de l'école cynique jusqu'à la fin de la cité* (Paris, 1933–43, repr. 1973).

periodization is appropriate to most Greek poleis (especially Athens), it does not reflect some of the most significant events in Spartan history. Furthermore, the usual framework does not take into account events that affected women. In any case, it is irrelevant insofar as Sparta's contribution to the material arts was negligible after the archaic period.

Perhaps most important for Spartan history were the political and social changes that occurred after the Second Messenian War. By the end of the seventh or in the early sixth century these changes created the distinctive Spartan way of life. Changes in the fifth and fourth century may have been significant, but these were not accompanied by sharp dislocations. A major turning point was the aftermath of the battle of Leuctra (371 B.C.E.), when enemy troops invaded Spartan territory for the first time, soundly defeated the Spartans, and brought about the liberation of Messenia. Though individual Spartans were tempted to work as mercenaries, Sparta declined to participate in the campaigns of Alexander and thus was not so immediately affected by the changes that produced the Hellenistic world. Sparta's relative isolation was not ended until the reign of Agis IV, which began ca. 244 B.C.E., when Sparta went through a series of political upheavals culminating in defeat by the Roman general Flamininus in 195 B.C.E. and inclusion in the Roman province of Achaea.

This simple time line does not reveal how the Spartans themselves manipulated, created, and recreated their own history. There were two successful programs to revive the traditional Lycurgan constitution and the social, educational, and religious institutions alleged to have existed in earlier times, one in the Hellenistic period, the second in the Roman period. At the time of both revivals, the sources refer explicitly to actions taken in accordance with the ancient customs and laws.[10] The impact of these revivals complicates the historian's task. For example, if the evidence for the authority of the priestess of Artemis Orthia is purely Roman, should we assume that she exercised exactly the same power in an earlier period? The Spartans believed (or at least wished others to believe) that she had. In the Roman period, they were known to be proud and pedantic about their heritage, and nostalgia would have encouraged them to accept or even promulgate myths as historical truth and exaggerate the virtues and distinctiveness of their past (see Appendix). Plutarch, one of our principle sources, is often not aware of the chronological problems, and in fact offers pieces of information about such important topics as marriage that are mutually contradictory unless the practices he refers to were not concurrent but occurred at different time periods. In his defense, in his works that deal with Sparta, he was writing biography and philosophy, not history. Although these problems will be discussed as they emerge, let me sketch them here. As a historian, I naturally try to use a chronological approach, but because of the ways in which the Spartans themselves revised their own history, I have found a straightforward chronological

---

10. E.g., *SEG* XI.626, lines 2–3, and see chap. 4, below.

framework unworkable. For this reason, the chapter titles are topical: the first three, however, follow the Spartan woman through the life cycle. Furthermore, the discussions of the topics are, as much as possible, chronological. Motherhood is the thread that links all the chapters. The reader should note in addition that B.C.E. or C.E. have been added to a date when necessary to avoid ambiguity. Otherwise, all dates should be understood as "Before Common Era." "Spartan women" applies only to women of the highest civic class, although I will discuss other women who lived in the territory controlled by Sparta and who interacted with the highest class.

Following the precedent of classical authors, I will refer to the legendary lawgiver Lycurgus and the Lycurgan constitution without implying a belief that this shadowy figure ever existed, or that Spartan customs or laws were the result of a single creative act. In the same way I will refer to the *rhetra* ("legislation") of Epitadeus without insisting that Epitadeus ever existed.[11] Plutarch (*Agis* 5) reports that sometime after the Peloponnesian War a certain ephor named Epitadeus proposed a rhetra that would permit a person to give or bequeath his *kleros* ("plot of land") and house to anyone he wished. Xenophon (*Lac. Pol.* 15) does not name Epitadeus, but observes that in his day the Spartans no longer obeyed the laws of Lycurgus. Aristotle (*Pol.* 1270a15–34) also does not mention Epitadeus. Whether or not Epitadeus ever existed, major economic changes associated with him occurred at the end of the fifth or in the early fourth century (see chap. 4). These changes began earlier, but the dramatic events after the Peloponnesian War precipitated the changes and made them perceptible. The changes are important because they increased women's potential to own immovable property. To establish the chronological framework, my book will attribute these changes to the rhetra of Epitadeus without lingering on the complexities of dating.

Another issue is whether the cult of Hera at Elis is directly relevant to Spartan women. We do not know if races in honor of Hera were restricted to local girls from Elis or were pan-Hellenic, like the competitions for men at neighboring Olympia. The latter seems more likely. Whatever the current political relationships in Greece, the games were usually held under conditions of a

---

11. Thus S. J. Hodkinson, s.v. Epitadeus, *OCD³*, describes him as fictitious, and in "'Blind Ploutos'? Contemporary Images of the Role of Wealth in Classical Sparta," in *The Shadow of Sparta*. ed. A. Powell and S. J. Hodkinson (London, 1994), 183–222, esp. 207, 214, he sees Epitadeus as part of the "mirage." Hodkinson, *Property and Wealth in Classical Sparta* (London, 2000), 90–94, reviews the scholarly debate on Epitadeus and change in property tenure. E. Schütrumpf, "The Rhetra of Epitadeus: A Platonist's Fiction," *GRBS* 28 (1987), 441–57, argues that Plutarch's report is adapted from Plato *Rep.* 8.555D–E. In contrast, J. Christien, "La loi d'Épitadeus: Un aspect de l'histoire économique et sociale à Sparte," *RD* 52 (1974), 197–221, and Evanghelos Karabélias, "L'épiclerat à Sparte," *Studi in onore di Arnaldo Biscardi* (Milan, 1982), vol. 2, 469–80, 471–72, express no doubt about the existence of Epitadeus and the impact of his reform. On Plutarch, see the Appendix to this book.

temporary peace,[12] and statuettes of the victors show girls dressed in the semi-nude costume associated only with Spartans. Since only Spartan women are known to have seriously pursued physical education, they would probably have been the most numerous among the competitors. Convenience of travel to nearby Elis probably ensured a strong presence for Spartan women in any female agonistic activity at Olympia. This volume therefore includes a discussion of the athletic events associated with the cult of Hera at Elis (see chap. 1).

I am grateful to the John Simon Guggenheim Memorial Foundation for a fellowship and to the Fellows of St Hilda's College, Oxford, and to the American Academy at Rome for their frequent hospitality while I was doing research for this book. I am also pleased to have the opportunity to thank Thomas Figueira, Nigel Kennell, Jo Ann MacNamara, H. Alan Shapiro, and the Family History Reading Group for their comments on the manuscript. I am also grateful to Georgia Tsouvala for research assitance, to David van Taylor for computer advice, and once again to Angela Blackburn for gracious and tactful editorial help.

12. But for the relationship between Sparta and Elis as a hindrance to Cynisca's entrance into the equestrian events at Olympia, see chap. 1.

CONTENTS

ILLUSTRATIONS

ABBREVIATIONS

With a few obvious exceptions, journal titles are abbreviated according to the form in *L'année philologique*. Accepted abbreviations are used for standard works. Lists of such abbreviations may be found in reference books such as the *Oxford Classical Dictionary*, 3d edn., and in the major Greek and Latin dictionaries.

Dawkins, *AO*   R. M. Dawkins et al. *The Sanctuary of Artemis Orthia at Sparta*. Society for the Promotion of Hellenic Studies Supplementary Papers, no. 5. London, 1929.

LGPN 3A   *A Lexicon of Greek Personal Names*. Vol. 3A. *The Peloponnese, Western Greece, and Magna Graecia*, ed. Peter M. Fraser and Elaine Matthews. Oxford, 1997.

Poralla²   Paul Poralla, *A Prosopography of Lacedaemonians from the Earliest Times to the Death of Alexander the Great (X–323 B.C.)*. 2d edn. Chicago, 1985.

PMGF   M. Davies, *Poetarum Melicorum Graecorum Fragmenta*. Vol. 1. Oxford, 1991.

Spartan Women

1

EDUCATION

The History of Childhood

In the modern western world, schooling is mandatory and the curriculum prescribed by state authorities who verify its effectiveness by examinations of students, teachers, and textbooks. In antiquity, parents alone were usually responsible for their children's upbringing. At Athens there was a little outside supervision: a boy was scrutinized at successive stages of life by his father's tribe.[1] In contrast, there was no outside surveillance of girls' upbringing, because a modest, well-brought-up young woman was hidden from the public eye. At home with her mother and other women in the household, a girl learned the skills that she would need to use as an adult. Wearing long dresses, and playing indoors with dolls and small animals, she learned to be nurturant and to perform household tasks.

Every well-governed state that comes into existence and evolves as the result of deliberate creative acts and legislation endorses the child-rearing practices and values it needs. The educational system is part of political organization, and each role in it, including parent, teacher, and pupil, is socially constructed. Only at Sparta did the state prescribe an educational program for both boys and girls beginning in childhood. Spartans themselves, of course, undertook most of the pedagogical tasks, but they also are known to have invited a few foreigners to teach the young.[2] Poets were the most revered teachers in archaic Greece. There were no travelling women poets: evidently the Spartan authorities determined that education was valuable, and there was no reason to be concerned about any inappropriate liaisons between a male teacher such as Alcman and female as well

---

1. See further Sarah B. Pomeroy, *Families in Classical and Hellenistic Greece* (Oxford, 1997), 141–42 and passim.

2. Terpander, Stesichorus, and other poets worked in archaic Sparta: Arist. fr. 551 Gigon, Plut. *Mor.* 1134b, Athen. 14.635e, etc.

as male pupils.³ Alcman's origin, variously said to be Lydian or slave, did not pose an insurmountable deterrent (see Appendix). The earliest datable evidence for the girls' official program is archaic and continues through the classical period. In the Hellenistic period, the traditional system for both boys and girls was discontinued. The boys' program (*agoge*) was fully revived by Cleomenes III: whether the girls' program was also restored at this time is not indisputable, but there are some hints that they were included, perhaps voluntarily rather than under the mandate of the state. When the revolution of Cleomenes failed, the agoge continued until it was abolished by Philopoemen in 188, to be later restored in an archaizing form in the Roman period. At that time as well, state supervision of girls' education was revived through the authority of the *gynaikonomos*.⁴

In archaic and classical Sparta, girls were raised to become the sort of mothers Sparta needed, just as boys were trained to become the kind of soldiers the state required. The boys' program was far more arduous than the girls'. Young boys left home to learn the survival techniques and skills they would need as hoplites. Their educational program was full time and competitive, and they were frequently examined by older boys and adult authorities appointed for this purpose (Xen. *Lac. Pol.* 2.2 4.1–6, Plut. *Lyc.* 16,18). The goal of the educational system devised for Spartan girls was to create mothers who would produce the best hoplites and mothers of hoplites. Because all the girls were expected to become the same kind of mothers, the educational system was uniform.⁵ This goal obviously did not require the full-time practice and scrutiny that was imposed upon the boys. Girls lived and ate at home with their mothers. Thus it would appear that they enjoyed some privacy and leisure denied to the boys (see below). We surmise that, compared to other Greek women, they had plenty of time to do whatever they wanted to do.

Literacy

The extent of literacy in Greece in general, and in Sparta in particular, has been much debated.⁶ It is generally agreed that literacy at Sparta was confined to a

---

3. Nevertheless, Alcman confesses his interest in women in *PMGF* 34, 59a, b, and see below on Megalostrata, who was not said to have been his pupil.

4. See further Nigel Kennell, "The Elite Women of Sparta," paper delivered at the annual meeting of the American Philological Association, December 28, 1998; abstract published in *American Philological Association 130th Annual Meeting: Abstracts*, 84. In this paper, Kennell is less willing to accept the evidence for a girls' agoge in the Roman period than he was in *The Gymnasium of Virtue: Education and Culture in Ancient Sparta* (Chapel Hill, N.C., 1995), 46.

5. Though no ancient source states that every girl participated in the system, the universality of the goal implies it. See further Jean Ducat, "Perspectives on Spartan Education in the Classical Period," in *Sparta: New Perspectives*, ed. S. Hodkinson and A. Powell (London, 1999), 57–58.

6. See William V. Harris, *Ancient Literacy* (Cambridge, 1989).

small elite, and lack of the ability to read and write did not hinder an ordinary citizen's ability to participate in government.[7] Paul Cartledge reports that major epigraphical sources in Sparta give the names of approximately twelve women as compared with one hundred men.[8] This sex ratio, however, is not direct evidence of levels of literacy for women and men respectively; rather, it is a reflection of the fact that men performed more deeds deemed worthy of commemoration and, at least until the end of the fifth century, generally had more funds at their disposal to pay for inscriptions. For example, athletic victories generated a substantial number of inscriptions, but no woman was victorious in horse racing until the fourth century (see below).

There is no reason, however, to assume that the sex ratio among literate Spartans was as skewed as it was elsewhere in the Greek world. In a democratic polis like Athens, there were strong incentives for men to learn how to read and and write;[9] since women did not participate in government, there was little reason for them to become literate, though some did. In Sparta, in contrast, the education of boys was devoted to developing military skills, leaving little time for the liberal arts. Girls, however, spent time with their mothers and older women. Furthermore, since they were married at eighteen—a substantially later age than their Athenian counterparts—they had as many years as most girls do in modern western societies to devote to their education. They could well have learned reading and writing, as well as other aspects of *mousike* (music, dancing, poetry) in such an all-female milieu.[10] Of course, in the days when poets such as Alcman were engaged to teach choirs of young maidens, they learned from the poets.[11] Though copies of the poems were probably preserved in state or private archives, the oral tradition was strong (see Appendix). Doubtless the girls committed most information to memory, and did not write it down, for surely they could not have sung and danced while dangling a papyrus roll. By repeating poems like those of Alcman at festivals, successive generations of Spartans learned both their content (including mythology, religion, courtship, and etiquette) and mousike. The repetition of this material tended to create children who thought

7. See further Paul Cartledge, "Literacy in the Spartan Oligarchy," *JHS* 98 (1978), 25–37, esp. 33–37.

8. From the sixth to the fourth century: Cartledge, "Spartan Wives: Liberation or Licence?" *CQ* 31 (1981), 84–105, esp. 93 n. 54.

9. Thus F. D. Harvey, "Literacy in the Athenian Democracy," *REG* 79 (1966), 585–635, esp. 623.

10. At Athens, respectable women who were literate learned their letters at home: Sarah B. Pomeroy, *Xenophon. Oeconomicus: A Social and Historical Commentary* (Oxford, 1994), 270, 283. For learning in an all-female milieu, cf. the young women in the circles of Sappho and other women poets in archaic Lesbos. The parallel is not exact, however, for several reasons, including the fact that Spartan girls were required to devote a good portion of their time to gymnastics.

11. There is evidence for male leaders of female choirs at Aegina, but the age of the females is not clear: Herod. 5.83.3.

and behaved as their parents did. Thus Spartan society remained conservative and conscious of its traditions.

The educational goals of the state and the girls' curriculum are reflected in lyrics written by Alcman for choirs of Spartan maidens:

Alcman, Partheneion 1 PMGF

Polydeuces.
Among the dead I do not take account of Lycaethus [but] of
   Enarsophorus and Thebrus the fast runner . . . and the violent
(5) . . . and wearing a helmet
[Euteiches], and king Areius, and . . . outstanding of demigods
   . . . the leader
   . . . great, and Eurytus
(10) . . . tumult
   . . . and the bravest
   . . . we shall pass over . . . . Destiny and Providence, of all [gods] . . . the
   oldest
(15) . . . strength [rushing] without shoes.
Let no man fly to heaven
   . . . [or] try to marry Aphrodite
   . . . . queen, or some
   . . . or a daughter of Porcus.
(20) The Graces . . . the house of Zeus
   . . . with love in their eyes
god . . . to friends . . .
(25) gave gifts . . . youth destroyed . . . vain . . .
(30) went, one of them [killed] by an arrow . . . [another] by a marble
   millstone
   . . . in the house of Hades . . . .
(35) They plotted evil deeds and suffered unforgettably. There is such a
   thing as vengeance from the gods, and blessed is the man who, being
   reasonable, weaves the web of the day without weeping.
(40) And I sing the light of Agido: I see her like the sun which Agido is
   now calling to shine as our witness. But the renowned choir leader
   does not allow me to praise or blame her [i.e., Agido] at all.
(45) For she herself is conspicuous, as if one set among the herds a
   strong horse with thundering hooves, a champion from dreams in
   caves.
(50) Don't you see? The mount is a Venetic: but the hair of my cousin
   Hagesichora blooms like pure gold;
(55) and her silvery face—why need I tell you clearly? There is
   Hagesichora herself; while the nearest rival in beauty to Agido will
   run as a Colaxian horse behind an Ibenian.
(60) For the Pleiades rise up like the Dog Star to challenge us as we bear
   the cloak to Orthria through the ambrosial night.
(65) There is no abundance of purple sufficient to protect us, nor our
   speckled serpent bracelet of solid gold, nor our Lydian cap,

adornment for tender-eyed girls, nor Nanno's hair, (70) nor Areta
who looks like a goddess, nor Thylacis and Cleesithera. Nor will you
go to Ainesimbrota's and say "I wish Astaphis were mine," and (75)
"I wish Philylla would look at me, and Demareta, and lovely
Vianthemis"—no, it is Hagesichora who exhausts me with love.

For Hagesichora with the pretty ankles is not here beside us. (80) She
waits with Agido and commends our feast to the gods. Gods, receive
it! For the accomplishment and fulfillment are up to the gods.

(85) Choir leader, I would say I myself am a girl who screeches in vain
like an owl from a roof beam; but I desire to please Aotis especially,
for she is the healer for us.

(90) However, because of Hagesichora girls come to lovely peace. For it
is necessary to obey the trace-horse and the driver.[12]

(95) Of course she is not a better singer than the Sirens, for they are
goddesses, and instead of their eleven, we are only ten, and children
who sing. (100) But we sound like a swan on the waters of Xanthos.
And she with her thick blond hair . . . .

Alcman, *Partheneion* 3 *PMGF*

Olympian Goddesses . . . about my heart . . . song and I . . . to hear the
voice of . . . (5) of girls singing a beautiful song . . . . will scatter sweet
sleep . . . from my eyelids and lead me to go to the contest where I
will surely toss my blond hair

(10) delicate feet . . . .

(61) with limb-loosening desire, and more meltingly than sleep and
death she gazes toward . . . nor is she sweet in vain. But Astymeloisa
does not answer me (65) while she holds the wreath, some star
falling through the gleaming sky, or a golden bough, or a soft feather
(70) she crossed on long feet. The moist grace of Cinyras [i.e., per-
fume] sits on the maiden's hair.

(73) Astumeloisa among a crowd, darling of the people . . . .

(75) taking . . .

I say . . . . If a silver . . . . I might see (80) if she would love me coming
near, and take me by the soft hand, at once I would worship her.

But now a child, heavyhearted . . . to a child, the girl-child

(85) grace[13]

As we have mentioned, Sparta was the only polis where the training of girls
was prescribed and supported by public authority. The spiritual and intellectual
education of girls is interesting, especially since apparently boys did not receive

12. Trans. Sarah B. Pomeroy. For further comments on these poems, and a photograph of a portion of one of the papyrus texts, see Appendix.

13. See *LSJ* s.v. kubernao 2 for associations with chariots and horses, rather than the common
interpretation of piloting a ship.

an education superior to that of girls (in contrast to the situation at Athens). Therefore the cultural level of girls may well have been superior to that of boys, inasmuch as the latter had to devote so much attention to military training. The intensity of the training of both sexes is unparalleled in the rest of the Greek world. Competitiveness was as much a part of the cultural curriculum as of the physical program. Alcman was hired to teach maidens to perform in choruses that stressed competition among its members both as individuals and as participants in groups of rival choruses, and his poems refer to ranking and contests.[14]

In the early classical period, some women could read. An anecdote about the precocious Gorgo (born in 506 B.C.E.), daughter and wife of kings, suggests that she knew how to read. When Demaratus, who was in exile, sent a secret message to Sparta by writing it on a wooden tablet and covering it with wax, Gorgo told the recipients to scrape the wax off and read the message (Herod. 7.239). While it is not reported that Gorgo herself read the message when it was uncovered, she realized that there might be writing on such a tablet. Other stories about her poise and precocity also indicate that she probably could read.[15] She will have acquired her skill not necessarily through formal tuition, but while in her indulgent father's presence, listening quietly or more likely (judging from what we are told about her assertiveness and self-confidence) piping up persistently to ask questions about the texts that poets, diplomats, bureaucrats, and other literate people consulted.[16] Anecdotes about Spartan mothers sending letters to their sons urging them to be brave also suggest that literacy was not unknown among women.[17] Though the source of the anecdotes is late and they can not be dated or verified, considering the fact that mothers were separated from their sons who were on military service for long periods of time, the idea that they communicated by letters is not unthinkable.

Dedications by women to female divinities that bear the name of the dedicator begin in the late seventh century. This date is consistent with the spread and use of the alphabet in the Greek world. Inscriptions, however, that include dedications do not constitute incontrovertible evidence of literacy inasmuch as they were likely to have been written by craftsmen, rather than by the dedicators themselves. Nevertheless, that inscriptions commemorating the deeds of individual women are found at sanctuaries frequented by women suggests that some women could read them (see below on the Heraea). Such inscriptions are consistent with the picture given by other sources and allow us to conclude that some women, at any rate, were literate.

---

14. *PMGF* TA 2.34–35, *PMGF* 1.58, 59, and passim, *PMGF* 3.8.

15. See chap. 3 nn. 25, 34, and chap. 4.

16. Cf. Agesilaus for another Spartan king who enjoyed the company of his young children, two daughters and a son: Plut. *Ages.* 25.6, *Sayings of Spartans*, 213.70.

17. Plut. *Sayings of Spartan Women*, 241a3, d10, 11. On this source see Appendix. Cf. the letters of Olympias to Alexander: Plut. *Alex.* 39.4–5.

Doubtless there was change over time in the rate of women's literacy and in its relationship to the literacy of men. After the Peloponnesian War, when Sparta was no longer isolated, Spartan women were probably as literate as aristocratic women elsewhere in the Greek world.[18] For example, *Anonymus Iamblichi*, a work written some time after the Peloponnesian War in a literary Doric, reports that the Spartans thought it was fine for their children not to learn mousike and letters.[19] He may, however, be referring to boys only.[20] In any case, by the middle of the fourth century, Plato describes women's curriculum as consisting of gymnastics and mousike and comments that this program leaves plenty of time for luxury, expense, and unstructured activity (*Laws* 806A, cf. *Rep.* 5.452A). He also states that in Crete and Sparta not only men, but also women, take pride in education and goes on to praise their skills in philosophical discussion (*Prot.* 342D: *paideusis*). This talent is an aspect of the women's ability to speak. Spartan women were encouraged and trained to speak in public, praising the brave, reviling cowards and bachelors (Plut. *Lyc.* 14.3–6). Aristotle thought it was natural for women to be silent (*Pol.* 1260a28–31), and almost five hundred years later Plutarch wrote: "A wife should speak only to her husband or through her husband."[21] In Athens, respectable women were encouraged not to speak. In Xenophon's *Oeconomicus* (7.10), a husband describes his young wife as having been brought up "under careful supervision so that she might see and hear and speak as little as possible." Her husband is unusual in believing that as an essential part of her education to be his partner and to supervise the household, he must first teach her how to speak (7.10).

Some Learned Women

Of course literacy is related to verbal ability, and in Greece, even among literate circles, poetry was often either sung or read aloud. According to hazy traditions, there were two female poets in Sparta. Both of them apparently worked in the archaic period, when Sappho and lesser-known women poets flourished in other parts of the Greek world. None of the work of the Spartan women poets is extant.

18. See further Sarah B. Pomeroy, "*Technikai kai Mousikai*: The Education of Women in the Fourth Century and in the Hellenistic Period," *AJAH* 2 (1977), 51–68, and *Women in Hellenistic Egypt: From Alexander to Cleopatra* (with a new foreword and addenda, Detroit, 1989), 59–72.

19. Diels-Kranz⁶, vol. 2, p. 408, 2.10, and see Kathleen Freeman, *The Pre-Socratic Philosophers* (Oxford, 1946), 418–19. For a translation, see Rosamond Kent Sprague, *The Older Sophists* (Columbia, S.C., 1972), "Dissoi Logoi," 282.

20. On the ambiguity of *paides*, which can mean "children," "boys," or "slaves," see below, Appendix n. 77.

21. *Advice to the Bride and Groom*, 32: see further Sarah B. Pomeroy, ed., *Plutarch's Advice to the Bride and Groom and A Consolation to His Wife* (New York, 1999), ad loc.

Megalostrata is mentioned by Alcman. He describes her as "a golden-haired maiden enjoying the gift of the Muses."[22] Several Muses were involved, for in this period poets not only wrote words, but also composed musical accompaniment, and in some cases choreography. Athenaeus (13.600f) reports that Megalostrata attracted lovers because of her conversation, and that Alcman was madly in love her. Though she is not specifically identified as Spartan, she is called a "maiden," and as we have seen, Alcman spent much time in Sparta creating poetry for unmarried girls. Furthermore, like Helen, she is blonde, and her name is suitable for a Spartan, for it means "large army." That she had a personal flirtation with Alcman is questionable. In Greek biographical tradition, written hundreds of years after the death of the subjects, it was common to hypothesize erotic links between creative women and men, rather than grant them an independent existence or a purely intellectual relationship with men.[23]

There was also a tradition about Cleitagora, a woman poet whose name was used to identify a *skolion* (drinking song).[24] The Cleitagora is mentioned in Aristophanes (*Lys.* 1237, *Wasps* 1246), and Cratinus (254 Kassel-Austin). The *Lysistrata* passage suggests that she was Spartan, whereas the *Wasps* offers the possibility that she was Thracian: the scholiast to each passage draws the obvious, and mutually opposing, conclusion. The former inference, however, is more likely to be correct for several reasons: first, in the context of the *Lysistrata* where the leading female characters are an Athenian and a Spartan visitor, it is more appropriate to sing a song by a Spartan woman. Hence the ambassador in *Lysistrata* says it not right to sing the song called the "Telamon," but rather the "Cleitagora."[25] Furthermore, of all Greek women, Spartans alone drank wine not only at festivals, but also as part of their daily fare.[26] Therefore it is natural to attribute a drinking song to a Spartan woman who probably composed it for a woman's festival.

The archaic period also produced at least one Spartan female philosopher. Chilonis, daughter of Chilon, one of the Seven Sages, was a follower of Pythagoras.[27] Iamblichus (*VP* 267) named seventeen or eighteen women among the 235 disciples of Pythagoras; nearly one-third of the women cited were

22. *PMGF* 59, Poralla² 510.

23. On traditions linking women philosophers to the men in their circle see Pomeroy, "*Technikai kai Mousikai,*" 58.

24. See further Denys Page, *PMG* 912; Jeffrey Henderson, *Aristophanes: Lysistrata*, ed. with introduction and commentary (Oxford, 1987), ad loc.; and Douglas M. MacDowell, *Aristophanes: Wasps*, ed. with introduction and commentary (Oxford, 1971), ad loc.

25. According to the Scholiast to *Lys.* 1237 Cleitagora was mentioned in Aristophanes, *Danaids* (= fr. 271 Kassel-Austin). According to Hesychius, s.v. Kleitagora (k 2913 Latte), she was from Lesbos.

26. Xen. *Lac. Pol.* 1.3, and below, chap. 6 nn. 3, 19, 21–22.

27. I.e., Cheilonis: Iambl. *VP* 267, Poralla² no. 760. For her father, who was ephor in 556, see Poralla² no. 230. See further Conrad M. Stibbe, *Das andere Sparta* (Mainz, 1996), 211.

Spartans. In contrast, only three of the 218 men were Spartans. Some of the pseudepigrapha attributed to women were in the Doric dialect, and these originated from the group of Pythagoreans around Tarentum, a Spartan colony.[28] In addition to Chilonis, Iamblichus mentions Nistheadousa[29] and Cleaichma, a sister of the Spartan Autocharidas.[30] Timycha, wife of Myllias of Croton, is singled out for her courage in resisting Dionysius, tyrant of Syracuse. Dionysius (r. 396–79) had her tortured when she was six months pregnant. Rather than reveal the secrets of the Pythagoreans, she bit her tongue off.[31] Cratesiclea as well was a Pythagorean who was married to Cleanor, a fellow Pythagorean.[32] Their dates are not known. Unlike Chilonis, who was said to be a contemporary of Pythagoras, Cratesiclea and Cleanor may have been neo-Pythagoreans. It was natural for members of the same family, especially a married couple, to become Pythagoreans, for the philosopher ordained rules for everyday life including dietary prohibitions and the proper seasons for sexual intercourse. The idea that prescribed commandments and structure might govern even the minutiae of life in an entire community doubtless was familiar to Spartans. Moreover, Sparta enjoyed cultural ties with Samos, Pythagoras's native land.

The interest in philosophy continued into the Hellenistic period. As we have mentioned, one of the Pythagorean women may have been a neo-Pythagorean. Stoicism also had some effect upon Spartan women, though this philosophy was directed toward men. Cleomenes III invited Sphaerus, a disciple of Cleanthes, to give lectures to the youths and ephebes.[33] When the Spartan revolutions failed, Cleomenes and his family sought aid, followed by asylum in Egypt (see chap. 4). Upon embarking as a hostage for her son's behavior, his mother Cratesicleia set an example of courageous behavior: "Let no one see us crying or doing anything unworthy of Sparta. For this is up to us alone. Our fortunes will be whatever the deity may bestow." She was not at all afraid of death.[34] Self-sacrifice, belief in a single all-powerful divinity, and courage in the face of death are all characteristics of Stoics.

28. See further Holger Thesleff, *An Introduction to the Pythagorean Writings of the Hellenistic Period* (Åbo, 1961), esp. 77–78, 99, 103–5, 114–16.

29. Manuscripts vary. Nistheadousa is listed with a question mark in Diels-Kranz 58, "Pythagoreische Schule: A. Katalog des Iamblichos," but not cited in Poralla² or in *LGPN*3A. On these women, see further Gilles Ménage, *Historia mulierum philosophorum* (1690–92), trans. B. H. Zedler as *The History of Women Philosophers* (Lanham, Md., 1984), chap. 11.

30. *LGPN*3A s.vv. dates Cleaichma to the sixth century, but Autocharidas to the fifth century.

31. Iambl. *VP* 267.31, see also Porphyry, *Pythag.* 61, Poralla² no. 702, and *LGPN*3A s.v.

32. Iambl. *VP* 267, Poralla² nos. 450, 420. On neo-Pythagorean women, see further Pomeroy, *Women in Hellenistic Egypt*, 61–65.

33. Plut. *Cleom.* 2, *FGrH* III.585, and see further Pomeroy, *Families*, 65–66.

34. Plut. *Cleom.* 22.6–7, 38.4. This vivid passage may not only record a real event, but may also reflect the Stoic leanings of Plutarch's source, Phylarchus: see chap. 4 n. 48, and Appendix.

Mousike

Musical performance was an essential feature of ancient religion, and Spartans were taught to sing, dance, and play musical instruments. Athenaeus (14.632f–633a) observes that the art of music was practiced more intensely in Sparta than elsewhere, for it was a pleasant relief from the self-control and austerity of everyday life. Votive figurines depict women playing various wind, string, and percussion instruments (see chap. 6). In Alcman, *Partheneion* 1 (97, 99), young girls display critical judgment about their own singing abilities: though they do not sing as well as the Sirens, they sing sweetly indeed. Most of the descriptions we have about women's practice of mousike concerns their dancing. Even Aristophanes, though he could not ever have been a witness, refers to the maidens dancing on the banks of the Eurotas (*Lys.* 1307–10). The hyporcheme, in which the chorus sings as it dances, was performed by Spartan men and women.[35] Athenaeus (14.630e) links the hyporcheme to the comic and vulgar dance called the kordax, and comments that both are funny. Spartan women also were famous for performing another undignified dance called the *bibasis* (Pollux 4.102, Aristoph. *Lys.* 82). This dance required physical prowess and coordination, for the dancer had to jump and thump her buttocks with her heels in competition for prizes. A bronze figurine that was once thought to represent a girl runner may represent a girl dancing vigorously (fig. 1).[36]

Physical Education

There is more evidence, both textual and archaeological, for athletics than for any other aspect of Spartan women's lives. Furthermore, there is more evidence for the athletic activities of Spartan women alone than for the athletics of all the women in the rest of the Greek world combined.[37] Clearly these activities caught the attention of writers and lead us to conclude that Spartan women's intense involvement in such activities was probably unique in the Greek world. Moreover, although there are relatively few high-quality works of art pertaining to the lives of Spartan women in other spheres, an impressive proportion are relevant to their athletic pursuits. Some of these artifacts are extant; others are known through descriptions by Pausanias and others.

Many of the athletic activities were part of religious festivals that were held in honor of female divinities. It is difficult to separate athletics from religion:

---

35. Athen. 14.631c, citing Pindar fr. 112 Snell.

36. S. Constantinidou, "Spartan Cult Dances," *Phoenix* 52 (1998), 15–30, esp. 24. For details of manufacture and interpretations, see Appendix, below.

37. Giampiera Arrigoni, "Donne e sport nel mondo greco: Religione e società," in *Le donne in Grecia*, ed. Giampiera Arrigoni (Bari, 1985), 55–201, devotes pp. 65–101 (of a total 73 of text [the remainder consists of illustrations and special exegeses]) and nn. 29–185 (of a total 259) to Sparta and uses Sparta as a touchstone throughout the article.

Fig. 1. Girl from Prizren or Dodona.

She is dressed as a runner. That she glances back, however, rather than keeping her gaze in the direction of her feet, also suggests that she is dancing. London, British Museum 208. Photo courtesy of the Trustees of the British Museum.

however, we will concentrate on the former in the present chapter and the latter in chapter 6.

Xenophon (*Lac. Pol.* 1.4) states with approval that Lycurgus instituted physical training for women no less than for men, including competitions in racing and trials of strength. Euripides (*Andr.* 595–601) specifically alludes to racing and wrestling. Plutarch (*Lyc.* 14.2) gives a more explicit account of the physical curriculum, mentioning running, wrestling, discus throwing, and hurling the javelin.[38] Skill in these activities is particularly useful for a soldier. The women's

38. B. B. Shefton, "Three Laconian Vase Painters," *ABSA* 49 (1954), 299–310, esp. 307, no. 17, for nymphs or girls swimming. Alcman also wrote a work titled "The Female Swimmers" (*Kolumbosai: PMGF* TB 1, fr. 158).

curriculum was a selective and less arduous version of the men's, but similar to it. As the girls in Theocritus announce: "we all run the same racecourse and rub ourselves with oil like men along the bathing places of the Eurotas."[39] The silvery face mentioned in Alcman, *Partheneion* 1 (55), may be the glistening effect of the oil in addition to beads of sweat resulting from vigorous exercise. Since boys' and girls' activities were similar, the question of whether they were educated together arises. In Plato's *Republic* 5, male and female guardians are trained for the same jobs in the government and the military: therefore they are educated together. In proposing co-ed education, Plato's idea is more radical than the Spartan reality of his time. Although sources agree that there was no shyness because of their nudity, it is not clear whether boys and girls used the same exercise ground and racecourse (*dromos*).[40] Xenophon and Plato discuss the education of boys and girls in separate sections and the *agelai* ("herds") are always described as single sex.[41] Given the relative strength and swiftness of men and women, co-ed competitions and trials of strength in most cases would not have been as efficient in training future hoplites as single-sex exercises. The following two nineteenth-century paintings set in the Platanistas respectively depict, first, the girls exercising separately (fig. 2), and second, provoking the boys to involve them in co-ed wrestling (fig. 3).

In figure 2, girls wrestle before a crowd of elders.[42] Members of the Council of Elders (Gerousia) stand alongside and serve as judges. Lycurgus, seated at top center, crowns a victorious girl. To his right at his feet sits a bearded old man recording the names of the victors on a tablet. Taygetus looms behind. The structure in the center is probably either the shrine of Alcon[43] or the sanctuary of Poseidon (cf. Paus. 3.14.8). The simple architecture of the monuments reflects Spartan austerity and restraint. Though the Spartan men do not leer at the girls, the modern viewer may find it difficult to distinguish between athletic and erotic nudity, and quite possibly the artist did not intend to make such a distinction.

---

39. *Idyll* 18.22–25. Theocritus, of course, is not an unassailable witness to practices in the classical period, but his report is consistent with those from earlier, more trustworthy sources.

40. There is no evidence for the Platanistas ("the grove of plane trees") before the Hellenistic period, when two teams of youths staged a mock battle.

41. Contra Cartledge, "Spartan Wives: Liberation or Licence?" 91. T. Scanlon, "Virgineum Gymnasium: Spartan Females and Early Greek Athletics," in *The Archaeology of the Olympics*, ed. W. Raschke (Madison, Wis., 1988), 185–216, esp. 190, also argues that education was co-ed, but the evidence he cites is tendentious (Eur. *Andr.* 99–100) and Roman (Ovid, *Her.* 16.149–52, Prop. 3.14), when sensationalism may have prompted or intensified participation in co-ed contact sports so that women's wrestling of the archaic and classical period became the pancration in the Roman period. Philostratus, *Imag.* 2.6.3, specifies the pancration as the pancration of men (*andron*). For *agele* (i.e., *agela* "herd") used of girls, see n. 110 below.

42. For a detailed description, see Giovanni Paludetti, *Giovanni de Min* (Udine, 1959), 290, 307. 310–11, 320, App. 1, and fig. 31.

43. A son of Hippocoön, older brother of Tyndareus, whose other sons are mentioned at the opening of the extant fragment of Alcman, *Partheneion* 1.

Fig. 2. Giovanni Demin, *La lotte delle Spartane* ("Spartans Wrestling").
Fresco, 1836. Villa Patt, Sedico. Photo, Zanfron.

Demin may have been influenced by Roman and late Greek traditions suggesting that while exercising Spartan girls were sexually provocative.

In figure 3, note that the third figure from the left caresses the breast of the second girl from the left and kisses her.[44] There is no ancient authority for the girls' costume: to the modern viewer it resembles the apron-like skirts worn by some Native Americans. In the group behind Lycurgus stands among the mothers. Degas himself said that the rock in the background is Taygetus, from which newborns who did not pass official scrutiny were thrown.[45] He had studied Greek and Latin and many years after completing the picture he stated that the source was Plutarch.[46] This reliance on Plutarch is doubtless a major factor in Degas's avoidance of the potentially more licentious interpretations of Demin's depiction.

Spartan women were not trained for actual combat; if they had engaged in co-ed athletics, they would have been more prepared. Plato (*Laws* 806A) and Aristotle (*Pol.* 1269b) complain that despite their physical education, they were no better than other Greek women when it came to defending their country.[47] When the Thebans invaded Sparta under Epaminondas in 369 B.C.E., the women were terrified and panicked because their country had never before suffered invasion.[48] It is necessary to point out that at that moment Spartan men were no better than other Greeks, for they had lost a battle. A century later, anticipating an attack by Pyrrhus, Archidamia, grandmother of Agis IV, rallied the other women to oppose the men's scheme to send them to safety in Crete. They declared they had no wish to continue living if Sparta were destroyed. They performed heavy manual labor in behalf of Sparta, assisting the men in digging a trench in a single night as a defense against the elephants of Pyrrhus.[49] Finally, they told the few soldiers who were present to go to sleep and finished the trench themselves. The next day they cheered the army on. Chilonis, wife of king Cleonymus, held a rope around her neck so she would not be taken alive (see chap. 4).

44. Carol Salus, "Degas' Young Spartans Exercising," *Art Bulletin* 67 (1985), 501–6, argues that the subject of the painting is courtship, and that the figure touching the girl's breast is male (504). However, Degas may be depicting the well-known homosexual relationship between females.

45. Martin Davies, *The French School* (London, 1957), 70, and see further M. H. Sykes, "Two Degas Historical Paintings: *Les jeunes spartiates s'exercent à la lutte* and *Les malheurs de la ville d'Orléans*" (Master's thesis, Columbia University, New York, 1964).

46. Phoebe Pool, "The History Pictures of Edgar Degas and Their Background," *Apollo* 80 (1964), 306–11, esp. 308.

47. Nicolas Richer, *Les éphores: Études sur l'histoire et sur l'image de Sparte (viiie–iiie siècle avant Jésus-Christ)* (Paris, 1998), esp. 83–84, sees a connection between the Partheniai ("children of unmarried women") who were sent to settle Tarentum and the Tresantes ("tremblers," "cowards"), for both are feminized. See further chap. 2 n. 45 below.

48. Xen. *Hell.* 6.5.27–8; Plut. *Ages.* 21.4–5; Arist. *Pol.* 1269b37–9.

49. 273–272 B.C.E.: Plut. *Pyrr.* 27.2–5, 29.6. Cf. Polyaen. 8.49 and 70 for the military assistance of the women of Cyrene. Jacoby *FGrH* 81, Komm. F 48, suggests that a similar passage of Pompeius Trogus in Justin is based on Phylarchus. See further David Schaps, "The Women of Greece in

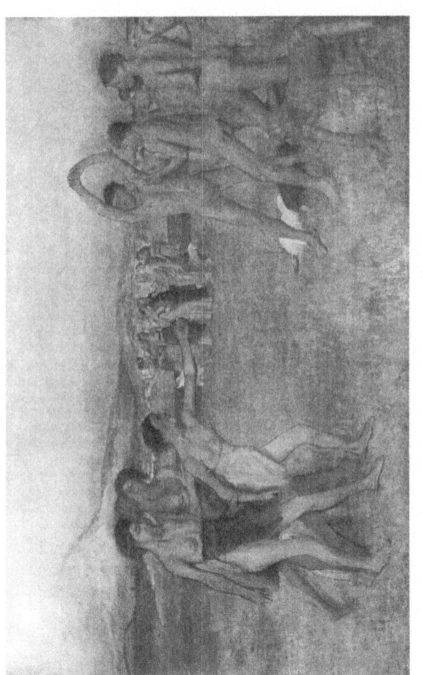

Fig. 3. Hilaire Germain Edgar Degas, *Les jeunes Spartiates s'exercent à la lutte*
("Young Spartans Exercising").

1860. London, National Gallery. Photo courtesy of the Trustees of the National Gallery.

One may speculate that Spartan women would have been better at defending themselves if need be, for Plutarch (*Mor.* 227d12) states that a goal of their physical education was to make them able to defend themselves, their children, and their country. At any rate, just as there is little evidence for illicit adultery at Sparta, there is little for the rape of individuals.[50] During the bitterly fought Second Messenian War, however, Aristomenes and his troops succeeded in carrying off some maidens who were dancing in a secluded place. During the night the guards attempted to rape the maidens, but Aristomenes slew the most aggressive men, saved the girls, and released them for a large ransom.[51] Spartan women were reputed to drag bachelors around the altar and to hit them to make them enter marriage at the appropriate time.[52] Although the source of this gossip is a writer who tends to exaggerate, the implication is that the women were very strong, in fact powerful enough to drag around a Spartan man in his prime, not an easy job even in a ritual when the man was not resisting; and perhaps the women worked in teams.

When athletic activities were not part of ritual for women, they were purely sports. Some of the skills were useful for hunters. Xenophon (*Cyn.* 13.18) reports that some women enjoyed hunting. Although the women he names were the mythical Atalanta and Procris, it is possible that Spartan women engaged in this sport as well (see below). They will not have had to go far, for the region of Mount Taygetus was rich in wild game (Paus. 3.20.4–5). Doubtless, like Spartan youths, they could have outraced and encircled a hare. As we have mentioned, they were taught to throw a javelin. In that case we speculate they will have increased their consumption of protein, for meat does not otherwise appear to have been a significant part of the female diet.[53] In any case, Spartan women were not anemic, and of course exercise does whet the appetite. A poet of middle comedy refers to a certain Helen who devoured a prodigious quantity of food. Helen's name suggests that she was Spartan, or at least wanted to seem to be, and her food consumption equaled that of male athletes.[54]

The education of Spartans apparently affected the social construction of their religion. Plutarch exaggerates when he states that all Spartan divinities

---

Wartime," *CPh* 77 (982), 193–213, and Maria Luisa Napolitano, "Le donne spartane e la guerra: Problemi di tradizione," *AION (archeol.)* 9 (Naples, 1987), 127–44.

50. Jerome para. 308 Migne relates several anecdotes about the rape of Spartan virgins in conditions of war. See also Orosius 1.21 and Justin 3.4.1–5.

51. Paus. 4.16.9–10, and see chap. 6 n. 11.

52. Clearchus of Soli (fl. ca. 250 B.C.E.) fr. 73 Wehrli = Athen. 13.555c. New York City firefighters, both male and female, are trained to be able to carry adults of both sexes.

53. See chap. 3 on liquid and dry food rations. Xen. *Lac. Pol.* 15.3 refers to men eating meat at the *syssition* (mess group). Spartiates did raise animals on their estates (Plut. *Alcib. I* 122d).

54. Athen. 10.414d quoting Heraclitus comicus (also known as Heraclides) in "The Host," Kassel-Austin *PCG* 5.560.

carried weapons.[55] Nevertheless, at Sparta many important divinities, including Athena of the Bronze House, Aphrodite Morpho, and Aphrodite Areia, were portrayed as as warriors.[56] Artemis Orthia was shown wearing a helmet and holding bow and spear. In contrast, in Athens, only one major goddess, Athena, was often shown fully armed. Despite the anthropomorphism of Greek divinities, it would be naive to postulate that goddesses were invariably a direct reflection of their female worshippers.[57] For example, Athena's helmet, shield, and spear had no implications for Athenian women, and other important gods and goddesses at Athens were not shown armed. On the other hand, the Spartan evidence, with its intense focus on martial prowess, does seem to have implications for women.[58]

Horsemanship

Horseback riding and chariot racing were not part of a traditional Greek physical curriculum for most boys, and certainly not for girls.[59] Throughout Greece, however, wealthy gentlemen were expected to be accomplished horsemen and to be able to serve in the cavalry.[60]

Sparta was known for breeding and racing horses. Riding horses requires skill rather than brute strength.[61] Of course, little is known about women's education in archaic and classical poleis other than Athens and Sparta, but there can be no doubt that Sparta's excellence in equestrian affairs had repercussions for Spartan women. Women as well as men were actively involved with horses, riding, driving horse-drawn vehicles, and engaging in competitive equestrian events. Archaeological and textual evidence from the archaic period testify to the long history of this involvement. Fragmentary terracotta figurines of Orthia

55. *Sayings of Spartans* 232d5, *Lac.* 239a (28).

56. Paus. 3.17.6, 3.15.10; *Greek Anthology*, Planudian Appendix 173–76, etc., and see further J. G. Frazer, *Pausanias's Description of Greece*, vol. 3 (London, 1913), 338.

57. *OCD³* s.v. Aphrodite considers the possibility that the armed Aphrodite was connected with women's education, but prefers to interpret the armor as alluding to Aphrodite considered to be the polar opposite of Ares. Robert Parker, "Spartan Religion," in *Classical Sparta*, ed. A. Powell (Norman, Okla. 1989), 142–72, esp. 146, suggests that the portrayals of divinities with armor were retained at Sparta from earlier primitive cult images. See further Fritz Graf, "Women, War, and Warlike Divinities," *ZPE* 55 (1984), 245–59, and chap. 6 n. 72 below.

58. On the armed Aphrodite: Julianus (sixth century C.E., *Anth. Pal.* 9.447), and Graf, "Women, War, and Warlike Divinities," 250–51.

59. For Plutarch's version see above. Arist. *Pol.* 1337b24–25 lists reading, writing, gymnastics, the musical arts, and possibly painting. In Plato, *Laws* (804E), riding is prescribed for women.

60. Xenophon, *On Horsemanship, Cavalry Commander*, and see further, Pomeroy, *Xenophon, Oeconomicus*, 2, 219, 226, 231, 243.

61. The owner of the horse ridden by Julie Krone, the first woman to win a Triple Crown, said of her: "She's got great finesse, beautiful hands on a horse, and good communication. You don't have to bully a horse—just talk to him." Joe Drape, "Krone Adds Another First to Her Accomplishments," *New York Times*, Aug. 8, 2000, sec. D, pp. 1, 5, esp. 5.

riding astride and side-saddle were found at the sanctuary.[62] More votives of horses than of all other animals combined were also found.[63] Figurines depicting Helen on horseback similar to those found at the sanctuary of Orthia were discovered at the Menelaion.[64] Bronze votives at both sanctuaries depict female figures identified either as mortals or as Artemis and Helen riding side-saddle. The habits of divinities are not always emulated by human beings, but, as the ambivalence in the identity of the figures makes clear, there does appear to be a direct connection between goddesses and women as riders.[65]

In Alcman, *Partheneion* 1, the girls compare themselves to horses that are ridden.[66] They comment that the Colaxian was inferior to the Venetic and Ibenian.[67] Because of the educational function of poetry, this remark suggests that the girls had specialized knowledge about the different strains of horses. The Colaxian was a sturdy pony, the Veneti used more for chariots than for riding, and the Ibenian perhaps Celtic or Ionian.[68] They also understood chariot racing and refer to the trace-horse and the driver (line 90). At the Hyacinthia, Spartan girls drove expensively decorated light carts, and had an opportunity to display their equestrian skills before the entire community. Some raced in chariots drawn by a yoke of horses.[69] For some processions, the girls rode in carriages shaped like griffins or goat-stags.[70] These Spartan girls apparently had much more fun than Nausicaa described in the *Odyssey* (6.37–38, 57–58, etc.), who had to beg permission from her father to drive a team of two mules while riding in a cart loaded with other women and sacks of dirty laundry.

Not only could Spartan women drive horses, but they also knew how to ride them. Agesilaus II used to like to play "pony on a stick" with his young children, Archidamus, Eupolia, and Prolyta (Plut. *Ages.* 25.6, *Sayings of Spartans* 213.70). This report indicates that girls played at riding astride, and that the hobby horse on a stick was not considered a "boys' toy." In 220/219, at the end of the reign of

62. Dawkins, *AO*, 146, all dates. Some riders on figurines dated 700–600 must have had to ride side-saddle: Dawkins, *AO*, 150.

63. Dawkins, *AO*, 157.

64. A. J. B. Wace, M. S. Thompson, J. P. Droop, "The Menelaion," *ABSA* 15 (1908), 108–57, esp. 124, all dates, and H. W. Catling, "Excavations at the Menelaion, Sparta, 1973–76," *AR* (1976–77), 24–42, esp. 38, and fig. 42.

65. Mary Voyatzis, "Votive Riders Seated Side-Saddle at Early Greek Sanctuaries," *ABSA* 87 (1992), 259–79, esp. 272, 274, for fourteen figures from the Orthia sanctuary, one seventh cent., the others sixth, and five from the Menelaion, all sixth cent.

66. *Parthenion* 1, 47–59; see also Aristoph. *Lys.* 1307. Theoc. *Id.* 18.30 compares Helen to a Thessalian horse, and see chap. 6 n. 47.

67. Scholion B, fr. 6, col. i (P.Oxy. 2389).

68. J. K. Anderson, *Ancient Greek Horsemanship* (Berkeley, 1961), 36–37.

69. Perhaps mules: Athenaeus' text is unclear. See further Kaibel (ed.), Athen. 1.317.

70. Athen. 4.139f, Xen. *Ages.* 8.7, Plut. *Ages.* 19.5–6.

Cleomenes III, the heroic wife of Panteus fled to the coast on a galloping horse.[71] Thence she embarked to join her husband who was in exile with Cleomenes in Alexandria (Plut. *Cleom.* 38). Like male landowners, Spartan women could drive or ride out to survey their property as men did.[72] Driving horses or riding them endowed Spartan women with an autonomy that was unique for women in the Greek world.

At Athens, in contrast, sumptuary laws and measures intended to curtail women's visibility in public proscribed women's opportunities to ride in carriages, and there is no evidence that they ever rode horses.[73] Women are rarely portrayed in art riding in carriages except in marriage processions. Sometimes, of course, it was necessary to travel for a funeral or a festival. According to traditional laws ascribed to Solon, they were not to travel at night except in a wagon with a torch shining in front (Plut. *Sol.* 21.4) At Rome, where much more wealth was available, the Lex Oppia, enacted as a sumptuary measure in 216 B.C.E., also forbade women from riding in chariots except for religious purposes.[74]

That a Spartan was the first female star in Greek athletics not surprising. Cynisca was a daughter of the Eurypontid king Archelaus II and sister of two kings, Agis II and Agesilaus. Her name, Cynisca, is unusual and may be a nickname for an especially tomboyish woman. Her paternal grandfather, Zeuxidemus, was also nicknamed Cyniscus (Herod. 6.71). The meaning "little hound" perhaps alludes to an interest in hunting.[75] The name of her mother and of her niece Eupolia ("well horsed"),[76] her sister's name Proauga ("flash of lightning"), and her niece's Prolyta ("she who is let loose in the forefront") allude to equestrian interests in the female line. Cynisca is the first woman whose horses were victorious at Olympia. She must have been close to fifty years old at the time.[77] The Eleans had banned the Spartans from Olympia in 420 (Thuc. 5.49–50). After the Peloponnesian War, Sparta attacked Elis, and Agis was able to offer sacrifices at Olympia in 397 (Xen. *Hell.* 3.2.21–31). Cynisca entered her horses at the earliest possible moment and won her victories in two successive Olympiads, in 396 and 392. No wonder Pausanias (3.8.2) calls her ambitious. Cynisca must have been champing at the bit herself for several years, hoping she would have an opportunity to race her horses at Olympia before she died.

71. For public models, note that Hellenistic queens were publicly honored by equestrian statues: see E. Fantham et al., *Women in the Classical World* (New York, 1994), 220, 222. At Rome, Cloelia was portrayed mounted on a horse, though her heroic deed involved swimming: Liv. 2.13.11.

72. Xen. *Hell.* 3.3.5 for Spartan men out on their country estates.

73. The sole exception is a woman who was dressed up to impersonate Athena and placed in a chariot. She may, however, have had a driver: Herod. 1.60.

74. Liv. 34.1–8; Tac. *Ann.* 3.34, Val. Max. 9.1.3, Oros. 4.20.14, Zonaras 9.17.1, and see further Sarah B. Pomeroy, *Goddesses, Whores, Wives, and Slaves: Women in Classical Antiquity* (New York, 1995), 178.

75. According to Arist. *HA* 608a25, female Laconian hounds are more clever than the males.

76. Poralla², no. 310.

77. According to Moretti, *IAG*, pp. 41, 43, Cynisca was born sometime before 427, probably around 440.

Cynisca's *quadriga* (four-horse chariot) was evidence of great wealth like that of some of her contemporaries who were victors, including tyrants in Sicily. Likewise Cynisca's commemorative monuments were examples of conspicuous consumption equal to those of men.[78] Like wealthy men who owned racehorses, Cynisca did not drive them herself but employed a jockey. Indeed, she would not even have been present at the victorious event inasmuch as women were not permitted to attend the games.[79] Her image, however, stood in the sanctuary. Apelleas, son of Callicles, of Megara, created a sculpture of her chariot, charioteer, and horses in bronze, and a statue of Cynisca herself.[80] He also made bronzes of her horses that were smaller than lifesize (Paus. 5.12.5). These were erected at Olympia. They were the first monuments dedicated by a woman to commemorate victories at pan-Hellenic competitions. The choice of Apelleas suggests that Cynisca had done some research to find a sculptor from an allied city who specialized in images of women. Apelleas was fond of depicting women praying.[81] Thus it is quite possible that Cynisca was portrayed expressing gratitude to the gods. The author of the epigram inscribed on the base of her statue is unknown. The poem is metrically competent; straightforward in the "Laconic" style; and of course written in the Doric dialect.

Cynisca herself is represented as speaking:

> My ancestors and brothers were kings of Sparta.
> I, Cynisca, victorious with a chariot of swift-footed horses,
> erected this statue. I declare that I am the only woman
> in all of Greece to have won this crown.[82]

78. For a dedication of a small votive by Cynisca to Helen at the Menelaion, see A. M. Woodward, "The Inscriptions," *ABSA* 15 (1908), 40–106, esp. 86–87, no. 90 = *IG* V.1.23.

79. Pausanias (5.6.7; 6.20.9) states that *parthenoi* (virgins, unmarried women) could view the games, but that married women were excluded. This provision seems extremely unlikely in view of the need to chaperone young girls. Matthew P. J. Dillon, "Did *Parthenoi* Attend the Olympic Games? Girls and Women Competing, Spectating, and Carrying Out Cult Roles at Greek Religious Festivals," *Hermes* 128 (2000), 457–80, esp. 461–62, suggests that fathers accompanied their girls. Pausanias may be thinking about the *parthenoi* who were present not as spectators, but because they participated in the races at Elis. The only exceptions (not mentioned by Pausanias) were the priestess of Demeter and a female envoy from Ephesus: see L. Robert, "Les femmes théores à Éphèse," *CRAI* (1974), 176–81 = *OMS* 5.669–74. Of course it is possible that even at her advanced age Cynisca was technically a *parthenos*. Perhaps she had been widowed at a young age. In any case, no husband nor children are recorded for her, and her brother's attempts to manipulate her (see below) suggest that she did not have a husband. Her single-minded devotion to racing may have not left any time for wifely duties.

80. Paus. 6.1.6: see further Bianchi-Bandinelli, *EAA* 1.460–61.

81. His name may have been Apelles. Bianchi-Bandinelli, *EAA* 1.460–61, Pliny *HN* 34.86. The manuscript variant *adornantes* ("adorning themselves") would probably make sense as well in the case of Cynisca, who seems to have been vain and by no means modest. On the commemorative monuments, see J. G. Frazer, *Pausanias's Description of Greece* (London, 1913), vols. 3, 4, ad loc.

82. Paus. 6.1.6 = *Anth. Pal.* 13.16 = *IG* V.1.1564a = *I. Olympia*, no.160 = Moretti, *IAG*, no. 17, and Moretti, *I. Olympia*, nos. 373, 381.

This epigram was only the second ever composed to commemorate a deed of the Spartan royalty (Paus. 3.8.2). The first one was written by Simonides and was inscribed at Delphi in honor of Pausanias, victor over the Persians at Plataea. Obviously Cynisca was thought of in very exalted company. She had won the most prestigious horserace twice at the most prestigious pan-Hellenic atheltic festival. Cynisca's commemorative sculptures at Elis stood between that of Troilus of Elis[83] and those of male Lacedemonians. Pausanias (6.2.1) includes Cynisca in his observation that after the Persian war, the Lacedaemonians were the keenest breeders of horses. No husband or children are recorded for Cynisca.[84] Xenophon and Plutarch, however, draw attention to her relationship with her brother the king, who had encouraged her to enter a chariot at Olympia in order to demonstrate that such victories were the result of wealth and expenditure, not of virtue (*andragathia*, "manly virtue").[85] Whether Agesilaus was actually inspired by mean-spiritedeness and sibling rivalry, or by the lofty motives Xenophon and Plutarch ascribe to him, the anecdote suggests that he thought his sister's horses had a good chance to win. Like some male owners of victorious racehorses,[86] Cynisca was not only extremely wealthy, but she was also an expert in equestrian matters. According to Pausanias (3.8.2), she had an ambition to be victorious at Olympia, and was the first woman to breed horses. With the increase in private wealth, much of it in the hands of women, and with their keen interest in athletics and knowledge of horses, it was natural that Spartan women would own racehorses. Cynisca was a member of the first group of extremely wealthy women who begin to become evident after the Peloponnesian War (see chap. 4).

A heroön was erected to Cynisca near the Platanistas where the athletic contests of young Spartans were staged. In Greece it was not uncommon to treat athletes as heroes, but Cynisca was the first woman to be elevated to this status. Her shrine was in the vicinity of the shrines of mythical heroes including the sons of Hippocoön. The heroön would have been built after her death and would have served as an inspiration to other women.[87]

Cynisca's example was soon followed by other women, especially Spartans; the author Pausanias (8.1) sees their victories as a trend. Among them was the Spartan Euryleonis, who was victorious at Olympia with a two-horse chariot in

---

83. Named for Troilus, famous for his horses, called by Homer *hippiocharmes* (*Il.* 24.257: "fighting from a chariot").

84. *LGPN* 3A s.v., and see n. 77 above.

85. Xen. *Ages.* 9.6, sim. *arete* in Plut. *Ages.* 20.1, and in *Sayings of Spartans*, Ages. 49.

86. See further Pomeroy, *Families*, 93–94. Like Cynisca, Bilistiche received divine honors, but this worship was part of the Hellenistic trend to divinize members of the royal families and some of their intimate associates.

87. Moretti, *IAG*, p. 44, suggests that the sculptures by Apelles were also erected after Cynisca's death, and commissioned either by her family or by the state.

368.[88] A statue of Euryleonis stood with those of other luminaries such as the general Pausanias in the vicinity of the Bronze House (Paus. 3.8.1, 3.17.6). In fact the Spartans Cynisca and Euryleonis were the first women whose chariots were victorious at Olympia. Approximately a century later they were followed by royal women and women connected with the courts of Alexander's successors (see below).[89]

Competitions

Competitive racing and trials of strength for women, no less than for men, were part of the physical education system instituted by Lycurgus (Xen. Lac. Pol. 1.3–4, cf. Arist. Pol. 1269b). Some of these contests were doubtless organized in a routine manner; but others took place as part of religious festivals. We are better informed about the latter.

Running races were the only athletic events for women that took place at festivals. There were races in honor of Helen,[90] Dionysus,[91] Hera,[92] and in honor of local deities called Driodones.[93] Theocritus reports in his *Epithalamium to Helen* (18.22–25) that 240 maidens rubbed their nude bodies with oil as men did and raced along the Eurotas. That the girls were said to be as old as Helen when she married Menelaus indicates that the races were associated with puberty. As Theocritus reports the event, there was a tacit beauty competition as well, with Helen winning the prize (see Conclusion). The women's race at the Heraea in Elis was the most prestigious, the equivalent for women of the Olympic competitions held for men:[94]

> Every fourth year the Sixteen Women weave a robe for Hera, and the same women also hold games called the Heraea. The games consist of a race between virgins. The virgins are not all of the same age; but the youngest run first, the

---

88. Moretti, *I. Olympia*, nos. 396, 418.

89. Bilistiche, mistress of Ptolemy II, who was said to be from Argos, Macedonia, or Phoenicia, was the next woman whose victories are recorded: see further Pomeroy, *Women in Hellenistic Egypt*, 53–55. Her victories were probably in 268 and 264: Moretti, *IAG*, p. 42. Berenice II was the next woman after Bilistiche whose horses were victorious. Berenice originally came from Cyrene. Her interest in equestrianship is additional testimony to cultural links between Cyrene and Sparta. For the horses of Cyrene see, e.g., Pindar, *Pyth.* 4.2. According to Strabo (17.3.21 [837]), Callimachus praised the horses of Cyrene. For an epigram attributed to Posidippus comparing Berenice to Cynisca see *P. Mil. Vogl.* VIII.309, xiii 31–34.

90. Schol. Theoc. 18. 22–5, 39–40: see A. S. F. Gow, *Theocritus*, vol. 2 (Cambridge, 1952), 354, 358.

91. See below. There was also a race called *en Drionas* about which little is known: see Hesych. s.v. E2823 (Latte).

92. Hesych. s.vv. Driodones, en Drionas.

93. See further T. Scanlon, "The Footrace of the *Heraia* at Olympia," *AncW* 9 (1984), 77–90.

94. On the connection between Spartan maidens and the races for Hera, see Preface, and Appendix, "Mirrors and Bronze Statuettes."

next in age run next, and the eldest virgins run last of all. They run thus: their hair hangs down, they wear a shirt that reaches to a little above the knee, the right shoulder is bare to the breast. The course assigned to them for the contest is the Olympic stadium; but the course is shortened by about a sixth of the stadium.[95] The winners receive crowns of olive and a share of the cow which is sacrificed to Hera; moreover, they are allowed to dedicate statues of themselves with their names engraved on them.[96]

Rather than actual portraits, the statues were doubtless images of girls running with the name of the honorand inscribed.[97] It is obvious that the victorious women, or their families, sought fame and immortality no less than victorious men, and were willing to pay the cost of a dedication.

Athletic Nudity

The Greek word *gymnos* means "nude" or "lightly dressed."[98] Nudity at Sparta may be explained in terms of religion, initiatory rites, erotic stimulation, and the requirements of athletic prowess. Though these strands are intertwined, for heuristic purposes we will separate them, and treat nudity as a costume for sports here. (For other implications, see chap. 2 and Conclusion.)

Not only did Spartan women wear a *peplos* (tunic) that revealed their thighs,[99] but they regularly exercised completely nude.[100] Mature women and pregnant women exercised.[101] Even older women exercised nude. As male athletes had discovered, light clothing or none at all is best for racing. Even nowadays (or at least before the adoption of lycra bodysuits), racers wear as little clothing as possible. Thucydides (1.6) credits the Spartans with being the first to exercise unclothed.

95. I.e., 160 meters. David G. Romano, "The Ancient Stadium: Athletics and *Arete*," *AncW* 7 (1983), 9–15, esp. 14, suggests that the length of the girls' race was correlated with the measurement of the stylobate of Hera's temple at Olympia, while the length of the boys' race was correlated with the stylobate of the temple of Zeus. According to Herod. 2.149, the length of the stadion was 6 plethra or 600 feet (168.6 m.). According to Romano's (p. 14) formula, the girls' stadion race would be ca. 128 meters.

96. Paus. 5.16.3: see Frazer, *Pausanias's Description of Greece*, vol. 3, 593.

97. The girl depicted in fig. 1, above, may be running as part of a dance, for she glances behind her. On the other hand, she may be looking to see if any competitor is catching up.

98. For a survey of nudity in antiquity, see Larissa Bonfante, "Nudity as a Costume in Classical Art," *AJA* 93 (1989), 558–68.

99. Ibycus, fr. 339 *PMGF*; Eur. *Andr.* 595–601, cf. *Hec.* 932–36; Soph. fr. 872 Lloyd-Jones, Aelius Dionysius (2d cent. c.e., 4.35 [140] Erbse), for girls wearing one himation only, without belt or chiton; similarly Moeris, a lexicographer (2d cent. c.e., d27).

100. Xen. *Lac. Pol.* 1.4; Plut. *Lyc.* 14.4–15.1; Nic. Dam. *FGrH* 103 F 90, cf. Anacreon fr. 99 (Page-Campbell).

101. Aristoph. *Lys.* 78–84, Critias fr. 32 (Diels-Kranz 2.1969).

The girls who raced at the Heraea lowered the right shoulder of the peplos and revealed their right breast.[102] This costume was peculiar to this festival. No ancient source specifies the ethnic identity of the girls who competed at Elis.[103] They may have been girls from the neighborhood, or at least originally so. It seems more likely, however, that the games became pan-Hellenic, though on a smaller scale than the men's events at Olympia.[104] In view of the tendency at Athens, for example, to seclude and protect young girls and to keep their names out of the public eye, it is unlikely that Athenian maidens would have been brought to race at Elis. At Athens (and probably elsewhere in Greece), girls were devalued, and the expenses involved in travelling were considerable. Therefore, if the Heraea were pan-Hellenic, only girls who lived fairly close by would have participated. Considering the likelihood that attention was not paid to women's athletics anywhere but Sparta, and given the historical evidence for Spartan domination of Elis in the archaic period, it is likely that the games were established along Spartan principles and that the majority of competitors and victors were Spartan. Many of the sculptures at the temple of Hera were the work of Lacedaemonian artists (Paus. 5.17.2). Finally, bronze figurines depict girl runners in short peploi baring the right breast. These figurines were manufactured in Sparta (see Appendix). As we have mentioned, the bare-breasted costume was worn only by girls who raced at the Heraea. Though some prepubescent Athenians raced nude at least once in their lives at the sanctuary of Artemis at Brauron, only Spartan girls regularly wore short dresses and exercised nude. Moreover, historical sources assign the earliest foundation of racing for girls anywhere in Greece to Lycurgus. For these reasons, it is generally assumed that, at least when the political relationship between Sparta and Elis was favorable, the girls who raced at the Heraea were mostly Spartans.

Nudity for women indicates that their athletic prowess was understood to be a high priority: it certainly attracted a great deal of attention, both artistic and prurient. Ibycus and later writers described the women as "thigh-flashers" (see above). In the *Andromache* (595–602), written in the early years of the Peloponnesian War, Euripides mentions the bare thighs and co-ed racing and wrestling. *Anonymus Iamblichi* reports that Spartan girls strip for exercise.[105] Plato apparently knew of the Spartan practice, for it is generally assumed that nude exercise for women in the *Republic* (457A) is based on the Spartan reality.

---

102. See further N. Serwint, "The Female Athletic Costume at the *Heraia* and Prenuptial Initiation Rites," *AJA* 97 (1993), 403–22. Beth Cohen, "Divesting the Female Breast of Clothes in Classical Sculpture," in *Naked Truths: Women, Sexuality and Gender in Classical Art and Archaeology*, ed. A. O. Koloski-Ostrow and C. L. Lyons (London, 1997), 84 n. 15, questions Serwint's fifth-cent. dating of the Vatican girl runner, otherwise considered a classicizing work of the Roman period.

103. See further Scanlon, "The Footrace of the *Heraia* at Olympia," 83, and Preface, above.

104. Serwint, "The Female Athletic Costume at the *Heraia* and Prenuptial Initiation Rites," 419, suggests that the change occurred ca. 580 when the festival was restructured.

105. Diels-Kranz 2.90.9, and see Freeman, *The Pre-Socratic Philosophers*, 418–19.

Plato refers to women who are natural athletes (*Rep.* 456A). He also suggests that the bodies of old women are laughable (*Rep.* 457B), and, indeed, retreats from nudity for adult women in the *Laws* (833D). In the *Republic* (452B), all women exercise naked, though the older ones are described as wrinkled and not good-looking. In *Laws* (833C), Plato prescribes nude racing only for prepubertal girls, and racing clothed for adolescents until marriage at eighteen to twenty years of age. Plato's distinction may be reflected in the artistic portrayals of Spartan girl runners, though a modern viewer may misinterpret clues to the age of subjects in ancient art.[106] Bronze mirrors and statuettes portraying girls completely nude seem to modeled on a prepubertal, slim-hipped girl. Those wearing the chiton show an adolescent with fully developed breasts. The older group may be dressed because they have already reached menarche and need to wear an undergarment to absorb menstrual blood.[107]

Upon marriage, girls graduated from the state-controlled educational system. Some of them, at least, still managed to stay in good physical shape. Non-Spartan authors report that adult women were physically fit. Lampito, a married woman, is in excellent condition and can touch her buttocks with her feet while jumping in the air (Aristoph. *Lys.* 82). Spartan women needed to be able to assume this position while dancing in certain religious rituals.[108] As we have just observed, in his *Republic* Plato states that even mature women will exercise in the nude: this ordinance may reflect some reality at Sparta. In any case, as we have seen, some mature women continued to be interested in horses and probably rode or drove to their country estates.

Education in Hellenistic and Roman Sparta

Was there an agoge for girls, and if so, was it parallel to or imitative of the boys' agoge? These questions are further complicated by historiographic issues surrounding the boys' agoge. According to revisionist history, the agoge as described in great detail by Plutarch was largely a Hellenistic invention that was revived in the Roman period.[109] Therefore, although Plutarch's description has enjoyed greater popularity and influence, Xenophon's report should be understood to be a more accurate account of the educational system of the classical period. In any case, ancient authors as well as modern scholars agree that some sort of

---

106. See further Christiane Sourvinou-Inwood, *Studies in Girls' Transitions: Aspects of the Arkteia and Age Representation in Attic Iconography* (Athens, 1988).

107. For a loincloth, see chap. 6 n. 59. My interpretation assumes that menstruation was not regarded as pollution restricting eligibility to compete at a religious ritual confined to females.

108. See further chap. 6 n. 16.

109. Nigel M. Kennell, *The Gymnasium of Virtue: Education and Culture in Ancient Sparta* (Chapel Hill, N.C., 1995), 98, 147, and passim.

institutionalized educational system for girls existed whenever such a system existed for boys.[110]

In the Hellenistic period the fortunes of Sparta declined (see chap. 4). Owning good racing teams was expensive. Nevertheless, the Panathenaic victor lists for 170 B.C.E. record the victory of a Spartan woman with a quadriga.[111] She is one of nineteen non-Athenian citizens, including seven women, whose names appear on victor lists for this period (170, 166, 162 B.C.E.). Her name, Olympio, is either prophetic of her deed or a nickname alluding to an Olympic victory not otherwise attested.

In the Roman period, because Sparta was a destination for tourists, the characteristics that made Sparta distinctive were emphasized. The athleticism of women was exaggerated. Foreigners were allowed to see what they had never before been able to witness: Spartan women engaged in athletics. There were other professional women athletes in the Roman world. Therefore, in order to attract an audience, the Spartans needed not only to be good athletes, but also to create a unique image. History and tradition were mined for publicity. Spartan athletics were authentic. The reports of Plutarch (see above) and Propertius (3.14) indicate that the curriculum for girls was firmly established and well articulated in Roman Sparta. Propertius mentions nude co-ed wrestling; ball playing; hoop rolling; the pancratium (wrestling with no holds barred); discus throwing; hunting; chariot driving; and wearing armor. Vergil (*Aen.* 1.314–24) also describes Spartan huntresses wearing short dresses, armed with bows and arrows, pursuing a wild boar. Ovid (*Her.* 16.151–52) writes of a nude Helen wrestling in the palaestra. Doubtless, like other Greeks, they continued to anoint themselves with oil. One Spartan woman in the first century B.C.E. is reported to have doused herself with so much butter that the odor made a Galatian princess ill (Plut. *Mor.* 1109b). The Spartan, in turn, was nauseated by the smell of the other woman's perfume, perhaps because she maintained the traditional Spartan ban on wearing perfume.

110. Pindar fr. 112 Snell: "Lakaina . . . parthenon" quoted by Athenaeus 14.631c, see n. 41 above; Xen. *Lac. Pol.* 1.4; Plut. *Lyc.* 14.2; Nic. Dam. *FGrH* 90 F 103; etc. See most recently Ellen Millender, "Exercise, Nudity and Spartan Female Sexual License: A Reconsideration" (paper delivered at the annual meeting of the American Philological Association, Dec. 28, 1998; abstract published in *American Philological Association 130th Annual Meeting: Abstracts*, 82), in agreement with Kennell, *The Gymnasium of Virtue*, 46, about an educational system for girls organized by the state. However, in "The Elite Women of Sparta" (paper delivered at the annual meeting of the American Philological Association, Dec. 28, 1998; abstract published in *American Philological Association 130th Annual Meeting: Abstracts*, 82), Kennell is less sanguine about the existence of a formal agoge for women in the Roman period. Jean Ducat, "Perspectives on Spartan Education in the Classical Period," in *Sparta: New Perspectives*, ed. S. Hodgkinson and A. Powell (London, 1999), 43–66, esp. 64 n. 31, argues that girls' *agelai* did not exist, but in "La femme de Sparte et la cité," *Ktèma* 23 (1998), 385–406, esp. 387, he notes that there was a system of initiation and education for girls, though it was not so structured as the boys' agoge. See also A. Brelich, *Paides e Parthenoi*, vol. 1 (Rome, 1969), 157–59.

111. Stephen V. Tracy and C. Habicht, "New and Old Panathenaic Victor Lists," *Hesperia* 60 (1991), 187–236, esp. 205, 213, 214.

Athletic competitions for respectable women were held under state supervision.[112] A fragmentary inscription of the second century C.E. indicates that the magistrates (*biduoi*) in charge of ephebic competitions also supervised twelve "female followers of Dionysus."[113] These Dionysiades were virgins; eleven of them ran a foot race at a festival of Dionysus.[114] Another inscription from a statue honors a woman racer who won a victory.[115] These games were founded under either Tiberius or Claudius.

Wrestling for women in Sparta had a long pedigree. Furthermore, since nudity often results from wrestling and other athletic endeavors, the performances of female wrestling were doubtless piquant (see fig. 3). In the days of Nero, a Spartan woman engaged in a wrestling match at Rome with a Roman senator, M. Palfurius Sura.[116] Athenaeus (13.602e) reports that Spartans displayed their girls to their guests unclothed. Athenaeus may well be exaggerating: the Greek tendency to understand the world in polarized categories may have prompted Athenaeus to interpret some nudity for specific acceptable purposes (as Plutarch understood it) into gratuitous indecent display. On the other hand, if this report is true, the practice may be understood as a shocking spectacle, in keeping with the tastes of the Roman world.

Social Construction of Sexual Behavior

Plutarch (*Lyc.* 18.4) reports that erotic ties between older and younger women were common. In Alcman, *Parthenion* 1.73, the girls mention visiting Aenesimbrota, who is probably a purveyor of love magic. She would provide drugs, spells, and magical devices to attract the object of desire.[117] Hagnon of Tarsus, an Academic philosopher of the second century B.C.E., states that before marriage it was customary for Spartans to associate with virgin girls as with *paidika* (young boyfriends).[118]

---

112. See P. A. Cartledge and A. J. S. Spawforth, *Hellenistic and Roman Sparta: A Tale of two Cities* (London, 1989), 205–6.

113. *SEG* XI (1954), no. 610, 1–4, and Paus. 3.11.2.

114. Hesych. s.v. Dionysiades, D1888 (Latte); Paus. 3.13.7 speaks of eleven (not twelve) runners. Kennell, *Gymnasium of Virtue*, 46–47, considers these events a legacy from an earlier girls' agoge.

115. *SEG* XI.830. Her name is indecipherable, but the editor suggests that she is Panthalida, daughter of Agis, attested in *IG* V.1.588, 2–3.

116. Schol. Juvenal 4.53: Moretti, *IAG*, p. 168 for the date.

117. See further M. L. West, "Alcmanica," *CQ* 15 (1965), 188–202, esp. 199–200.

118. In Athen. 13.602d–e: see further C. Calame, *Les chœurs de jeunes filles en Grèce archaïque*, vol. 1 (Rome, 1977), 434, and Jan Bremmer, "An Enigmatic Indo-European Rite: Paederasty," *Arethusa* 13 (1980), 279–98, esp. 292–93. K. Dover, *Greek Homosexuality* (London, 1978), 188, interprets the passage as anal penetration of girls by boys, and states that "the original sexual meaning of 'lakonize' will have been 'have anal intercourse,' irrespective of the sex of the person penetrated."

Weaving

According to Xenophon (*Lac. Pol.* 1.1), Lycurgus wisely decided that the labor of slave women (*doulai*) sufficed to weave the clothing that the Spartans required. Nevertheless, doulai were not the only women in Sparta who knew how to weave. To make the point about the difference between Spartans and other Greek women, Xenophon and Plato (*Laws* 806A) exaggerate the Spartans' liberation from weaving. Furthermore, weaving served as a "catch-all" term for the domestic work usually performed by Greek women. In fact, Spartan women could weave and supervise their slaves' work, but they were not encouraged to weave endlessly, nor did their reputation depend upon it. One of the *Sayings* attributed to Spartan women underlines this ethnic distinction:

> When an Ionian woman was proud of something she had woven (which was very valuable), a Spartan woman showed off her four well-behaved sons and said these should be the work of a noble and honorable woman, and she should swell with pride and boast of them. (Plut. *Sayings of Spartan Women* 241.9)

Although servile women did the routine weaving, freeborn women wove for ritual purposes. Paraphernalia for weaving and hundreds of plaques depicting textiles were discovered at the shrine of Artemis Orthia.[119] These offerings date from the archaic to the Hellenistic period, but most are probably sixth to fifth century.[120] Literary testimony conplements the archaeological finds. Ten young girls in a choir for whom Alcman wrote a *Partheneion* (1.61) sing about bringing a cloak to Artemis Orthia. Presumably, like the Arrephoroi who began the weaving for the peplos of Athena at Athens, they had participated in making the cloak.[121] Pausanias (3.16.2) reports that every year women wove a chiton for Apollo of Amyclae in a room designated as the chitona.[122]

---

119. Miniature weaving implements: Dawkins, *AO*, pl. 185, nos. 14, 15, 17, 23, 24; usable implements: Dawkins, *AO*, 242, pl. 174, no. 2; plaques: Dawkins, *AO*, pl. 181, 27, 28; pl. 185, nos. 12, 21, 22; pl. 186, nos. 20, 21.

120. On these votives, see most recently Lin Foxhall, "The Women of Artemis Orthia, Sparta" (paper delivered at the annual meeting of the American Philological Association, Dec. 28, 1998; abstract published in *American Philological Association 130th Annual Meeting: Abstracts*, 83).

121. Similarly, every four years sixteen women from Elis wove a peplos for the xoanon of Hera and organized the Heraion games: Paus. 5.16.2, 6.24.10. The weaving of Hera's peplos may have begun only ca. 575 simultaneously with the introduction of the Sixteen Women at the Heraia: Paus. 1.16.5, John Magruder Mansfield, "The Robe of Athena and the Panathenaic *Peplos*," (Ph.D. diss., University of California, Berkeley, 1985), 470.

122. Whether this practice was begun in the archaic period is doubtful, for statues of Apollo traditionally were nude. See further Irene Bald Romano, "Early Greek Cult Images" (Ph.D. diss., University of Pennsylvania, 1980), 103, who doubts that a garment appropriate for a 30 cubit column-shaped statue of Apollo was woven annually. On clothing for statues, see Frazer, *Pausanias's Description of Greece*, vol. 2, 574–75, and see now Irene Bald Romano, "Early Greek Cult Images and

The *xoanon* (wooden image) of Artemis Orthia wore a *polos* (head-dress representing the celestial sphere) and a woven dress reaching to the feet.[123] The figure must have been small and light, for the priestess held it during the whipping ceremony (Paus. 34.16.10).[124] Therefore annual or quadrennial weaving of garments for the divinities could not have been a great burden to Spartan women. Furthermore, weaving garments need not have entailed the obligation to prepare the wool and the performance of messy, tedious tasks including washing, beating, combing, carding, dyeing, and spinning. Rather, like Helen who spun with her golden distaff[125] (one suspects not very energetically), Spartan women were not required to expend much labor in producing clothing for their cult images. At least ten girls are named in Alcman, *Partheneion* 1, and they wove only one cloak. Clothing the xoanon of Artemis was like dressing a large doll.

In contrast, Athenian women not only wove for the *oikos* (family, household, estate), but also were responsible for weaving a peplos for Athena annually. The wooden image was probably less than lifesize, and the cloth depicted on the Panathenaic frieze around 2.0–2.5 × 1.8–2.3 meters.[126] Every four years, however, they had much more work. The peplos woven by Athenian women for the greater Panathenaea was an elaborate tapestry, so large that it was fixed as a sail on the Panathenaic ship.[127] This peplos was probably about 4–8 meters square,[128] and all who attended the festival could admire or criticize the result.

Since Spartan clothing was less elaborate than Athenian, the women who wove in Sparta had less to do. Young boys wore a chiton or went nude: they were allocated only one cloak to wear throughout the year, and did not sleep on mattresses, but on straw which they gathered themselves (Plut. *Lyc.*16.6–7). Adult men wore a short red cloak and were buried with only such a cloak and a chaplet of olive leaves.[129] Since the cloaks constituted a kind of uniform, they may have been distributed by the state. Women's peploi were short and scanty: for racing they wore the *chiton exomis* (tunic with one sleeve) which barely reached the knee (Paus. 5.16.3). Unlike Athenian women, they did not normally wear many

Cult Practices," in *Early Greek Cult Practice: Proceedings of the Fifth International Symposium at the Swedish Institute at Athens, 26–29 June, 1986*, ed. R. Hägg, N. Marinatos, and G. C. Nordquist (Stockholm, 1988), 127–34.

123. An ivory plaque with an image of the cult figure displays incised textile patterns. For the plaque: Dawkins, *AO*, 208, and pl. 96, no. 2. For the weaving: Romano, "Early Greek Cult Images," 123, contra P. Ziehen, "Sparta," *RE* 18.3 (1949), col. 1466.

124. The cult statue of Hera was probably seven feet tall, or less: Romano, "Early Greek Cult Images," 441. Pausanias (5.17.1) refers to it as an *agalma* (image).

125. Homer, *Od.* 4.131–35. Theoc. (18.33–34) describes Helen as an accomplished spinner and weaver.

126. Mansfield, "The Robe of Athena," 6, 23 n. 14.

127. Mansfield, "The Robe of Athena," 58, 89 n. 26.

128. Mansfield, "The Robe of Athena," 58.

129. Aristoph. *Lys.* 1138–41, Xen. *Lac. Pol.* 11.3, Plut. *Lyc.* 27.2–4, *Mor.* 238d, Ael. *VH* 6.6.

layers of clothing. They probably wore whatever the weather required (see chap. 2, fig. 4, Vix crater, and Conclusion). Such dress did not command attention; but their skimpy attire did. When the women were preparing to dig a trench against the attack of Pyrrhus, some wore outer dresses (*himatia*) over their tunics, and some wore only their tunics (*monochitones*, Plut. *Pyrrh.* 27.3). Dionysius, the clever tyrant of Syracuse, assumed that expensive Sicilian chitons for Lysander's daughters would constitute an irresistible bribe. At first Lysander refused to accept them, but later on, when a Sicilian ambassador showed him two dresses and asked him to choose one for a daughter, Lysander took both, for he had more than one daughter (Plut. *Lys.* 2.5). Doubtless the increase in visible private property that took place after the Peloponnesian War also affected women's wardrobes.

The brief chiton exomis worn by Spartan women caused as much consternation to other Greeks as the miniskirt. Artemis, when she was portrayed as a huntress, and the Amazons were the only other females known to the Greeks who wore such short skirts, and they were visible only in art, not in real life. Because Spartan women were in fine physical condition, their skimpy clothing must have been flattering. In contrast, respectable Athenian women exercised only by doing housework, mostly indoors or in the courtyard of their house. The visual arts portray Athenian women as heavily covered in many layers of cloth, with skirts reaching to the ankles. Even little girls wore long dresses. In the sumptuary laws attributed to Solon, it was deemed necessary to specify limits to the amount of clothing Athenian women might include in their dowries, or wear at funerals, or use to wrap the dead.[130]

Weaving was the only activity of women that most Greeks recognized as productive.[131] In prosperous households, more fabrics than could ever be used by the household were woven. These were stored up, to be given as gifts or part of dowries, or, if times were hard, to be sold or traded at the marketplace. At Sparta, neither women nor men engaged in activities that produced objects for use or sale. In fact, such work was prohibited.

Not until the Hellenistic period were the names of the Athenian women who had woven the peplos for Athena announced. In contrast, like Greek men who had always sought fame, Spartan women had a consciousness of themselves that is conveyed to the observer. Their pride shines forth in Alcman's poetry, in Plutarch's *Sayings of Spartan Women*, and in the dedications of victors' images at the sanctuary of Hera at Elis and of Zeus at Olympia. As girls and women, Spartans left their mark on the historical record in pan-Hellenic contexts.

130. Plut. *Sol.* 20.8, 21.4–5, and see further Pomeroy, *Families*, 101.

131. On women and weaving see further Pomeroy, *Xenophon: Oeconomicus*, 60–64, 270, 274, 284, 297, 307.

2

BECOMING A WIFE

And I was thinking that Sparta among cities of few citizens proved to be the most powerful and famous, and I wondered in what way this had come about. When, however, I thought about the Spartans' way of life, I no longer wondered. I admired Lycurgus, their lawgiver, whose laws they were fortunate in obeying, and I think him extremely wise. He did not imitate other cities, but thinking the opposite of most, he made his country outstandingly fortunate.

Now, to begin at the beginning, I will discuss the breeding of children. In other states the girls who are destined to become mothers and are brought up in the approved manner live on the most modest amount of food, with the smallest possible allowance of delicacies. They are either totally deprived of wine, or drink it mixed with water. The rest of the Greeks think it right that their girls keep silent and work wool, like sedentary craftsmen. How, then, ought we expect that women brought up in such a way will bear a sturdy child?

But Lycurgus thought that slave women were able to supply clothing, and he believed motherhood was most important for freeborn women. Therefore first he ordered the female sex to exercise no less than the male; moreover, he created competitions in racing and trials of strength for women as for men, believing that healthier children will be born if both parents are strong.

(Xenophon, *Lac. Pol.* 1.1–4)

Eugenics: Nature in Alliance with Nurture

In highlighting women in the following discussion of marriage and reproduction, we are not engaging in affirmative action or compensatory scholarship. Rather, we are following the best ancient precedent: the intention of the revered founder of the Spartan way of life. Xenophon points out that Lycurgus devoted a great deal of attention to motherhood and marital intercourse. He also observes that Spartans were the only Greek girls who were generously fed, draws attention to the physical training for females that was unique in Greece, and supplies as the motivation the belief that strong parents produce stronger children. (According to Aristotle and other medical writers, acquired characteristics, as well as those with which a person was born, were widely thought to be inherited.)[1] Xenophon's account of the raising of girls makes it clear that the "Lycurgan" system—insofar as it was concerned with health and eugenics—was not merely a Hellenistic or Plutarchean invention.

Girls and boys exercised nude. Not only nude youths but young women as well may have participated in the Gymnopaidia ("Festival of Nude Youths"). Plutarch (*Lyc.* 15.1) writes that confirmed bachelors were dishonored: they were excluded from viewing the young women and men exercising in the nude (*tais gymnopaidiais*).[2] Perhaps the bachelors preferred nonproductive sexual liaisons with boys to the exclusion of reproductive sex with females and this prohibition of viewing, which meant that they were barred from attending a major festival, was the state's punishment. In any case, while engaged in these activities, nubile Spartans had an opportunity to view the bodies of potential spouses.[3] Although Plutarch (*Lyc.* 4.4) argues that women's nudity was not intentionally erotic, it would have been difficult to prevent some viewers from becoming stimulated.[4] Sometimes, women did parade nude in order to whet the appetite of unmarried men for marriage.[5] Doubtless they attracted other women as well (see chap. 1).

Infanticide

Patriarchy exercises authority over men as well as women, and in Sparta apparently even more over men. Males, from the moment of birth, were examined, tested, and evaluated according to eugenic standards by older men:

> The father did not decide whether to raise a baby; rather he took it and carried it to some place called Lesche where the elders of the tribes sat and examined

1. See further Sarah B. Pomeroy, *Families in Classical and Hellenistic Greece* (Oxford, 1997), 96–99.

2. On the ambiguity of this word, see Appendix n. 77.

3. See further David Leitao, "The Exclusion of *Agamoi* from the *Gymnopaidiai* and the Politics of Viewing in Sparta" (paper delivered at the annual meeting of the American Philological Association, Dec. 29, 1997; Abstract published in *American Philological Association 129th Annual Meeting: Abstracts*, 171). Contra Michael Pettersson, *Cults of Apollo at Sparta: The Hyakinthia, the Gymnopaidiai, and the Karneia* (Stockholm, 1992), 76. See Preface, above.

4. Compare a male reaction to the first sculpture of the nude Aphrodite at Cnidus: according to Pliny, *HN* 36.20, a man embraced the statue and ejaculated on it.

5. Plut. *Lyc.* 15.1. Athen. 13.566e exaggerates the erotic or leering aspect when he reports that Spartans strip virgins before strangers.

the infant, and if it was well built and sturdy, they ordered the father to rear it, and assigned it one of the nine thousand lots of land; but if it was ill born and misshapen, they sent it to the so-called "Apothetae," a chasm-like place at the foot of Mount Taygetus, thinking that any baby which was not naturally created at the very beginning to be healthy and strong was of no good either to itself or the state. Therefore the women used to bathe their newborn babies not with water but with wine, thus making a sort of test of their constitutions. For it is said that epileptic and sickly infants are thrown into convulsions by the unmixed wine and lose their senses, while the healthy ones are rather hardened by it, and given a strong constitution. (Plut. *Lyc.* 16.1–2)

Plutarch is our only source for the practice of systematic male infanticide. As we have seen, in the sentence immediately following his statement on infanticide he describes the allocation of a *kleros* (lot of land) to every infant.[6] The Greek words Plutarch uses for infant (*to gennethen, to paidarion, ta brephe)* are neuter; even the pronoun *autôi* can be understood as neuter or masculine. On the basis of this passage alone, it could be deduced that newborn girls were subjected to exposure and infanticide and were given kleroi. However, other passages in Plutarch (*Lyc.* 8.4) and Xenophon (*Lac. Pol.* 9.5) make it clear that girls were supported by the kleroi of their male kinsmen (see below). Pierre Roussel[7] sees a connection between infanticide and allocation of a kleros and argues that the state was involved with infanticide exclusively in connection with males. Considering their concern over the decline in size of the population, it is likely that the magistrates understood that the number of Spartiates was directly related to the number of child-bearers (not inseminators) and therefore did not cull female infants.

Male infanticide was wasteful only of the mother's nine-month investment. By eliminating unpromising male infants, the community was not obliged to pay the costs of rearing a boy who would not, as Plutarch (*Lyc.* 16.1–2) puts it, be of use to himself or to the state. The decision ostensibly satisfied eugenic considerations. The infant who failed the initial inspection was eliminated before he could produce children who were likely to inherit his undesirable characteristics.

A question that is often raised is whether at Sparta girls as well as boys,were vulnerable to infanticide. Nowadays few scholars doubt that girls were regularly exposed in Athens.[8] The need to furnish a dowry at, or even before, puberty, and the general devaluation of women, were probably among the reasons why a

6. On Hodkinson's criticism of this passage, see chap. 4 nn. 61–62 and Appendix n. 90.

7. "L'exposition des enfants à Sparte," *REA* 45 (1943), 5–17, in agreement with G. Glotz, "L'exposition des enfants," *Études sociales et juridiques sur l'antiquité grecque* (Paris, 1906), 187–227, esp. 188, 192, 217–19, who mentioned only sons.

8. See further Sarah B. Pomeroy, *Goddesses, Whores, Wives, and Slaves: Women in Classical Antiquity* (New York, 1995), 69–70, 164–65, 227, etc., and *Families,* 118, 120–21, etc. Mark Golden, in "Demography and The Exposure of Girls at Athens," *Phoenix* 35 (1981), 316–31, argues that the female infanticide rate was as high as 20 percent.

father might choose not to raise a daughter. Was Sparta the antithesis of Athens? Did Sparta expose all boys who did not appear to have the potential for becoming excellent soldiers, but raise all girls—except, one would suspect, those with obvious and debilitating physical abnormalities?[9]

We may deduce from Plutarch's description that at birth girls were simply handed over to the women. This conclusion is *ex silentio*; on the other hand, it can be argued that Plutarch was unusually scrupulous among Greek authors in remembering to mention women where it was appropriate. It seems that girls were not subjected to official scrutiny as were Spartan boys, nor, apparently, did fathers make a determination about rearing or exposing them, as they did in Athens. The women would test the babies for epilepsy or sickliness by seeing if a bath in undiluted wine would throw them into convulsions. Plutarch does not state whether the immersion ordeal was part of the official evaluation process, nor does he indicate the fate of the infants, presumably both male and female, who failed the wine-immersion test. He does not tell us whether the women took any action in the case of infants who had failed the test, but if they did not, then what was the point? If the decision to expose apparent weaklings was up to the women, they would have exercised a power usually reserved for men in the Greco-Roman world.

There probably was change over time, with private citizens taking upon themselves the right to judge the male infant's viability that had previously been a monopoly of the community.[10] Such changes were correlated with the right to dower and to alienate and bequeath property. The individual father's decision may have followed the verdict of the tribal elders, or the former supplanted the latter totally. At any rate, there is no indication of systematic female infanticide or neglect of girls at Sparta, nor is there any indirect evidence, such as skewed sex ratios. It seems likely that because in Sparta there was no money and women could own land, they could more easily be given a dowry.[11] At Athens, where women could not own land, a father would have to furnish cash or movables, and this obligation might well be a deterrent to rearing girls.

Eugenic principles, such as existed in that era, underlie much of Spartan demographic engineering. The Spartans were celebrated for breeding fine hounds and racehorses, so it is not surprising to see them transfer these notions to human beings. By eliminating weak male infants, they tried to give natural evolution a boost, and through the subsequent rigorous training of boys, they

9. Cf. Conclusion, below, on "ugly" daughters. Daniel Ogden, "Crooked Speech: The Genesis of the Spartan Rhetra," *JHS* 14 (1994), 85–102, esp. 91–98, follows M. Delcourt, *Stérilités mystérieuses et naissances maléfiques dans l'antiquité classique* (Liège, 1938), in stressing the exposure of infants with marks of divine disfavor such as clubfeet.

10. Roussel, "L'exposition des enfants à Sparte," 17, alludes to such changes, though he is unable to determine exactly when they occurred.

11. See further Pomeroy, *Families*, 55.

assured the survival of the fittest and future reproduction by them. A mistake might be made, and a man might prove to be a coward. Such tremblers were most likely to be younger men facing their first real conflict, rather than hardened veterans. Anecdotes about Spartan mothers show that they are concerned lest their sons prove to be cowards (see chap. 3). In any case, cowards did not reproduce, for they were socially ostracized, and neither they nor their sisters (presumably young and not married) could find spouses (Xen. *Lac. Pol.* 9.5). Eugenic motivations may also be detected in the choices made in wife-sharing or husband-doubling arrangements (see below). Plutarch (*Lyc.* 15.7) agrees with Xenophon that a man could ask a husband if he might plant his seed in a wife who had already produced children, but he also attributes the initiative to the husband. For example an elderly man with a young wife might offer her a handsome, noble young man, and then adopt the children born of this union (Plut. *Lyc.* 15.12). Daniel Ogden has speculated that Spartans believed that in the process of wife-lending, male sperm could mingle and produce offspring who were thought to have descended from two male parents.[12] Though the male contribution to the embryo was usually thought to dominate, it is also necessary to pay sufficient attention to the female contribution. The rejection of cowards' sisters and of some wives in favor of married women who were *euteknos* ("blessed with good children") and *gennaia* ("well born") reveals a belief that the mother was more than merely a fertile field for the father's seed, and that each woman continued to make her own particular contribution to the offspring. Indeed, in Plutarch's *Sayings of Spartan Women* (e.g., 240e, 241d), the mothers take all the credit for the way their sons turn out. Of course this is an exaggeration that results from the author's effort to prove that Sparta was very different in this respect from other Greek cities where mothers had little to do with the rearing of sons after the age of seven. Xenophon (*Lac. Pol.* 6.2) reports that at Sparta fathers were involved in their children's upbringing. Nevertheless, Plutarch's view on the strong influence of mothers is corroborated by other sources (see chap. 3).

Husband-Doubling, Wife-Sharing

Sarah Blaffer Hrdy has questioned the assumption of anthropologists that women prefer monogamy when raising the human infant, who is helpless for a long period, while men prefer polygamy in order to increase the possibility of creating offspring and perpetuating their own genetic legacy.[13] Hrdy argues persuasively that polyandry can be beneficial to mothers, for it increases the number

12. Daniel Ogden, *Greek Bastardy* (Oxford, 1996), 230, 234–35. Cf. Plut. *Cat. Min.* 25 on Cato's sharing his wife Marcia with Hortensius for the purpose of bearing children. The arrangement was a result of the profound friendship between the two men.

13. "The Optimal Number of Fathers: Evolution, Demography, and History in the Shaping of Female Mate Preferences," *Annals of the New York Academy of Sciences* 907 (2000), 75–96.

of possible fathers who will help with the care of infants and thus perpetuate the mother's genetic legacy. The presence of more than one father who believes that a child may be his own is a kind of assurance of help for mother and infant. Multiple fathers increase the possibility of survival and wellbeing of offspring.[14] The shared mother thus forges alliances between half siblings, more so than the father whose role both the primary sources and secondary scholarship has acknowledged. The concept of "partible paternity" which Ogden proposed in terms of benefits to the husband and the male lover or *genitor* (i.e., biological father) needs to be reexamined from the perspective of benefits to mother and child. Partible paternity was certainly useful in a society like Sparta, where male mortality and the absence rate of men from the home were relatively high and women were seldom at physical or economic risk. That Spartiates reproduce was certainly a goal of the community. That they treat all children as though they were their own was also an explicit goal (Xen. *Lac. Pol.* 2.10, Plut. *Lyc.* 17.1). That two men treat a child as though it belonged to each of them was certainly a step in this direction.

In most patriarchal and patrilineal states in antiquity, husbands enjoyed exclusive access to the reproductive potential of wives, using legal remedies or even violence to exclude intruders. At Sparta, the authoritarian patriarchy impinged upon the husband's monopoly of sexual access to his wife. Not only were the Spartan man's rights as a husband less than those of husbands elsewhere in Greece, but his rights as a father were less. As we have mentioned above, the state also usurped the father's right to determine whether his son was to be reared.

Primary sources generally view reproduction from the father's perspective. In a typical nineteenth-century attempt to interpret the development of marriage and society in prehistory, Engels painted a picture of the introduction of strict sexual restraints on women coinciding with the development of private property and the father's wish to know for certain that he was both *pater* (i.e., legally father and husband of the child's mother) and genitor of his heir.[15] Engels ranked the "pairing marriage" that he found at Sparta as more archaic than marriage in Homeric times, but he believed that Spartan marriage customs allowed greater freedom to women.

Darwin, who wrote at about the same time as Engels, at least was largely correct in his views, but there is no doubt that he was influenced by Victorian assumptions about male and female sexuality.[16] Darwin asserted that "the female

---

14. See S. Beckerman, R. Lizarralde, et al., "The Bari Partible Paternity Project: Preliminary Results," *Current Anthropology* 39, 1 (1998), 164–67, esp. 166, and Sarah Blaffer Hrdy, *Mother Nature* (New York, 1999), 246–49.

15. F. Engels, *The Origin of the Family, Private Property, and the State* (1884), with introd. by Eleanor Burke Leacock (New York, 1972), 125–28.

16. See Sarah Blaffer Hrdy, "Raising Darwin's Consciousness," *Human Nature* 8.1 (1997), 1–49, esp. 6–9.

is less eager (to copulate) than the male . . . and may often be seen endeavoring for a long time to escape from the male."[17] Scholars of Greek demography and society have long been influenced by Darwinian theories about the promiscuous human male and the coy female whose behaviors were considered advantageous for human evolution.[18] Xenophon (*Lac. Pol.* 1.9) spelled out some but not all the benefits of having, in effect, two husbands when he wrote: "for the wives want to get possession of two oikoi, and the husbands want to get brothers for their sons." Plutarch's report mentions the benefits to the husband of impregnation of his wife by a vigorous lover, but the modern feminist scholar can extend the concept to the wife. Surely she, too, benefited both genetically and perceptibly from producing strong children. Her investment in nine months of pregnancy would not be wasted by a decision of male elders to toss the offspring off Taygetus. If she was an heiress, she would sooner fulfill her obligation to produce an heir for her father. Because Greek gynecologists were uncertain about the period of gestation, it would be easy to attribute paternity to more than one father.[19]

Marriage

Spartans were reputed to have chosen their spouses by several systems, some similar to those practiced in other poleis, others unique. The former were based on the oikos system and the goal was the perpetuation and prosperity of the individual family; the latter evolved from the communal ideal of equality and the goal was the production of children for the good of the state.[20] In the former system, personal inclinations and ambitions determined the choice of a spouse; in the latter system the state provided incentives for marriage. Women were active players in both systems.

Xenophon's description shows that in his day the two systems overlapped. Although there was an oikos system in place, the welfare of society was fostered by means of what is commonly referred to by scholars as 'wife-sharing' for reproductive purposes. Although it is not always obvious that Xenophon is reporting an entirely logical system, it is apparent from his language that the wife is an

---

17. *The Descent of Man* (London, 1871, repr. Princeton, 1974), 273.

18. See, e.g., Paul Cartledge, "Spartan Wives: Liberation or Licence?" *CQ* 31 (1981), 84–105, esp. 105: "the modern feminist is unlikely to be over-impressed by the way in which Spartan women . . . were 'seized' and 'had' as wives in the domicile of their husbands, who could 'lend' them for extra-marital procreation; finally, and perhaps least of all, by the overriding emphasis placed on their child-bearing potential and maternal roles by men who monopolized the political direction of a peculiarly masculine society." On Cartledge's place in the historiography of Spartan women, see Appendix, below.

19. See, on Timaea, chap. 4, and Ann Ellis Hanson, "The Eight-Months' Child and the Etiquette of Birth," *Bulletin of the History of Medicine* 61 (1987), 589–602, esp. 589–92, 596.

20. Pomeroy, *Families*, 48–50, 54–56, 59–62.

active participant in the arrangement whereby she produces children for a partner in addition to her husband. This practice should therefore be called "husband-doubling" or "male-partner duplication" or "nonexclusive monogamy," or, at any rate, some term that does not suggest passivity on the wife's part:[21]

> He [Lycurgus] saw, too, that during the time immediately following marriage, it was usual elsewhere for husbands to have unlimited intercourse with wives. He decreed the opposite of this: for he ruled that the husband should be embarrassed to be seen visiting his wife or leaving her. Thus the desire for intercourse was more fervent in both of them, and if there should be a child, it would be more sturdy than if they were satiated with one another. In addition to this, he took away from men the right to take a wife whenever they wanted to, and ordered that they marry in their prime, believing that this too was conducive to the production of fine children. If, however, it happened that an old man had a young wife—seeing that men of that age guard their wives—he thought the opposite. He required the elderly husband to bring in some man whose body and spirit he admired, in order to beget children. On the other hand, in case a man did not want to have intercourse with his wife[22] but wanted children of whom he could be proud, he made it legal for him to choose a woman who was the mother of a fine family and well born, and if he persuaded her husband, he produced children with her. Many such arrangements developed. For the wives want to get possession of two oikoi, and the husbands want to get brothers for their sons who will share their lineage and power, but claim no part of the property. Thus in regard to the breeding of children he thought the opposite to those of other states. And anyone who wishes to may see whether it turned out that the men in Sparta are distinctive in their size and strength. (Xen. *Lac. Pol.* 1.5–10)

Plutarch also describes marriage customs appropriate for a utopian society in which reproduction is the primary goal of marriage and the economic aspects of the private oikos are deemphasized in favor of the common good. Though he reiterates much of Xenophon's report on husband-doubling, in Xenophon the child born of extramarital intercourse would have no claim on the estate of the

---

21. Thus Bella Zweig, "The Only Women Who Give Birth to Men: A Gynocentric, Cross-Cultural View of Women in Ancient Sparta," in *Woman's Power, Man's Game: Essays on Classical Antiquity in Honor of Joy K. King,* ed. Mary DeForest (Wauconda, Il., 1993), 32–53. Cartledge, "Spartan Wives: Liberation or Licence?" 103, 105, and Cynthia B. Patterson, *The Family in Greek History* (Cambridge, Mass., 1998), 73, 77–78, take cognizance only of the first part of Xenophon's report on husband-doubling (to 1.8), thus suppressing the second part stating that the women want to control two oikoi. Both emphasize "lending" the wife, rather than husband-doubling. In this way, the wrong impression is given that Spartan women are merely passed around between men to be used as baby-making devices.

22. For this translation, see n. 38 below.

biological mother's husband.[23] It appears that the Spartans were not concerned with the legal issue of illegitimate birth: rather, arrangements between consenting males, with the practical consent of the woman involved, were valid in assigning paternity. Children belonged to the oikos of the father and therefore the biological mother would have no legal claim on the newborn, except after adoption. Plutarch introduces the new idea that the biological mother and her husband might adopt the child born from extramarital intercourse, and then, of course, the child would inherit from them:

> There were also these incentives to marry. I mean the processions of girls, and the nudity, and the competitions in view of the young men, who were attracted by a compulsion not of an intellectual type, but (as Plato says)[24] a sexual one. In addition he [Lycurgus] decreed that those who did not marry would lose a civic right, for they were excluded from the spectacle of the Gymnopaidiai ["Nude Youth"] ....
>
> They used to marry by capture, not when the women were small or immature, but when they were in their prime and fully ripe for it. The so-called "bridesmaid" took the captured girl. She shaved her head to the scalp, then dressed her in a man's cloak and sandals, and laid her down alone on a mattress in the dark. The bridegroom, who was not drunk and thus not impotent, but was sober as always, having dined with his mess group, then would slip in, untie her belt, lift her, and carry her to the bed. After spending only a short time with her, he would depart discreetly so as to sleep wherever he usually did with the other young men. And he continued to do this thereafter. While spending the days with his contemporaries, and going to sleep with them, he would cautiously visit his bride in secret, embarrassed and fearful in case someone in the house might notice him. His bride at the same time was scheming and helping to plan how they might meet each other unobserved at a suitable time. They did this not just for a short period, but for long enough that some might even have children before they saw their own wives in the day. Such intercourse was not only an exercise in self-control and moderation, but also meant that partners were fertile physically, always fresh for love, and ready for intercourse rather than being satiated and impotent from unlimited sexual activity. Moreover, some lingering spark of desire and affection always remained in both.

23. J. Christien Tregaro, "Les bâtards spartiates," in *Mélanges Pierre Lévêque*, ed. M.-M. Mactoux and E. Geny (Paris, 1993), 33–40, esp. 36, argues that the Xenophon passage means that the child born of the union of a lover ("amant," i.e., genitor) and another man's wife would be a member of the lover's family but have no claim on the lover's property, because such a child was illegitimate. Since Tregaro (35–36) also argues that the lover was a bachelor, it is difficult to understand the lover's motivation in such a scenario. The passage is ambiguous. The common interpretation, however, that Xenophon is referring to the husband's motivation (i.e., getting allies for his children free of charge), seems more sensible. On the domicile of the married woman who has produced children for more than one oikos, see chap. 3.

24. *Rep.* 458D.

After making marriage as modest and orderly as this, he showed equal concern for removing empty womanish jealousy. Banning from marriage every
kind of outrageous and disorderly behavior, he made it honorable for worthy
men to share children and their begetting, and derided people who think that
there can be no combination or sharing of such things, and who resort to mur-
ders and wars. Thus if an older man with a young wife should take a liking to
one of the handsome and virtuous young men and approve of him, he might
well introduce him to her so that he might fill her with noble sperm and then
adopt the child for themselves. On the other hand, a respectable man who
admired someone else's wife noted for her lovely children and her self-control
might persuade the husband that he have intercourse with her—thereby
planting in fruitful soil, and producing fine children who would be linked to
fine ancestors by blood and kinship. (Plut. *Lyc.* 15.1, 3–7)

Some of the bizarre customs Plutarch mentions, such as the cutting of the
bride's hair and the secret marriage, could not have existed simultaneously, certainly not where women regularly spent much time out of doors. Nor are they
mentioned by Xenophon. We can only speculate that they were created over time
like other reforms attributed to Lycurgus, were enforced by the ongoing fear of
oliganthropia (sparse population) after the Second Messenian War (see below) or
even later, and relaxed when the Spartans realized that they were able to win the
Peloponnesian War despite their small population. Another possibility is that
these customs were revived or invented in the Hellenistic period either in connection with the reforms of Agis IV and Cleomenes III or under the influence of
some other utopian philosophical program.

The "capture" of the bride was a ritual enactment of a prearranged
betrothal.[25] The bridesmaid was ready and waiting with the bride's costume. The
bride herself, full grown, would have been able to put up a good struggle if she
truly objected and the groom was really raping her. An abduction rather than a
joyous spectacular wedding ceremony may serve to ward off the jealous evil eye.
The shaving of the head and dressing of the bride as a man (Plut. *Lyc.* 15.8) may
have been part of a rite of passage that signalled her entrance into a new life. As a
maiden she wore her hair long and uncovered, as a wife she wore it short, and
covered by a veil (see fig. 4).[26] In some sense, she was transformed into a youth in

25. See further Judith Evans-Grubbs, "Abduction Marriage in Antiquity: A Law of Constantine
(*CTh* ix.24.1) and Its Social Context," *JRS* 79 (1989), 59–83, esp. 62–63.

26. Heracl. Lembus, *Excerpta Politiarum*, 373.13 (Dilts); Lucian, *Fug.* 27; cf. Xenophon of
Ephesus 5.1.7 (Dalmeyda). Plutarch's explanation is that unmarried girls need to find husbands; the
married women need to keep the men who have them (*Sayings of Spartans*, 232c2). Pliny *HN* 8.164
states that the libido of mares is extinguished once the mane is cut. Horace *Od.* 2.11.24 writes of a
woman with hair tied back in a twist in the Laconian style. This style was simple and appropriate for
women who spent time outdoors. Propertius 3.14.28 associates unscented hair with Spartan women.
See further R. G. M. Nisbet and M. Hubbard, *A Commentary on Horace, Odes, Book II* (Oxford, 1978,
pbk. 1991), 178–79. I am grateful to Nicholas Horsfall for this reference. For elaborate hair-cutting

Fig. 4. Married woman.

Mature woman with head and shoulders covered by a mantle. Rim of the Vix crater. Bronze volute crater from a tomb at Vix. Total height 1.64 m. Châtillon-sur-Seine. Ca. 530. See Appendix n. 102, and most recently C. M. Stibbe, *Das andere Sparta* (Mainz, 1996), fig. 8 and pp. 137, 152, for a date of 570–560.

the agoge. Since participation in the agoge was a prerequisite to becoming a full-fledged citizen, the transvestism may have been symbolic of the bride's inclusion in the citizen body.[27] It may also have been an attempt to ward off the evil eye or the supernatural spirits who were deemed to be jealous of the bride's fortune. The bride's costume may have also helped to ease the husband's transition to procreative sex from the homosexual intercourse to which he was accustomed.[28]

---

protocols marking ages and marital status, see Ellen N. Davis, "Youth and Age in the Thera Frescoes," *AJA* 90 (1986), 399–406.

    27. See further Ephraim David, "Dress in Spartan Society," *AncW* 19 (1989), 3–13, esp. 7, and "Sparta's Social Hair," *Eranos* 90 (1992), 11–21, esp. 17.

    28. See further G. Devereux, "Greek Pseudo-Homosexuality and the 'Greek Miracle'," *Symb. Oslo.* 42 (1968), 69–92, esp. 83–84. On the potential for extramarital intercourse with lower-class women, see chap. 5.

We may ask if there were any analogous comforts for the bride who had been accustomed to female caresses. At Athens, vases depicting weddings often show Erotes ("Cupids"), an attempt to enlist the services of the supernatural in making the bride receptive to the bridegroom. The Athenian bride, however, was much more in need of help than the Spartan. The Athenian was not quite fifteen: she married a stranger nearly twice her age, moved to a new house, and rarely saw her friends and relatives again.[29] The Spartan, in contrast, married a young man close in age. The couple had seen each other nude at festivals and during exercise since childhood. Because the marriage was secret until the bride became pregnant, she did not change domicile for a while (see below). Since the bride and groom were around eighteen and the groom was obliged to live with his army group until the age of thirty, the wife would not have been obliged to adapt to her husband's personality; she raised the children and managed the household for the most part by herself. These responsibilities made it necessary that the bride be mature, not an adolescent like the Athenian bride. Furthermore, the Spartan bride's principal source of companionship and sentimental attachments would continue to be other women. In cases where the bridegroom was older than normal, the scenario would be quite different, for the husband would no longer be sleeping with his army group.

Yet, even in such households the husband probably did not completely dominate the wife. If he was impotent or infertile, he nevertheless was obliged to participate in the social goal of reproduction as well as to consider wife's desires. Xenophon implies that her wishes and ambitions were consulted in cases where she was to be inseminated by a younger man to whom she was not married. Marriage between an older man and a younger woman could be the consequence of the epiklerate.[30] Though Spartan law is not so well understood as Athenian, some form of the epiklerate may have existed, for it appears that when a daughter was the sole survivor and heiress in a family, she was under some obligation to marry a close kinsman of her father, though he might have been elderly. In such cases, nevertheless, the pressure to produce an heir was intense.

Sexuality

There is no reason to assume that the sexuality of Spartan women was repressed or indeed less assertive than that of the men, or, of course, to assume the contrary. If we rely on the judgment of Teiresias, who had been both male and female, women's capacity to enjoy sex was nine times greater than men's. Xenophon and

29. For the Athenian marriage at best, see Xen. *Oec.* 7–10 and Sarah B. Pomeroy, *Xenophon, Oeconomicus: A Social and Political Commentary* (Oxford, 1994), ad loc.

30. Thus E. Karabélias, "L'épiclérat à Sparte," *Studi in onore di Arnaldo Biscardi*, vol. 2 (Milan, 1982), 469–80, esp. 479.

Plutarch speak of desire for intercourse on the part of both spouses, though within the limits of modesty.[31] Plutarch (*Lyc.* 15.1) also refers to flirtatious behavior when the girls parade nude before the bachelors, trying to interest them in marriage. Perhaps this competition for men continued after marriage. Xenophon at first reports the incitement for wife-lending or husband-doubling from the male perspective: "a man could choose a woman who was already mother of a fine family and of high birth." Since the goal of the liaison was only reproduction, it made sense for the potential genitor to choose a mature woman who had already proven her ability to reproduce, rather than a young virgin. Plutarch (*Lyc.* 15.7) agrees with Xenophon, and draws attention to the age and impotence of the husband and the attractiveness and nobility of the lover. Though no ancient source mentions that any woman actively chose her surrogate husband, we suggest that a lively young wife would be able to exert influence on a feeble old husband. Why should a modern scholar assume that women were passive in these arrangements? And why did the attractive man in question choose one woman rather than another? It is not improbable that she solicited his attention. One revered example of a Spartan woman who chose a man younger than her husband is of course Helen. Spartans, because of their respect for tradition, took their mythical exempla seriously, and Helen must have been a major figure in a Spartan woman's thoughts even before marriage (see chap. 6).

In cases where the husband was old, the young man who was allowed to have intercourse with the wife was physically and morally attractive. Though eugenic goals were primary, we need not assume that the wife's experience with her surrogate husband was unpleasant.

The Economics of Marriage

Xenophon depicts the Spartans as careful, if not calculating, in their selection of spouses and family planning. Herodotus (6.57, 71) refers to fathers betrothing daughters and giving them in marriage. Contradicting Herodotus is the report of Hermippus (late third century B.C.E.) that cohorts of nubile men and women found spouses by groping randomly in a dark room, and that the women were without dowries.[32] Likewise, the enactment of the marriage as an abduction suggests a lack of dowry, but does not definitely preclude one. This method of spouse selection reflected the ideal of equality among potential partners. It was a casualty of the manifest advent of private property. The men who were engaged to marry Lysander's daughters attempted to break their engagements when they

---

31. Xen. *Lac. Pol.* 1.5, Plut. *Lyc.* 15.1.4–5; see also Plut. *Advice to the Bride and Groom*, 18.

32. Of course, the nubile men and women were not equally endowed with good looks. On Lysander's bad luck in this selection process, see: Athen. 13.555b–c citing Hermippus = *FGrH* IV.3 1026 F 6 = F. Wehrli, *Die Schule des Aristoteles*, suppl. 1 (Basel, 1974), fr. 87. J.-F. Bommelaer, *Lysandre de Sparte: Histoire et Traditions* (Athens, 1981), 58, finds the anecdote suspect for chronological reasons, unless Lysander married twice. See also chap. 3 n. 18 and Conclusion.

discovered that Lysander was poor. They were fined for marrying badly, for their primary goal was to marry wealthy, rather than virtuous, women.[33] Xenophon does not mention the random selection of spouses, but he does describe husband-doubling, a practice that was unique in the Greek world and doubtless contributed to the racy reputation of Spartan women. This breach of sexual exclusivity was introduced after the rhetra of Epitadeus, which permitted a man to give his house and kleros to whomever he wished while he was alive, or to bequeath them in his will.[34] By the classical period (if not earlier), in addition to the land designated for distribution as kleroi, some was held as private property.[35] It is clear that with more property openly in private hands Spartan men and women had increased incentives to develop heirship strategies. They may have limited the number of their offspring to increase the patrimony and social mobility of their heirs.[36] Wives and husbands evidently shared the same views about family planning and attempted to further the special interests of the oikos within the context of an authoritarian patriarchy.

Sex Ratio and Polyandry

Xenophon (*Lac. Pol.* 1.8), Polybius,[37] Plutarch (*Lyc.* 15.12–13), and Nicolaus of Damascus (*FGrH* 90 F 103Z) refer to polyandry at Sparta. This practice is not necessarily indicative of a paucity of women, which, in turn, could be a symptom of female infanticide. Xenophon (*Lac. Pol.* 1.8) mentions the case of the married man who has no desire to *synoikein* with his own wife, but prefers to produce offspring by a married woman who has already proven her procreative gifts. Some scholars understand *synoikein* as "marry" rather than in its common sense of "cohabit," "live with," or "have intercourse with."[38] The two interpretations, of

---

33. Plut. *Lys.* 30.5. On the traditions concerning Lysander's daughters, see Bommelaer, *Lysandre de Sparte*, 57–58.

34. Cf. Plut. *Agis* 5.2–5. On the rhetra, see Preface n. 11 and chap. 4 nn. 61–62.

35. See further Ephraim David, "The Influx of Money into Sparta at the End of the Fifth Century B.C.," *Scripta Israelica* 5 (1979/80), 30–45, and chap. 4.

36. Thus Thomas J. Figueira, "Population Patterns in Late Archaic and Classical Sparta," *TAPA* 116 (1986), 165–213, esp. 195.

37. Polyb. 12.6b.8. F. W. Walbank, *A Historical Commentary on Polybius*, vol. 2 (Oxford, 1967), 340 ad loc., suggests that fraternal polyandry was an adaptation to the absence of men.

38. Pace Ogden, *Greek Bastardy*, 239, and Tregaro, "Les bâtards spartiates," 35–36, who take *synoikein* as "marry" rather than as "live with" or "have intercourse with." For the latter meaning, see E. C. Marchant, *Xenophon*, vol. 7, *Scripta Minora* (Cambridge, Mass., 1968), 139; F. Ollier, *Le mirage spartiate* (Paris, 1933–43), vol. 1, 379, and *Xénophon: La république des Lacédémoniens* (Lyons, 1934), commentary, 34.8; W. den Boer, *Laconian Studies* (Amsterdam, 1954), 223; and Liana Bogino, "Note sul matrimonio a Sparta," *Sileno* 17 (1991), 221–33, esp. 229. F. W. Sturtz, *Lexicon Xenophonteum* (1801–4, repr. Hildesheim, 1964), vol. 4, 190, s.v. synoikein, gives as a primary translation, "Consuetudinem habere, coire." Only secondarily, citing other scholars, Sturtz gives, "Dicitur autem non de sola tori, sed de tota consuetudine, de matrimonio in universum," thus allowing for the possibility that the

course, overlap: it is a question of emphasis and the writer's usage. Xenophon uses *lambano* of a man who takes a wife, and *synoikein* for "having intercourse with." Furthermore, as we will see, there were other childless women in addition to those whose husbands rejected them (see below). In another variation on this theme, Polybius states that several brothers would share one wife. Fraternal polyandry was also a form of family limitation, for one shared wife could not have produced as many children for the brothers as individual wives might have. When each of these matrimonial experiments began and how long they lasted is unclear. Xenophon's description of husband-doubling postdates the rhetra attributed to Epitadeus, the victory in the Peloponnesian War, and perhaps the disaster at Leuctra—undoubtedly a period in Spartan history of such turbulence as to stimulate radical social change (see Appendix).

Infanticide and Sex Ratio

The answer to the question whether Spartans practiced female infanticide is not the same for all time periods. There is little data and few dates. Certainly by the Hellenistic period, when the Spartan ideal was thoroughly contaminated by alien arrangements and the "Lycurgan" economic system was embattled, and there is plenty of evidence for infanticide in the Greek world,[39] beleaguered and impoverished fathers may have decided to do away with female as well as male infants. The reports of fraternal polyandry in Polybius (12.6b.8), and of husband-doubling in Plutarch (*Lyc.* 15.7, see also Xen. *Lac. Pol.* 1.5–9) and Nicolaus of Damascus (*FGrH* 90 F 103), may actually indicate a scarcity of marriageable women at that time. On the other hand, if these arrangements were also found in the archaic period, that would suggest the simultaneous practice of female infanticide even then. In the light of the changing demographic picture at Sparta, it is interesting that Polybius (12.6b. 8) refers to polyandry as an "ancestral" custom: however, the Spartans instituted many novel social practices in the fourth century and Hellenistic period, for which they gained credence by referring to them as "ancestral" (see Preface).[40] Furthermore, Polybius was not favorably disposed to

---

genitor may have been a man who declined to cohabit, not only with a wife, but with any woman at all (except obviously, in the context being discussed, for the encounter necessary for insemination).

39. Sarah B. Pomeroy, "Infanticide in Hellenistic Greece," in *Images of Women in Antiquity*, ed. A. Cameron and A. Kuhrt (London, 1983), 207–22.

40. Michael Flower, "The Invention of Tradition in Classical and Hellenistic Sparta" (paper delivered at the Celtic Conference in Classics, National University of Ireland, Maynooth, Sept. 7, 2000), suggests that "husband-doubling" was introduced at a time when Spartiates were concerned about their falling population. He suggests that this may have happened towards the end of the fifth century.

Sparta and not averse to attributing customs to the Spartans that his readers would consider barbarous.[41] Some elite families in Hellenistic and Roman Sparta raised as many as three daughters, and in some cases daughters outnumber sons.[42] Women are well represented in these stemmata, owing in part to the fact that these families often resorted to claiming descent through matrilineal succession from Bronze Age heroes and heroines, including Helen and the Dioscuri.[43]

We may speculate that if female infanticide were not common, polyandry would have left some women unmarried. There was, however, so much movement out of the Spartiate class downward that the resultant sex ratio becomes unfathomable. We may also speculate about the possibility of intermarriage between full-blooded Spartan women and members of the various subordinate classes in Laconia, though there is little evidence for such arrangements, with one exception. A story about the founding of Tarentum is worth discussing, though its veracity has been questioned for many reasons.[44] During the archaic period, when the army was in the field for many years and it was uncertain whether the men would ever return safely, the Ephors ("Overseers," elected magistrates) directed that the women have intercourse with helots in order to produce a new crop of children who could replace the men in case they never came home. When the army did return to Sparta, the children born of miscegenation were sent off to found the colony that became known as Tarentum. This episode—if it actually occurred—was exceptional, and clearly an emergency measure. Furthermore, that Greek women would be forced to have intercourse with their social inferiors, who were simultaneously at war with their polis, is difficult to believe, though the eugenics program perhaps was not yet in place.[45] If these liaisons ever occurred, it is no suprise that the Spartans sent the offspring off to a colony. It is also reported that after many Spartans died in the war with the Messenians, they made some helots go to bed with the widows of the dead men so that their lack of manpower would not be apparent. They made these helots citizens.[46] In general, hypogamy

41. See Appendix. For polyandry and multiple sexual partners among barbarian women, see Herod. 1.216; 4.172, 176, 180; 5.6.

42. A. J. S. Spawforth, "Families at Roman Sparta and Epidaurus: Some Prosopographical Notes," *ABSA* 80 (1985), 191–258, esp. 234, 238, for the descendants of Tib. Claudius Eudamus and Claudia Damostheneia. Androtelia had at least four daughters: *SEG* IX.677c (add. et corr.), 2d–1st cent. B.C.E.

43. Spawforth, "Families at Roman Sparta and Epidaurus," 195–96, 219, 221.

44. Polyb. 12.6b5, Strabo 6.3.3 (279–80), etc. The probable source of this anecdote was Ephorus. Irad Malkin, *Myth and Territory in the Spartan Mediterranean* (Cambridge, 1994), esp. 139–42, understands it as aetiological, derived from the fact that the colonists were called "Partheniai."

45. Ogden, *Greek Bastardy*, 242, admits the possibility of procreative unions between Spartan women and helot men, though not in the context of the foundation of Tarentum. But this is highly unlikely for eugenic reasons among others. Acting on the theory of the inheritance of acquired characteristics, helots were bred for docility. A liaison between a Spartan woman and a male helot would not have produced the ideal Spartan; but see chap. 5.

46. Athen. 6.271c quoting Theopompus *Hist.* 32 = *FGrH* 115 F 171.

was not an option for elite Greek women, and there is nothing in the education of Spartan women that prepared them for such a possibility. Polybius' (12.6.5) version of the official insemination program is more credible: the Lacedaemonians sent back to their country men in their prime of life for the purpose of begetting children.

Limiting our discussion to the upper class, unmarried or childless Spartan women include those in the following five categories: the sisters of cowards, whom no man will marry; the wives Xenophon mentions, whose husbands prefer to reproduce by other men's wives; those to whom the state forbids marriage;[47] those like Lysander's daughters, whose lack of wealth does not make them attractive partners, particularly in a period of economic instability for men; and those to whom Cicero refers as refusing to bear children (see chap. 3). It must have taken a great deal of determination and self-will to belong to the latter group in a state that so cherished motherhood.

47. Plut. *Am. narr.* 775d gives one undatable example of the daughters of Alcippus and Damocrita. Their father's enemies had a vote passed forbidding the daughters from marrying. The damning nature of this vote shows that central to the values of marriage and motherhood was the capacity to create alliances between males. The family of Alcippus and Damocrita was prevented from acquiring sons-in-law who would be allies, and, like the families of cowards, it was doomed to extinction.

3

THE CREATION OF MOTHERS

Spartans were the only Greek mothers who were famous in antiquity qua mothers, and who served as paradigms in later periods of history. Xenophon and Plutarch are our main authorities for the exaltation of motherhood. As well-traveled, cosmopolitan reporters, they declare that nowhere else in the Greek world did the state lavish such attention on women.

The oikos is usually described as a unit for reproduction and production.[1] At Athens, the wives of citizens were distinguished from other women as "mothers of legitimate children and faithful housekeepers" (Ps.-Demos. 59.122). Because before the fourth century the economy at Sparta more than elsewhere in the Greek world depended upon the labor of those who were not free, not citizens, and not household residents, the "production" aspect of the oikos was minimal. Textual and archaeological evidence indicates that before the Roman period, Spartan houses were insubstantial: they need not have been used for long-term storage, since helots were required to supply agricultural products annually. Therefore housekeeping was not a time-consuming job for women, though, as we have demonstrated (see chap. 1), not only did they supervise domestics, but they also could weave and took pride in their skills. Nevertheless, there is no evidence that their textiles were exchanged or sold, or that the women were obliged to weave in order to provide clothing for their families. Wives were, above all, mothers. For these reasons, in this chapter we treat the Spartan family principally as a locus for reproduction and confine our examination of the economy of the oikos to inheritance and dowry and to the relationship of reproduction to economic concerns.

1. On the oikos and family, see further Sarah B. Pomeroy, *Xenophon, Oeconomicus: A Social and Historical Commentary* (Oxford, 1994), passim, and *Families in Classical and Hellenistic Greece* (Oxford, 1997), passim. I presented this material first in "The Spartan Family" (paper delivered at the University of Cambridge, Oct. 13, 1998), and much of the discussion of reproduction in "Spartan Wives and their Strategies" (paper delivered at the Celtic Conference in Classics, National University of Ireland, Maynooth, Sept. 7, 2000).

As a result of the emphasis on reproduction, girls were raised to become the type of mothers Sparta needed (see chap. 1). A mother had to be healthy, properly educated, and well versed in Spartan values. In the absence of fathers during children's formative years, women, including mothers, older sisters, and nurses, were the principal, if not the sole, influence in the creation of Spartan citizens.[2] Sparta recognized the services of mothers by permitting only women who had died in childbirth (like men who had died in battle) to be commemorated by grave markers.[3] Religion, especially the cults of Apollo and of Artemis (with whom Eileithyia was associated), provided a spiritual foundation for politically approved family values (see chap. 6).

Creating Childbearers

The mistress of the house supervised the conversion of raw food into edibles. The relationship between mother and daughter was strong.[4] Since the father dined with his syssition, the mother would have been in charge of food distribution in the home. I suspect that mothers were responsible for seeing to it that girls were well fed, though of course, like other Greek women in comfortable circumstance, they did not prepare the food themselves. This nourishment was so superior to what other Greek girls received that Xenophon comments on it.[5] Spartan girls

2. See most recently Valerie French, "The Spartan Family and the Spartan Decline," in *Polis and Polemos: Essays on Politics, War, and History in Ancient Greece in Honor of Donald Kagan*, ed. C. D. Hamilton and P. Krentz (Claremont, Calif., 1997), 241–74.

3. Plut. *Lyc.* 27.2, *Mor.* 238d, Paus. 3.12.8, 3.14.1, 3.16.6, 6.1.9. The reference to childbirth depends upon Latte's emendation of Plut. *Lyc.* 27.2. See W. K. Pritchett, *The Greek State at War*, vol. 4 (Berkeley, 1985), 244 n. 430, and most recently M. Toher, "On the *Eidolon* of a Spartan King," *RhM* n.s. 142 (1999), 113–27, esp. 122–26. W. den Boer, *Laconian Studies* (Amsterdam, 1954), 299–300, favors a Greek text that means: "except a man fallen in war or a woman if they were *hieroi* [priests or priestesses]." N. Richer, "Aspects des funerailles à Sparte," *Cahiers du Centre G. Glotz*, 5 (1994), 51–96, revives the criticism raised by C. Le Roy, "Lakonika," *BCH* 85 (1961), 228–32, esp. 231 n. 4, of Latte's emendation as "violente," and argues that only priests who had died in battle and women who were members of the *hieroi* (i.e., priestesses) were awarded epitaphs. This argument is unconvincing, however, in view of the inscriptions commemorating women who died *en lecho* (*IG* V.1.713, 714; from Geronthrai *IG* V.1128; from Hippola *IG* V.1277), and the total lack of such inscriptions commemorating priestesses. See D. H. Kelly, "Thucydides and Herodotus on the Pitanate *Lochos*," *GRBS* 22 (1980), 31–38, esp. 33–34, for a convincing rejection of this awkward Greek. Richer does not refer to Kelly's arguments. Margherita Guarducci, *Epigrafia greca*, vol. 2 (Rome, 1967–68), 173 n. 1, considers the women's epitaphs pre-Hellenistic. See further Mario Manfredini and Luigi Piccirilli, *Plutarco: Le vite di Licurgo e di Numa*, 2d edn. (Milan, 1990), 94 (app. crit.) and 276–77.

4. See further Barton Lee Kunstler, "Women and the Development of the Spartan Polis" (Ph.D. diss., Boston University, 1983), 459.

5. *Lac. Pol.* 1.4, and see chap. 1. Arist. *HA* 608b declares that the female eats less. Note that in Persepolis as part of a pronatalistic policy nursing women received extra rations: see R. T. Hallock, *The Persepolis Fortification Tablets* (Chicago, 1969), 344–53; Maria Brosius, *Women in Ancient Persia, 559–331 B.C.* (Oxford, 1996), 171–78; and Sarah B. Pomeroy, *Goddesses, Whores, Wives, and Slaves: Women in Classical Antiquity* (New York, 1995), 85.

may, in fact, have been given more food than their male counterparts, for the boys were deliberately given inadequate rations which they needed to supplement themselves.[6] The Spartan diet was distinctive and evoked comment from diverse sources.[7] Food was supplied in the form of a family wage allotted to male citizens from their kleroi. According to Plutarch (*Lyc.* 8.4), each kleros was sufficient to provide a rent of seventy *medimni* (bushels) of barley for a man, and twelve for his wife, along with proportionate quantities of fresh produce. Every Spartan was required to contribute one medimnus each month to his syssition (mess group). If we suppose that the husband consumed his twelve medimni at the syssition while the wife had the same amount at home, the basic diet of men and women was the same. Because Plutarch does not specify the amount of perishables, we do not have sufficient data to enable us to calculate the complete Spartan diet, but if it is true that a wife received twelve medimni of barley, a Spartan woman would have had, as a minimum, more than one and a half *choinixes* daily (approximately 0.839 kg, or one and a half times an Athenian man's daily grain ration), an adequate diet of staples even for an athletic, or pregnant, or nursing woman This amount of grain yielded approximately 3,416 calories daily.[8] A very active adult female twenty to thirty-nine years old requires 2,434 calories.[9]

Plutarch is our only source for the specific details of the food allotment. His report refers to a stable kleros system, which, however, was not in operation throughout Spartan history as private property increased in importance (see chap. 4 and Appendix). Nevertheless, Plutarch provides evidence for a generous dietary standard, and is consistent with what we know from Xenophon and others. In Aristophanes' *Lysistrata*,[10] Spartan women conform to the ethnic stereotype and are notably robust: Lampito complains that the other women are judging how plump she is just as they would assess an animal to be sacrificed. Fifty-eight medimni a year would have generously fed at least five or six children of various ages, or fewer children and some domestics. Furthermore, in addition to the minimum supplied by the kleros (when the system was functioning), property holders would have had access to additional grain, wine, olives, and animal and plant food grown on their private estates. Unmarried women would be supported by their male relatives and their private resources (Xen. *Lac. Pol.* 9.5). We note in passing that the man who was newly elected to the Gerousia (Council

6. Xen. *Lac. Pol.* 2.6, 7.8, describes the effort to keep boys and men slender, doubtless due to the warrior image. See also Plut. *Lyc.* 17.4.

7. R. W. V. Catling, "The Archaic and Classical Pottery," in *Continuity and Change in a Greek Rural Landscape: The Laconia Survey*, vol. 2, *Archaeological Data*, by W. G. Cavanagh, J. Crouwel, R. W. V. Catling, and G. Shipley (*ABSA* suppl. vol. 27) (London, 1996), 33–89, esp. 77, suggests that the peculiar shapes of Laconian pots reflect a diet different from that of most Greeks.

8. Lin Foxhall and H. A. Forbes, "*Sitometreia*: The Role of Grain as a Staple Food in Classical Antiquity," *Chiron* 12 (1982), 41–90, esp. 59.

9. Foxhall and Forbes, "*Sitometreia*," 49.

10. *Lys.* 80–84, and see further Conclusion.

of Elders) was given a second portion by his syssition. He was to give this as a gift to one of his female relatives (Plut. *Lyc.* 26). The relationship between such a man and woman imitated the relationship of king and subject. Spartan kings were regularly given a double portion so that they could bind various subjects to them by offering the extra food to them (Xen. *Lac. Pol.* 15.4). In short, Spartiate women were never underfed. To be sure, some people lost status in the late fifth century through the loss of property, but so long as the kleros supported these dues, they could supply the wife of the kleros holder.[11]

The subject of diet leads us to consider whether Spartan girls reached puberty later than their Athenian counterparts. If so, late marriage could have been an adaptation to delayed menarche, which has been observed in young female gymnasts preparing for the Olympics nowadays.[12] Spartan women, however, are unlikely to have exercised as vigorously as their modern counterparts, inasmuch as athletic standards and rewards for women are higher now than they have ever been. Moreover, ideas of beauty were different.[13] To the modern eye, the figures of the girls depicted in Laconian bronzes appear slim and athletic, but not pathologically emaciated. One doubts whether Spartans were told that "no woman is ever thin enough." In fact, a robust or sturdy body might have been seen as better for childbearing.

Fertility

Homosexuality and nonreproductive forms of heterosexual copulation also reduced fertility. Homosexual ties among Spartans were common.[14] Although Aristophanes depicts Spartan husbands as just as sex-starved in wartime as the rest of the Greeks and cowed by their wives' refusal to have intercourse,[15] he also makes some jokes about the Spartan males' homosexual activities and predilection for anal intercourse.[16] According to Xenophon (*Lac. Pol.* 2.13) and Plutarch

---

11. See further Thomas J. Figueira, "Mess Contributions and Subsistence at Sparta," *TAPA* 114 (1984), 87–109, esp. 98–100.

12. Natalie Anger, "Chemical Tied to Fat Control Could Help Trigger Puberty," *New York Times*, Jan. 7, 1997, sec. C, pp. 1, 3, reports studies demonstrating that fat is necessary for reproductive maturity and athletic women with little body fat experience late puberty.

13. We observe that Athenian vases depict brides as plump: see John H. Oakley and Rebecca H. Sinos, *The Wedding in Ancient Athens* (Madison, Wis., 1993), passim. In the Eleusinian votive relief depicting Demeter, Triptolemus, and Kore, the mother is thinner than her daughter (Athens, National Museum, no. 126 and New York, Metropolitan Museum of Art, acc. no. 14.130.9 A–K [Rogers Fund, 1914], Roman copy).

14. See P. Cartledge, "The Politics of Spartan Pederasty," *PCPS* n.s. 27 (1981), 17–36, and F. D. Harvey, "Laconica: Aristophanes and the Spartans," in *The Shadow of Sparta*, ed. A. Powell and S. Hodkinson (London, 1994), 35–58, esp. 41–42.

15. *Lys.* 78–85.

16. *Lys.* 1105, 1148, 1162, 1173–74.

(*Inst. Lac. 7*), the erotic relationships between men were purely spiritual. Elsewhere, Plutarch (*Lyc.* 18) emphasizes the spritual aspect, but does not specifically rule out the physical relationship. Xenophon and Plutarch also praised Lycurgus' directives limiting the frequency with which the newlyweds engaged in intercourse.[17] Bridegrooms were permitted only limited visits to their brides. Inasmuch as the Greeks were utterly ignorant about the days in the menstrual cycle when women were fertile, late marriage and infrequent intercourse in the early years of marriage must have reduced by at least one or two the total number of children borne by each woman. On the other hand, the secret marriage, which only pregnancy made public, produced more positive results, for presumably it allowed an infertile couple to find other partners with whom they may have been able to reproduce.

The state formally supported child production through rewards to fathers. A man with three sons was not obliged to serve garrison duty, and a man with five was exempt from liturgies (financial obligations to the state or citizen body).[18] These goals, however, were unrealistic. The demographic likelihood of any man having four, let alone five, sons is slim, except in families with eight to ten children, or by sheer luck. There is no indication that the state rewarded fathers of girls, nor were there tangible rewards for the mothers who would endure the pregnancies. The Spartan incentive invites comparison with Augustus's *ius trium liberorum* ("law of three children"), which granted social and legal rewards to many men and women, for it did not specify the sex of the children and rewarded both mothers and fathers.[19]

The pronatalist aims of the state were at variance with the economic ambitions of individual families. Like other Greeks, Spartans practiced diverging devolution, but the Spartans alone adopted unusual practices in their attempt to counter the decrease in the economic status that large families would naturally experience when the paternal estate was divided. Diverging devolution works only in a capitalistic economy with ever-expanding resources. Sparta's economy, agriculturally based, had a limited capability to expand.[20]

---

17. Xen, *Lac.Pol.* 1.5, Plut. *Lyc.* 15.5.

18. Aelian, *VH* 6.6, also states that the father of five sons could marry his daughters without dowry (see on dowries chap. 4). Perhaps such daughters had found their future husbands in the "lottery" in the dark room, and the men were obliged to marry them, or the state awarded dowries to them. See further chap. 2 n. 33.

19. Among the Roman upper classes, childbearing became so unpopular that Augustus decided to offer incentives to those who became parents and penalize those who remained childless: see further Suzanne Dixon, *The Roman Mother* (Norman, Okla., 1988), 71–103.

20. Arist. *Pol.* 1270b1– 4, and see further Thomas Figueira, "Population Patterns in Late Archaic and Classical Sparta," *TAPA* 116 (1968), 182 n. 43.

The Oikos and the Family Economy

The script for the secret marriage, in which the bridegroom stealthily visits the bride and the marriage is not made public until she is pregnant, indicates that the bride did not have to endure the trauma of losing her virginity and moving to a new home simultaneously. We do not have conclusive evidence about the couple's domicile during all stages of the marriage.[21] It seems likely that after a while, perhaps after the birth of a child, the bride left her parent's house to live with her husband. We do not know if the marriage was neolocal. Since the couple married when the bride was in her late teens and the groom slightly older,[22] there was a strong possibility that their parents would still be living. Xenophon does not indicate the domicile of a wife who took a male partner in addition to her husband so that she could control two oikoi (see chap. 2). Perhaps she used both residences so as to be better able to manage them. How the kleros system affected the pattern is difficult to envisage. Heiresses (brotherless women), of whom there were many, may have remained in their ancestral homes. Women in a matrilocal situation certainly enjoy more domestic power.[23] In any case, the possibility of a change of domicile is not as important as it was in a polis like Athens in view of the fact that Sparta was a "closed" society without distant cleruchies (land allotments in a foreign country) or numerous colonies. As we have noted above, marriage was highly endogamous and although the territory of Sparta was extensive, a bride did not run the same risk as her Athenian counterpart of being separated from her family by a long sea voyage. Furthermore, Plutarch's report (*Lyc.* 18) on the pederastic relationships between respectable adult women and unmarried girls refers to a multigenerational female social milieu in which, we may assume, family members would continue to mingle.

Affective Relationships: Daughters and Fathers

The fact that there were many heiresses in Sparta indicates that many families had no surviving sons. Because of the scarcity of male heirs, and perhaps owing to parents' personal inclinations, adoptions were rare. Even in families with children of both sexes, the father probably enjoyed a close relationship with his daughter, in fact closer than he had with his son, since the latter was living out of the house by the age of seven, in many cases while the father was still living with

---

21. S. Perentidis, "Réflexions sur la polyandrie à Sparte dans l'Antiquité," *RHD* 75 (1997), 7–31, esp. 22–25, for sensible speculations about the domicile of the Spartan couple.

22. The ages may be inferred from Plutarch's allusion (*Lyc.* 15.3) to the bride's maturity and from Plato, *Rep.* 5.452, 5.460E, who states that females should become parents for the first time at twenty and males at thirty.

23. Sarah B. Pomeroy, *Women in Hellenistic Egypt: From Alexander to Cleopatra* (New York, 1984), 17; Sarah Blaffer Hrdy, *Mother Nature* (New York, 1999), 248, 252.

his army group.[24] Children born to an older father, of course, would have had a better opportunity to develop a relationship with him. Examples of the close relationship between father and daughter include Gorgo and Cleomenes I,[25] Prolyta and Agesilaus II,[26] and Chilonis and Leonidas.[27] Gorgo and Chilonis became assertive women whose activities are recorded in the historical sources. As a little girl of eight or nine, Gorgo was present when an ambassador from the Greek cities in Ionia came to persuade Cleomenes to support their rebellion against Persia. When he offered Cleomenes a huge bribe, Gorgo advised her father not to stray from the path of virtue (Herod. 5.51). He followed her advice. Even if the veracity of this anecdote can not be tested, the general idea that a father encouraged his clever young daughter to give her opinion on serious matters rings true enough for readers who have enjoyed such dialogues. Cynisca became an Olympic victor (see chap. 1). Chilonis left her husband in order to show support for her father, who had taken asylum, but then, as the political situation changed, she pleaded with her father in behalf of her husband.

Unfortunately, owing to the problems scholars confront in reconstructing the history of ancient women, much of what we suppose about the relationships of Spartan daughters and their parents is based on assumptions. In contrast, there is textual evidence for the relationships with sons.

Mothers and Sons: Ideology of Motherhood

In order to inculcate her offspring with patriotism, the mother had to have the correct attitude herself. Spartan women were renowned for enthusiastically sacrificing their sons for the welfare of the state. Instead of lamenting at the death of their sons, they took pride in the bravery that had led to that fate. Perhaps the delay in bonding with a son, caused by the necessity to await the verdict of the elders as to whether the infant was fit to be reared, created a psychological distance between a mother and her male offspring. In Athens, women mourned the dead, lavished grave goods upon them, and visited funerary monuments; but in Sparta, grave goods and mourning were controlled, restricted in some circumstances and mandated in others. For example, when a king died, one man and one woman from each family were obliged to lament.[28] When the Spartans conquered Messenia, they forced the freeborn women to mourn over men who were not related or connected to them (Aelian, VH 6.1).

Modern psychology and sociobiology has taught us not to consider any particular version of human maternal behavior as "natural"; motherhood is

---

24. Thus Kunstler, "Family Dynamics and Female Power in Ancient Sparta," in *Rescuing Creusa*, ed. M. Skinner, *Helios* 13.2 (Lubbock, Tex., 1986), 31–48, esp. 458–59, and see chap. 1.

25. Herod. 5.50–53, Plut. *Sayings of Spartan Women*, 240d.

26. See chap. 1 n. 16.

27. Plut. *Agis* 11.5, 17–18.1, *Cleom.* 18, *Sayings of Spartan Women*, 1, and see chap. 4.

28. Herod. 6.58, and see further Pomeroy, *Families*, 50–51, and chap. 5 below.

socially as well as biologically constructed. Spartan women did not travel, and the family lives of *perioikoi* (free, but noncitizens) and helots were inappropriate for citizens. The only alternative model for the rearing of sons that was available to Spartan mothers was that for the rearing of daughters, and the latter would not have produced fine specimens of Spartan manhood. Thus, doubtless, Spartan mothers did rear their sons according to the customs and expectations of their state and society.

At least at some time, not only did women sanction the official ideology of motherhood, but several, in fact, were architects of it. The first example is Theano, mother of the traitor Pausanias. When her son had sought asylum in a building that was part of the sanctuary of Athena of the Bronze House, and the Ephors were in a quandary, Theano did not plead for his life. Instead, she placed a brick at the door of the temple and left. Following her example, the Ephors then blocked up the doors, leaving Pausanias inside.[29] Aelian reports (*VH* 12.21) that Spartan mothers lamented in private if a son's corpse bore the majority of wounds on the back.[30] That these anecdotes are not mere exaggeration and correspond to some historical reality is confirmed by the behavior of the Spartans after their defeat at Leuctra. The women were ordered not to mourn, but to suffer in silence. The next day, kinsfolk of those who had been killed in the battle wore happy faces, while the kinsfolk of the soldiers who had survived were sad (Xen. *Hell.* 6.4.16, Plut. *Ages.* 29.4–7).

Quotations in Plutarch's *Sayings of Spartan Women* also indicate that women promoted the ideal of Spartan motherhood. These aphorisms were attributed to famous women who lived in the classical and Hellenistic period, including Gorgo, daughter of Cleomenes and wife of Leonidas; Argileonis, mother of Brasidas; Gyrtias, mother of Acrotatus (who died at Megalopolis in 265 B.C.E.); and to undatable or anonymous women as well.[31] Spartans were the only Greek women whose statements were deemed worthy of quotation. I doubt that what we have here is propaganda actually written by men but ascribed to women in order to make the statements more dramatic and persuasive. The quotations were probably collected not only because of their wit and pithiness, but because they revealed familial attitudes that non-Spartans deemed amazing and noteworthy. For example:

29. Nepos, *Paus.* 5.3, Diodorus 11.45.6, Polyaenus 8.51. Poralla², 16–17, no. 55, calls her Alcathoa. Theano may have been her "professional" name, for it was often used by priestesses: see Blaise Nagy, "The Naming of Athenian Girls: A Case in Point," *CJ* 74 (1979), 60–64, and Pomeroy, *Families*, 157. Thucydides does not tell the tale of Theano and Pausanias. Omitting women's personal involvement is typical of Thucydides. We need not conclude that the story was a Hellenistic invention. Nepos, Diodorus, and Polyaenus may have read it in some other classical source less fastidious than Thucydides.

30. Perhaps catering to the Roman taste for blood, mothers and fathers witnessed the flogging of the boys at the altar of Artemis Orthia, encouraging them to endure the pain.

31. See Appendix. Though there are very few datable women, we do observe the obvious absence of any in Aristotle's period—the time of *anesis* ("licence," *Pol.* 1269b–1270a).

Because Damatria heard that her son was a coward and not worthy of her, she killed him when he arrived. This is the epigram about her:

His mother killed Damatrius who broke the laws,
She a Spartan lady, he a Spartan youth. (*Sayings of Spartan Women*, 240.f2)

Another Spartan woman killed her son, who had deserted his post because he was unworthy of Sparta. She declared: "He was not my offspring . . . for I did not bear one unworthy of Sparta." (*Sayings of Spartan Women*, 241.1)

Another, hearing that her son had fallen at his post, said: "Let the cowards be mourned. I, however, bury you without a tear, my son and Sparta's." (*Sayings of Spartan Women*, 241.2)

Another, hearing that her son had been saved and had fled from the enemy, wrote to him: "A bad rumor about you is circulating. Either absolve yourself at once, or cease to exist." (*Sayings of Spartan Women*, 241.3)

Another, when her sons had run away from a battle and come to her, said: "Wretched runaway slaves, where have you come to? Or do you plan to steal back in here whence you emerged?" And she pulled up her clothes and exposed herself to them. (*Sayings of Spartan Women*, 241.4)

A woman, when she saw her son approaching, asked: "How does our country fare?" And when he said: "All are dead," she picked up a tile, threw it at him, and killed him, saying: "Then did they send you to bring us the bad news?" (*Sayings of Spartan Women* 241.5)

These exemplary mothers would not tolerate a son's act of cowardice. Such behavior tainted with dishonor not only the soldier but his female relatives as well. In the case of Damatria and Damatrius, the son's name echoed his mother's.[32] Perhaps owing in part to the belief that acquired characteristics could be inherited, his sisters (note that his brothers are not mentioned), like the coward himself, could not find anyone willing to marry them, and his mother (note, not his father) might take his life for it. In view of the Spartan equation of womanhood with marriage and motherhood, the sisters received a harsh sentence. There was a strong likelihood that the family would become extinct. That mothers were reputed to enjoy the patriarchal power of Roman fathers and could kill their adult offspring who had disgraced them by their lack of patriotism is unprecedented in the ancient world.[33] It is striking that both Greek and Roman

32. Cf. Tac. *Germ.* 8 for the presence of the warrior's family on the battlefield as a goad to courage.

33. *Sayings of Spartan Women.* 240.f2, 241.1, 3, 5, 12; cf. 241.11.

traditions assert that the Spartan mother could pass judgment on an adult son unilaterally and behave so violently against her own offspring.

Some mothers appear to have actively sought their son's martyrdom, as we see again in Plutarch:

> As a woman was burying her son, a shabby old woman came up to her and said, "You poor woman, what a misfortune!" "No, by the two goddesses, what a good fortune," she replied, "because I bore him so that he might die for Sparta, and that is what has happened for me." (*Sayings of Spartan Women*, 241.8)

> Another woman handed her son his shield and exhorted him: "Son, either with this or on this." (*Sayings of Spartan Women*, 241.16)

Since Spartan women could manage their own property and lived close to their kinsmen and friends in a relatively well-protected territory, widowhood and the loss of a son were probably not such frightening and dreary prospects as the comparable situations were at Athens. Defeat by the helots or by a foreign power and the ensuing rape, slavery, or even death were more terrifying.

Most of the *Sayings of Spartan Women* concerning mothers and sons (or in the case of Gyrtias, a grandson) focus on the son's bravery; in fifteen quotations he shows himself worthy, in nine unworthy, and in one saying (242.19) one son is brave, another a coward. There are other themes as well. One saying draws attention to the pride of a mother of many sons as a well-known feature of Spartan ethnicity:

> When an Ionian woman was boasting about one of the tapestries she had woven (which was indeed of great value), a Spartan woman showed off her four most dutiful sons and said they were the kind of thing a noble and good woman ought to produce and she should boast of them and take pride in them. (*Sayings of Spartan Women*, 241.9)

Another saying emphasizes motherhood as the podium from which Spartan women dominated men:

> When a woman from Attica asked "Why is it that you Spartans are the only women who can rule men?" Gorgo replied, "Because we are the only ones who give birth to men." (*Sayings of Spartan Women*, 240.5)[34]

As the last two quotations discussed above suggest, motherhood could be a fulfilling experience for women, especially, a modern woman imagines, where

---

34. Sim. Plut. *Lyc.* 14.8. Annalisa Paradiso, "Gorgo, la Spartana," in *Grecia al femminile*, ed. Nicole Loraux (Bari, 1993), 107–22, emphasizes motherhood as the chief feature through which Spartan women gained power.

Fig. 5. Louis Jean François Lagrenée the Elder, *Spartan Mother and Son.*

Mother bids farewell to son in classicizing portrayal titled "Rapporte ce bouclier ou que ce bouclier te rapporte" ("Bring back your shield or let this shield bring you back"). 1771. Elizabeth Rawson, *The Spartan Tradition in European Thought* (Oxford, 1969), 265, points out that Spartan subjects first appear in French art in this period. Stourhead, Hoare Collection, National Trust. Photo, Photographic Survey, Courtauld Institute of Art.

nurses are available and the mother has no domestic chores.[35] Women's pro-creative role can contribute to their feelings of self-esteem as well as to a position of prestige not only in the family, but within the state. Some states in more recent times have sought to include women in this way, thus linking private with public. As an example, I will discuss not Nazi Germany, but the United States of America.

Excursus 1. Spartan Motherhood: Precedent and Proof

In the young American Republic, motherhood was designed as a political role for women: their assignment was to produce public-minded children. Republican motherhood functioned in several ways like Spartan motherhood and can serve as a heuristic model for the latter. Here, private and the public spheres intersect. Women were encouraged to display patriotism by sacrificing the men whom they loved. They were proud of their role in shaping a new generation of citizens. Women's history was marshaled into service to promote this view. According to Julia Sargent Murray, who lived from 1751 to 1820 and wrote essays on a variety of subjects including women's education:

> The character of the Spartan women is marked with uncommon firmness. At the shrine of patriotism they immolated nature. Undaunted bravery and unimpeached honor was, in their estimation, far beyond affection. The name of Citizen possessed, for them, greater charms than that of Mother; and so highly did they prize the warrior's meed, that they are said to have shed tears of joy over the bleeding bodies of their wounded sons.[36]

Three-quarters of a century later, the Confederate States of America displayed their conservatism by retaining not only slavery but also some features of Republican motherhood. During the American Civil War, inspired by patriotic propaganda, some southern women behaved in ways similar to those Plutarch attributes to Spartans. Women would leave bonnets and hoopskirts at the homes of young men who had not enlisted, with a letter commanding them to volunteer or be stigmatized as unmanly. They exhorted the troops to come home only if they wore laurel crowns of victory or were carried on shields of honor.[37] A mother wrote in the *Winchester Virginian*: "I am ready to offer you up in defense of your country's rights and honor and I now offer you, a beardless boy of 17 summers, —not with grief, but thanking God that I have a son to offer."[38]

35. Bella Zweig, "The Only Women Who Give Birth to Men: A Gynocentric, Cross-Cultural View of Women in Ancient Sparta," in *Women's Power, Man's Game*, ed. Mary DeForest (Wauconda, Ill., 1993), 32–53, has drawn attention to the positive aspects of motherhood at Sparta.

36. *The Gleaner* (1798, repr. Schenectady, N.Y., 1992), 706.

37. Page Gilpin Faust, *Mothers of Invention* (Chapel Hill, N.C., 1996), 14–15, 17.

38. Faust, *Mothers of Invention*, 15–16.

Upper-class southerners were familiar with Greek and Roman history. It would be ironic if they were influenced by ancient propaganda that had failed to sway the women toward whom it was originally directed. At any rate, these examples from the more recent past persuade me that there is no universal maternal instinct which inspires mothers to save their son's life without hesitation.[39] Some—even many—Spartan women might have harbored sentiments similar to those of women in southern American states and conformed to the ideal of motherhood prevalent at the time, especially since the consequences of defeat were horrendous. Of course, not all American women in the early Republic, or all Confederate women, embraced this particular patriotic ideology enthusiastically. Some women were more reluctant to sacrifice their menfolk on behalf of slavery or "states' rights."

Family Planning

The United States is a nation that derives "its just power from the consent of the governed." The "socialization" at Sparta was surely more effective. There is no comparable evidence for Spartan women rejecting the ideal until quite late (see below).

As a return on the investment in feeding and educating girls, the state expected them to produce children when they were mature. Yet, as Aristotle (*Pol.* 1269b–1270a) suggested, the authoritarian system placed more constraints on men than on women. There is no evidence that unmarried or infertile women (except the sisters of cowards) suffered any social pressure or disabilities similar to those experienced by bachelors and childless men.[40] The state did offer some rewards to mothers: prolific mothers of strong male citizens enjoyed prestige in life, and the names of women who had died in childbirth were recorded on tombstones.[41]

Neither Production nor Reproduction

Apud Lacaenas virgines,
Quibus magis palaestra, Eurota, sol, pulvis, labor
Militiae studio est quam fertilitas barbara.

Spartan maidens care more for wrestling, the [river] Eurotas, the sun, dust, and military exercise than for barbarous fertility. (Cicero, *Tusc.* 2.36)

39. On the biological and social aspects of the maternal "instinct" in primates, see Hrdy, *Mother Nature*.

40. The concepts of "late marriage" and "bad marriage" seem to apply only to men. See Stobaeus 22, "On Marriage," 1.16, and Pollux 3.40, 48 (Bethe).

41. See n. 3.

As Cicero reports, women did reject the burden of continuous child production that was the long-range goal of their physical education. Contraception is discussed in the Greek medical tradition dating from the classical period, but Spartans are the only respectable Greek women we know of who are specifically reported to have exercised control over their fertility. This report reflects the autonomy of Spartan women acting not in secret, as might be necessary for an individual, but assertively as a group whose behavior attracted notice. That they were not married until they were mature gave them an advantage over the more passive child brides in Athens.

Feminist historians have argued that the number of children a woman bears has a greater effect on the quality of her life than almost any other ongoing condition (that is, excluding such dramatic events as war and natural disaster). Like married women nowadays who remain childless out of choice, Spartan women were thought to be motivated by selfish desires.[42] In the history of the premodern world, refusal to bear children has usually been considered unpatriotic. Before the advent of modern medicine, abundant fertility was fundamental to the survival of the community. That after only one year of war and before the devastation of the plague Pericles urged Athenian women to bear more children underlines this necessity.[43] In order to alleviate the continuing and ominous population decline, Spartiate men produced children by helot women (see chap. 5). These mixed-blood children, called *mothakes*, were given some modified form of citizenship. We may speculate that the two practices were related: when the citizen women noticed their childbearing was no longer absolutely essential for the welfare of the state, and motherhood was consequently downgraded, they could well have decided it was not worth the trouble to bear many children.[44] Cicero's phrase, "fertilitas barbara," indicates that bearing children was considered unsophisticated. He was probably evaluating Spartan women by the standard of upper-class Roman women, and his judgment here was shrewd. Both Spartans and Romans enjoyed wealth, high status, and access to contraceptive methods (through formal medical care or word of mouth) which, though primitive, were not ineffective. The Hippocratics do not mention Sparta, but they do not write about Athens either, and we know from other sources that there were physicians in Athens. At Sparta they would have been important for military reasons. Archagathus, who in 219 B.C.E. was the first Greek physician to go to Rome, came from Laconia (Pliny, *HN* 29.12). Plutarch (*Sayings of Spartan Women*, 242.26) mentions a Spartan girl who brought on an abortion in secret. A fourth-century inscription from the sanctuary of Asclepius at Epidaurus reports that a Spartan

---

42. For modern parallels, see Elaine Tyler May, *Barren in the Promised Land: Childless Americans and the Pursuit of Happiness* (New York, 1995), esp. 71, 196–99.

43. Thuc. 2.44.3, and see further Pomeroy, *Families*, 39.

44. Hippocrates, *On Generation*, 5.1, states that a woman's volition controls whether or not she conceives.

mother came to find a cure for her daughter's case of dropsy. She slept at the shrine, saw a vision, and when she returned home she discovered that her daughter had seen the same vision and was cured.[45] Since women in Sparta were neither secluded nor silenced, as some women were elsewhere in Greece, and since Spartans spent much of their time in the company of women, it would be only reasonable to assume that they had at least the same knowledge of contraception as other Greek women.

With the exception of Cicero, ancient and modern authorities have offered social and economic, rather than biological, theories to explain the population decline at Sparta.[46] Among all the theories advanced about the reasons for the decline, we must give serious consideration to Cicero's (the most obvious one): women's control over reproduction.

Since the source of the verse Cicero quotes is not known,[47] we can only speculate about the reason for Cicero's remark, and whether it is relevant to women throughout Spartan history, or only to the Hellenistic period. Earlier, they probably bore children ungrudgingly, and gladly contributed their sons to the military, as tradition preserved, for example in Plutarch, *Sayings of Spartan Women*, asserts. Cicero may record disillusionment with the Spartan female ideal in the Hellenistic period, when women had become aware of other ways of life.

The drastic reduction in the amount of territory controlled by Sparta after the liberation of Messenia in 369 B.C.E. inspires some Malthusian speculations.[48] Since the Spartan economy was based on agriculture, they will not have wanted

45. *IG* IV.2.121–22 = E. J. Edelstein and L. Edelstein, *Asclepius: A Collection and Interpretation of the Testimonies*, vol. 1 (Baltimore, Md., 1945), 423, stele II, para. 21. The cure by proxy was unusual.

46. A sanctuary of Zeus Messapeus at Tsakona, 4 km north of Sparta, has recently been identified. The finds, including numerous nonidentical archaic ithyphallic terracotta votives and a smaller number of figurines of women, some of whom are pregnant, a larger number with legs spread to expose genitalia, suggest that the divinity was worshipped in connection with the Spartan concern for human fertility. The shrine was active until the early Hellenistic period with some resumption of interest in the 3d–4th cent. C.E. See H. W. Catling, "Excavations at the Menelaion, 1985," *Lak. Spoud.* 8 (1986), 205–16, esp. 211–12 and fig. 13; Catling, "A Sanctuary of Zeus Messapeus: Excavations at Aphyssou, Tsakona, 1989," *ABSA* 85 (1990), 15–35, esp. 21, 34; Catling, "The Work of the British School at Athens at Sparta and in Laconia," in *Sparta in Laconia: Proceedings of the 19th British Museum Classical Colloquium*, ed. W. G. Cavanagh and S. E. C. Walker, British School at Athens Studies, vol. 4 (London, 1998), 27. M. Overbeek, "The Small Finds," in *Continuity and Change in a Rural Landscape: The Laconia Survey*, vol. 2, *Archaeological Data*, by W. G. Cavanagh et al., *ABSA* suppl. vol. 27 (London, 1996), 183–98, esp. 190, mentions 15 female figurines: the most complete ones have arms and legs akimbo and genitals exposed, with no indication of breasts, suggesting a lack of emphasis on nurturance. See Catling, in a postscript on Tsakona in David Blackman, "Archaeology in Greece, 1999–2000: Lakonia," *AR* 46 (2000), 38–43, esp. 43,

47. Thus the Budé, ad loc. M. Pohlenz, *Ciceronis tusculanorum disputationum: Libri V* (Stuttgart, 1957), 158, conjectures that the source is Accius, *Meleager.*

48. For socioeconomic theories of reproduction, see, e.g., R. M. McInnis, "Childbearing and Land Availability: Some Evidence from Individual Household Data," in *Population Patterns in the Past*, ed. R. D. Lee (New York, 1977), 201–27.

to reproduce at the same rate as before the defeat at Leuctra, because if they did so after the loss of such a major resource they would reduce the economic status of individuals. Though their population did not fall immediately after Leuctra, despite the casualties, once the realities of the new limited territory had set in, Spartans may have adopted more strict family limitation policies.[49]

More consistent with Plutarch's account of women's cooperation in child production is Xenophon's observation that women agreed to take part in husband-doubling or wife-sharing arrangements, not as passive agents, but because of their own ambitions to dominate two oikoi and to improve the economic status of their children. These novel arrangements may have encouraged women to bear more children than they would have done in conventional monogamous families, since they could distribute them in two oikoi. In any case, if we suppose that Xenophon's comment that wives willingly participated in these arrangements contradicts Cicero's report that the women refused to bear children, we must reject one of these reports, or hypothesize that some women participated while others refused, or posit change over time, or speculate that Xenophon and Cicero had different purposes in drawing attention to these issues.

Throughout Spartan history there must have been some women who did not reproduce. Among any group of women or of couples, some will be infertile for all or some portion of their adult lives. There is the case of Anaxandridas, who resorted to bigamy rather than adultery or divorce, because his first wife had not produced an heir.[50] After he married a second wife, the first wife bore children. Among nonroyals, as we have mentioned, the secret marriage described by Plutarch, in which the bridegroom makes stealthy visits to the bride,[51] or divorce and remarriage would allow them to sample partners with whom they could have fertile unions. In addition, some women who may have been fertile were in marital situations that would not allow them to bear children because their husbands rejected them. Others remained spinsters. For example, the sisters of cowards could not find bridegrooms.[52] Daughters of wealthy men were more in demand than daughters of the poor. The fiancés of Lysander's daughters broke their engagements when they discovered that their prospective father-in-law was poor (Plut. *Lys.* 30.5).

Womanpower and Oliganthropia

Analyses of the population decline at Sparta make repeated references to "man-power" and to the numbers of males of all ages at various dates, but, with minor

49. G. Shipley, "The Extent of Spartan Territory in the Late Classical and Hellenistic Periods," *ABSA* 95 (2000), 367–90, esp. 385, points out that although Sparta lost most of Messenia after Leuctra, the southern part with its settlements and ports were retained.

50. Herod. 5.39–41.

51. *Lyc.* 15.3, sim. Athen. 13.555c, citing Hermippus (fl. late 3d cent.).

52. Xen. *Lac. Pol.* 9.5.

exceptions, they ignore women's reproductive failures or successes and their numbers relative to the number of males.[53] Yet there is no dearth of information. Surprisingly, the ancient sources give more direct data and commentary on reproduction and demography for Sparta than for other Greek communities.

Our knowledge of reproduction depends chiefly on Xenophon, Aristotle, Polybius, Cicero, and Plutarch. In the first sentence of the *Spartan Constitution*, Xenophon mentions *oliganthropia* (sparse citizen population), and in the next paragraph he discusses *teknopoiia* (child production), highlighting the role of women in this process (see chap. 1). This emphasis on women seems eminently sensible from a modern viewpoint, but considering the alternative theories of reproduction that were current in Xenophon's day—theories that minimized women's contribution to the embryo—Xenophon shows unusual insight.

Aristotle refers to women when he states that half of Spartan society was ungoverned. He sees a connection between women's ownership of two-thirds of the land and oliganthropia. *Anthropoi* may refer to either men or women, or both, and Aristotle could have used *oligandria* or a similar term if he had wanted to specify males. Yet the context indicates that Aristotle, more than Xenophon, considers oliganthropia as a lack of male citizens (*Pol.* 1270a33–34). With the exception of Ludwig Ziehen, scholars generally follow Aristotle in this interpretation.[54] Studies of the decline in Spartan manpower naturally draw attention to losses inflicted by a devastating earthquake around 464:[55] Ziehen speculated about the number of women lost in this calamity.[56] He argues that more women than men were killed because they were indoors, and points out that only five houses were reported to have withstood the earthquake.[57] No ancient source, however, reports that the earthquake was more catastrophic for women than for men. Ziehen is not convincing for several reasons: Spartan women were often out of doors and may not have suffered when the roofs of their houses caved in, and, secondly, from what we can deduce about Spartan architecture, their domestic quarters were so flimsy that a robust adult could have survived a collapse.

53. The material in this section was presented in Sarah B. Pomeroy, "Spartan Womanpower," paper delivered at the Annual Meeting of the American Philological Association, Dec. 28, 1998; abstract published in *American Philological Association 130th Annual Meeting: Abstracts*, 81.

54. The late David Asheri, in a personal communication.

55. Plut. *Cim.* 16.4–5: *neaniskoi* (youths) survived, but the ephebes (approximately eighteen to twenty years old) died when a gymnasium was destroyed.

56. See L. Ziehen, "Das spartanische Bevölkerungsproblem," *Hermes* 68 (1933), 218–37, esp. 232–35, 237. Stephen Hodkinson, "Inheritance, Marriage and Demography: Perspectives upon the Success and Decline of Classical Sparta," in *Classical Sparta: Techniques Behind Her Success*, ed. Anton Powell (Norman, Okla., 1989), 79–121, esp. 103, follows Ziehen.

57. Polyaen 1.41.3; Ael. *VH* 6.7.2; Diod. 11.63.

Demographic Speculations

The sources report the number of male citizens present at various battles as well as the number of male citizens in general at various points in the classical and Hellenistic periods, but, in general, numerical data from antiquity is unreliable. We have no information either on the absolute number of female Spartans or on the number relative to the number of males.[58] We may, however, speculate that, as a consequence of selective male infanticide and the death of men in battle, women outnumbered men fairly frequently, and that the sex ratio was further skewed by male emigration after the Peloponnesian War. Moreover, since Spartans lived a more healthy life than other Greek women, ate well, exercised out of doors, did not become pregnant before their bodies were ready for child-bearing, and, at least by the Hellenistic period if not earlier, limited the number of children they bore, they probably lived longer than other Greek women and had a better life expectancy than Spartan men. While it is true that relatively few grave markers have been found in Sparta because only men who died in war and women who died in childbirth were awarded this distinction, men who died might be buried at the battlefield, as were the heroes who died at Thermopylae. In contrast, all the women whose deaths were the result of childbirth would have been commemorated at Sparta. Though it is an argument *ex silentio*, it is worth pointing out that few such inscriptions have been discovered.[59] Xenophobia, lack of foreign trade and of an overseas empire, and not living in crowded urban spaces (as their Athenian counterparts did) will, in general, have had a beneficial effect on Spartan health. The men, however, traveled to foreign soil and were exposed to disease. These factors must have contributed to the large number of heiresses, or brotherless orphans, noted by Aristotle. There would have been a substantial number of widows, as well. A consequence of the unbalanced sex ratio was that not all adult women could be married simultaneously. Nevertheless, these excess women were not forced to become child producers. Moreover, because a Spartan woman shared in the paternal inheritance, she was not a burden to her family if she remained unwed. Since her portion of the patrimony would revert to her family of origin when she died, an unmarried daughter or sister would have been a financial, if not a social, asset. Perhaps Cicero included unmarried women when he stated that the women did not want to bear children.

Thirty years ago, without resorting to statistics and cliometrics, W. K. Lacey wrote in the style of Jane Austen:

> One feature which seems common to all societies is that rich men want to marry their daughters (especially only daughters) to the sons of rich men, and

---

58. Note the 240 adolescent girls in Theocritus, *Idyll*, 18.25.
59. See n. 3.

the Spartans seem to have been no exception. A shortage of eligible men leads to a competition for husbands. . . . Rich women, moreover, do not commonly bear large families, especially when, as in Sparta, they are independent and not subordinated to their husbands.[60]

Lacey, however, fails to draw the conclusion that a shortage of eligible men would leave some Spartan women husbandless, and hence childless.

Oikos and Polis

Private and public spheres were interlocking. The mother constituted a bridge between private and public. The state determined the character of the family; the reverse was true, as well. For example, women were expected to scold and humiliate cowards and bachelors. They had to be informed about public events to know which men deserved this treatment.

Aristotle saw that the polis was constituted of oikoi, but he did not distinguish the different sorts of oikoi that must exist for the creation of different sorts of poleis. According to Aristotle (*Pol.* 1252b10–12), the essential elements in the oikos were father, mother, child, and slave. Because the father alone of the members possessed a fully functioning deliberative faculty, he was the authority figure in all three relationships. Though appropriate to Athens, and doubtless to most other places in the Greek world, this model does not fit Sparta neatly throughout its history. In husband-doubling arrangements, the role of mother was distinct from the role of wife, and the role of father was distinct from the role of husband. According to the *Sayings of Spartan Women*, the women dominated their sons in certain settings, and according to Aristotle (*Pol.* 1269b12–1270a6), they even ruled their husbands. Xenophon (*Lac. Pol.* 1.9) reports that they managed the oikos, sometimes even more than one. Furthermore the major portion of the productive, or "slave," element of the Aristotelian formula was owned by the state, not by the individual oikos, and, for the most part, lived some distance from it (see chap. 5). All these differences between Spartan oikoi and those that at Athens contributed to creating a polis that was different from the Athenian polis.

There were also many elements of similarity between both poleis. Reproduction was universally the goal of marriage. At Athens, the marriage formula was explicit: the bride was given to the groom for the sowing of legitimate children. Yet we do not know of any Spartan politician who ever, like Pericles, directed mothers who had just lost adult sons in war to produce more children.

60. *The Family in Classical Greece* (Ithaca, N.Y., 1968), 205. S. J. Hodkinson, "Inheritance, Marriage, and Demography," uses cliometrics and a utilitarian view of women to come to the same conclusion. He also (106–9) speculates about the detrimental effects of incest on the Spartan population, but withdraws this hypothesis in Hodkinson, *Property and Wealth in Classical Sparta* (London, 2000), 444 n. 23.

Nor do we hear of any situation parallel to that at Athens during the second half of the Peloponnesian War, where a married man who already had children was encouraged to sire additional children by another citizen woman. In one of the examples that is cited of Socrates and Myrto, a dowerless daughter of Aristides, such a liaison could only have produced financial and personal misery for all concerned.[61] As we have mentioned, in facing the population decline, the Spartans chose to reproduce by helot women rather than press unwed female Spartans into service.

Change over Time

The degree and quality of the differences between the Spartan family and others in the Greek world changed over time. Scholarly interpretation has shifted as well. Previous generations of scholars, relying on Plutarch's report and influenced by the mirage, have emphasized differences. In the 1990s, Xenophon's testimony gained authority.[62]

Many features of the Spartan family—especially as described by Plutarch—either were in existence only in the archaic period, or were part of the mirage. This family owed its origin not principally to biology, but to human legislation. In this fictive family, the men were like "brothers" with equal economic resources.[63] They disciplined younger males and were in turn respected by them as fathers. Relationships between older and younger men were governed by the same incest taboos as if they really had been blood relatives (Plut. *Lyc.* 6.2, 8.4, 15.2; Xen. *Lac. Pol.* 2.10,13). This is also the community in which state officials exercised the prerogatives of fathers elsewhere in Greece, deciding which infants to rear and how to educate them (Xen. *Lac. Pol.* 2.2, 10). Women were excluded from managing the economic resources of the state and participating in the administrative processes of this public family, but that was true of all women (with the exception of some Hellenistic queens) in antiquity. Interestingly enough, just after Plutarch's lifetime, Roman Sparta honored some elite women by granting them titles that certified inclusion in the civic family. These titles included "daughter of the city" and "mother of the Boule and the people."[64]

Simone de Beauvoir envisioned the life of Spartan women as utopian:

> Since the oppression of woman has its cause in the will to perpetuate the family and to keep the patrimony intact, woman escapes complete dependency to the degree in which she escapes from the family. If a society that forbids private

---

61. See further Pomeroy, *Goddesses, Whores, Wives, and Slaves,* 66–67.

62. See Appendix n. 25.

63. Perhaps the references to other girls as "cousins" in Alcman, *Partheneion* 1.52, are fictitious.

64. A. J. S. Spawforth, "Families at Roman Sparta and Epidaurus: Some Prosopographical Notes," *ABSA* 80 (1985), 241, and see chap. 6 below.

property also rejects the family, the lot of women in it is found to be considerably ameliorated. In Sparta the communal regime was in force, and it was the only Greek city in which woman was treated almost on an equality with man. The girls were raised like the boys. The wife was not confined in her husband's domicile: indeed, he was allowed to visit her only furtively, by night; and his wife was so little his property that on eugenic grounds another man could demand union with her. The very idea of adultery disappeared when the patrimony disappeared. All children belonged in common to the city as a whole, and women were no longer jealously enslaved to one master; or, inversely, one may say that the citizen, possessing neither private wealth nor specific ancestry, was no longer in possession of woman. Women underwent the servitude of maternity as did men the servitude of war; but beyond the fulfilling of this civic duty, no restraint was put on their freedom.[65]

Nowadays feminist theory has encouraged historians to shift from a narrow focus on the androgynous educational system to an appreciation of Spartan motherhood and to criticism of societies based on Communist or totalitarian programs. Perhaps in reaction to earlier views, the current scholarly consensus is more nuanced and less influenced by information emanating from the mirage.

By the end of the fifth century, if not earlier, the Spartans did not even pay lip service to the all-male public family. The freedom to give kleros and house to anyone, or bequeath them by testament, signaled state acceptance of the private family and its fluctuating economy at the expense of the public family of men of equal status (Plut. *Agis* 5.1, and see chap. 4).

At Sparta, the patriarchal state was gradually supplanted by the nuclear family, which, however, was not dominated by men to the same extent as at Athens. In the fourth century, if not slightly earlier, the family at Sparta (like the family elsewhere in the Greek world) had its own economic base and reproductive agenda. It is clear that with more property openly in private hands, more Spartans, including women, had increased incentives to develop inheritance strategies and to regulate their fertility.

In their discussions of reproduction, Xenophon, Cicero, and to some extent Aristotle emphasize women's influence and volition. Xenophon's report on wife-lending or husband-doubling indicates that both parents concurred in limiting the size of the family so as not to reduce the share of the inheritance that would eventually be distributed to their heirs. As wives and mothers, women were active players in making arrangements beneficial to their families and to themselves.

65. *The Second Sex* (New York, 1952), 82.

4

ELITE WOMEN

Royal Women

More specific information is available about royal women than about any other group. It is clear, however, that a historian must not generalize from information about the female kin of kings to women of lesser social status. For example, because of concern about the legitimacy of the succession, only royal women are named in tales of adultery, but the ancient sources often do not distinguish between royal and upper-class women. Many Spartiates had Heraclid blood. Aristotle writes about wealthy women, but only Plutarch gives details about particular wealthy women and they are all members of the royal houses (see below). Furthermore, the Spartiates were an elite, an aristocracy, and women of the upper classes tend to imitate the most elite among them.

Marriage

Social and economic endogamy was characteristic of royal marriage. This pattern of selection of spouses was also common elsewhere in the Greek world, with uncle-niece and first-cousin marriage being common patterns.[1] Endogamy is a relative concept. Since the Spartan population was small and xenophobic, it could be characterized as endogamous in general. There were never more than 10,000 *homoioi* (men of equal status or similars) or, consequently, more than 500 elite. Marriages among the wealthy accelerated the concentration of wealth in fewer and fewer families, despite the presence of countervailing forces. The problem of finding a suitable spouse was intensified in the case of the kings: the small pool of eligible brides included members of the royal families and daughters or widows of wealthy or influential men, or in the case of Ariston, who at first had

---

1. Plut. *Roman Questions*, 108, and see further Sarah B. Pomeroy, *Goddesses, Whores, Wives, and Slaves: Women in Classical Antiquity* (New York, 1995), 64.

two barren wives, the extremely beautiful wife of a friend (Herod. 6.61 and Conclusion). Like Ariston, Demaratus married a woman who was claimed by another man. He carried off Percalus, the fiancée of Leotychidas II, who was his enemy, kinsman, and future successor, and married her himself (Herod. 6.65.2). Examples of royal endogamy are plentiful. The first wife of King Anaxandridas was the daughter of his sister (Herod. 5.39). Leonidas married his step-niece Gorgo, daughter of Cleomenes I (Herod. 7.205.1). King Archidamus V married the daughter of his cousin Hippomedon (Polyb. 4.35.13). Lampito, daughter of Leotychidas II, married his grandson, Archidamus II (Herod. 6.71.2). Sometimes a king chose to marry a daughter of a wealthy or influential man. An heiress from a royal family was certainly desirable. The elderly Cleomenes married Chilonis, a young Eurypontid heiress. Agiatis, who inherited the great wealth of her father Gylippus, was married first to Agis IV and, when widowed, to Cleomenes III (Plut. *Cleom.* 1.2). Eugenics also influenced spouse selection. The Ephors fined Archidamus for marrying a short wife, for she would bear short kings (Plut. *Ages.* 2).

The Succession

One of the earliest female members of the royal house about whom a story is told is Argeia, a Theban who was married to king Aristodemus, probably in the mid-tenth century B.C.E.[2] After she bore twin sons, her husband died. She would not disclose which son was the elder because she wanted both to rule as equals. Nevertheless, she revealed that Eurysthenes was older than Procles by bathing and feeding him first. Of course, any story about the tenth century must be treated with caution. Nevertheless, it is conceivable that in those early days or even when the story was first told, a mother, even a queen, looked after her babies herself, or at least was on hand to supervise servants who did the actual work.

Adultery and Bigamy

In the *Life of Lycurgus* (15.10, sim. *Mor.* 228b20), Plutarch passes on the proverbial notion that adultery was unknown at Sparta, but in other texts he tells of extra-marital liaisons, mostly in the form of anecdotes about individual royal women.

Such adulterous affairs are recorded because of concern over the legitimacy of the heir. Like Spartan men, the women, evidently, were thought to be capable of duplicity concerning affairs of state. Ephors watched the first wife of Anaxandridas give birth, since she had not been able to conceive until he took a second wife (Herod. 5.41). They suspected that she would sneak in a suppositious child, but she confounded them by giving birth to male triplets. Timaea, wife of

---

2. Herod. 6.52, 4.147; Paus. 3.1.5–9. See Deborah Gera, *Warrior Women: The Anonymous Tractatus de Mulieribus* (Leiden, 1997), no. 5 and pp. 121–25.

Agis II, was accused of having had a secret affair with Alcibiades and of conceiving Leotychidas by him.[3] Herodotus (5.40) comments that bigamy was "not Spartan." The Agiad Anaxandridas, however, resorted to bigamy rather than adultery because he had not produced any children with his first wife, and did not want to divorce her since he was fond of her.[4] The Eurypontid Ariston practiced bigamy, if not trigamy (Herod. 6.61–63). His third wife, whom, as we have noted, he took away from a friend, bore a son in less than nine months (Paus. 3.7.7). The legitimacy of this son, Demaratus, and his right to rule were questioned (Herod. 6.65–69). Demaratus himself confronted his mother and accused her of having had an affair with a stablehand (Herod. 6.68). (We have already observed [chap. 1] that Spartan women were interested in horses.) His mother replied that either Ariston or the legendary hero Astrobacus, whose shrine was in the courtyard, had engendered him. Of course, royal families are subject to greater constraints than commoners because of the need to have an heir, and one who was a blood heir for the kingship to be justified.

Chilonis, a Eurypontid who was the wife of Cleonymus, was involved in an adulterous liaison with Acrotatus, son of Areus I, by 272 when her elderly husband had left to persuade Pyrrhus to attack Sparta (Plut. *Pyrr.* 26.15–29.12). It was said that everyone in Sparta knew how she felt about her husband, but she was not ostracized, probably because her husband was utterly despicable, while her lover defended Sparta against Pyrrhus. Plutarch portrays her as a heroine who threatened suicide if Cleonymus and Pyrrhus were victorious. That her equally heroic granddaughter was named after her indicates that Chilonis did not suffer *damnatio memoriae*.[5]

We know of no penalty for adultery, nothing to compare with the Athenian laws requiring the husband to divorce a wife who had been raped or seduced, and prohibiting the adulterous woman from wearing jewelry and attending religious ceremonies. Perhaps the task of proving adultery at Sparta was so daunting that it was practically unpunishable. At Sparta, the only consequence of adultery apparently was an aspersion that political opponents of a potential king might cast upon his legitimacy.

Authority

The wives and daughters of Spartan kings could not be styled "queens" and "princesses," for they had no special role to play in society or religion. "Queen," at

---

3. Plut. *Lys.* 22.3–4, *Alcib.* 23.7–8, *Ages.* 3.1–2, and see further P. A. Cartledge, *Agesilaos and the Crisis of Sparta* (London, 1987), 115, and chap. 3, above.

4. Herod. 5.39–41. On the familial strife that ensued, see C. Dewald, "Women and Culture in Herodotus' Histories," in *Reflections of Women in Antiquity*, ed. H. Foley (New York, 1981), 91–125, esp. 108–9.

5. See further Alfred S. Bradford, "*Gynaikokratoumenoi*: Did Spartan Women Rule Spartan Men?" *AncW* 14 (1986), 13–18, esp. 14.

least as a title used by non-Spartans of one woman, emerged only in the late Hellenistic period.[6] Some of the royal women at Sparta did, however, wield a great deal of authority because of their influence on the kings. There was a long tradition of the involvement of women in politics, beginning with the child Gorgo, who advised her father the king about how he should treat a foreign ambassador (Herod. 5.51, 7.239). Her advice shows that she understood well the Spartan policy of avoidance of strangers (*xenelasia*). Women's influence was most apparent in Hellenistic dynastic politics as it was in much of the Greek world at that time. The women were often widows and older than the men they swayed. In the middle of the third century, when Agis IV promulgated his reforms, Agesistrata[7] was in her late fifties and Archidamia in her early eighties (see below).[8] It is rare in Greek history to find a grandmother and mother both not only alive, but active, at such advanced ages.[9] Cratesicleia remarried when old to give her son a stepfather as an ally (Plut. *Cleom.* 22.4). Agiatis was older than Cleomenes III when she converted him to the revolutionary program of her former husband Agis IV. Xenopeithia was the mother of Lysanoridas, who was a commander at Thebes. His father is not named; therefore we deduce that she was a widow, and important enough for her son's political enemies to want to murder her and her sister Chryse.[10] Cynisca was around sixty years old when she defied her brother, who was then king (see chap. 1).

Wealth

The wealth of Spartan women was fabled before reliable evidence for it appears in historical times. In Homer, Helen spins with a golden distaff, brings a hoard of valuable clothing to Troy, and obtains even more when there (*Od.* 4.131–35,

---

6. An honorary inscription at Delphi (*SIG*³ 430) identifies Areus as the son of King Acrotatus and Queen Chilonis. If this inscription refers to Areus I and to his mother Chilonis, the date is 267 B.C.E., though the parents of Areus I had not been king and queen. If the inscription refers to Areus II, posthumous child of Chilonis and Acrotatus, the date is 262–254. See R. Flacelière, *Les aitoliens à Delphes* (Paris, 1937), 84 n. 2, 457–58; Linda J. Piper, *Spartan Twilight* (New Rochelle, N.Y., 1986), 22; Bradford, "*Gynaikokratoumenoi*: Did Spartan Women Rule Spartan Men?" 14; *LGPN* 3A s.v. Areus 4 (ca. 330–265), 6 (ca. 262–254) for the posthumous child, and s.v. Chilonis 3.1, daughter of Leotychidas (i.e., Latuchidas) and 4 daughter of Leonidas and Cratesclea, and see chap. 3 n. 27. See also on Apega, below, although a tyrant's wife is technically not a queen, despite behaving like one. On the title of "queen" in general see Elizabeth Carney, "'What's in a Name?' The Emergence of a Title for Royal Women in the Hellenistic Period," in *Women's History and Ancient History*, ed. Sarah B. Pomeroy (Chapel Hill, N.C., 1991), 154–72.

7. *LGPN* 3A s.v. Agesistrata dates her ca. 295–241.

8. *LGPN* 3A s.v. Archidamia dates her ca. c. 310–241, and see below.

9. For Nicippia, a wealthy great-grandmother who is also probably a widow, see *SEG* XI.677, 1st cent. C.E., and see further chap. 6 nn. 54, 80.

10. Her sister Chryse was probably close to her in age. See Conclusion n. 2.

Il. 6.289–92). The young girls in Alcman's oeuvre allude to valuable jewelry and objects, including purple garments, golden mitres and bracelets, perfume, silver, ivory,[11] and racehorses. Euripides (*Andr.* 147–53) refers to the golden ornaments Helen wore in her hair, her embroidered dresses, and her wedding presents.

Archaeological evidence confirms the poets' reports. Gold and silver jewelry, mostly dating from the seventh century, was dedicated at the sanctuary of Artemis Orthia.[12] The pieces include fibulae, pendants, and beads (see further chap. 6).

Sometime after the Second Messenian War, when an austere discipline was imposed, the use of gold and silver was forbidden. We do not know what happened to women's valuable possessions when precious metals were outlawed and houses were searched to make certain that none were hidden within (Xen. *Lac. Pol.* 7.6, 14.3). Perhaps they were dedicated to the gods. Thereafter, women were not permitted to wear ornaments or gold.[13] Until the Hellenistic period, Sparta did not have coined money, or, consequently, a cash economy. When King Polydorus died and the Spartans purchased his house from his widow, they payed with oxen (eighth century B.C.E.: Paus. 12.3). Of course this purchase predated the invention of coinage, but even though foreign coins became available, such awkward transactions must have continued at Sparta long after other Greeks were using coins (see chap. 5 n. 9).

Land Tenure

Land was the most valuable commodity in the ancient world, and the land of Laconia was among the most fertile in Greece. The ownership of land connotes permanence. In Athens and some other Greek states, women were not permitted to own land or to manage substantial amounts of wealth.[14] These limitations draw attention to the impermanence of Athenian women in the family and state and their lack of access to the most valuable economic resources. The dowries of Athenian women consisted of movables and money. They were like metics (resident aliens), who also could own only movables and money. The type of

11. *Parth.* 1.64, 66–67; 3, fr. 3.71, 77; 162 fr. 2.c 3,5S elephantin, conj. D. A. Campbell, *Greek Lyric*, vol. 2 (Cambridge, Mass., 1988), 498 line 5, and see chap. 1 n. 123 for ivory plaques, and Appendix for ivory artifacts possibly portraying Helen.

12. J. P. Droop, "The Bronzes," in Dawkins, *AO*, 196–202, esp. 200, refers to "several silver specimens and two of gold with silver bulbs joined by a chain." See also R. M. Dawkins, "Artemis Orthia: Some Additions and a Correction," *JHS* 50 (1930), 298–99 and pl. XI.1, for another bronze fibula. Of course, there is no way to ascertain whether these items were worn by or dedicated by women. Men could have purchased them and given them immediately as gifts to the goddess, but (at least judging from inscribed dedications to Artemis elsewhere in Greece) women seem more likely to have done so.

13. Heraclides Lembus, *Excerpta Politiarum*, 373.13 (Dilts).

14. See further David Schaps, *The Economic Rights of Women in Ancient Greece* (Edinburgh, 1979), 6–7.

property women could hold was due not only to their low status, but also to the possibility that they might marry out of the polis. Moreover, Athenian women did not manage their own property; rather, the dowry passed from a woman's father to her husband. Unlike Spartan women, however, Athenians could produce wealth. The Athenian oikos was a locus of production as well as reproduction. Respectable citizen women contributed directly to the economic prosperity of the oikos by weaving and shrewd management.[15] Poor or lower-class women made money, often by working outside the home, and slave women contributed to their owner's economic prosperity by working as domestics or in manufacture or in service industries such as prostitution. Against this background, Spartan women (like Spartan men) can be viewed not as versatile producers, but essentially as owners, managers, and consumers of wealth based on land (see chap. 3).

The system of land tenure at Sparta is poorly understood.[16] Moreover, it changed drastically over time. Our knowledge of the laws governing the ownership of property at Sparta is uncertain, and in any case the laws may not reflect the actual historical situation at all times (Xen. *Lac. Pol.* 14.1, and see Appendix). In the following discussion, I will sketch a likely scenario and will concentrate in particular on the role women played in the evolving economy.

There were two systems of land tenure in Sparta, one private, the other public. The story just above about the house of the widow of Polydorus indicates that women owned property in Sparta from earliest times, and they continued to do so. The story also indicates that her property was private property.

Much of the land in Sparta was owned by the state. The participation of both men and women in this publicly owned land system changed over time. In archaic Greece, it was common for the founder of a colony to measure the territory and distribute it in equal shares to the male colonists. The Spartans, in effect, colonized their neighbors in Messenia and Laconia, though they themselves did not settle in the conquered territory and continued to live in the Spartan polis. The state distributed parcels of land to be used only for a man's lifetime.[17]

---

15. See further Pomeroy, *Goddesses, Whores, Wives, and Slaves,* 63, 72–73, and *Xenophon, Oeconomicus: A Social and Historical Commentary* (Oxford, 1994), passim.

16. See further David Asheri, "Laws of Inheritance, Distribution of Land, and Political Constitutions in Ancient Greece," *Historia* 12 (1963), 1–21, esp. 5–6, 12–15, 18–20, and for recent interpretations see S. Hodkinson, "Inheritance, Marriage, and Demography: Perspectives upon the Success and Decline of Classical Sparta," in *Classical Sparta: Techniques Behind Her Success,* ed. A. Powell (Norman, Okla., 1989); Hodkinson, *Property and Wealth in Classical Sparta* (London, 2000); and Sarah B. Pomeroy, *Families in Classical and Hellenistic Greece* (Oxford, 1997), 51–54, and *Property and Wealth in Classical Sparta.* The views Hodkinson expresses in *Property and Wealth in Classical Sparta* on women and the development of Spartan society have not changed fundamentally since the publication of his earlier articles on this subject, although, like Cartledge, he is now more firmly convinced that the economic system Plutarch attributed to Lycurgus and to archaic Sparta was really an invention of Hellenistic reformers. See Appendix n. 90, below.

17. According to Diod. Sic. 10.34.8, the Spartans did not receive wealth from their fathers, but inherited zeal to die in behalf of freedom and glory.

According to Plutarch (*Lyc.* 8), Lycurgus distributed 9,000 lots (kleroi) of state-owned land in equal shares. The conquered people became helots and worked the land (see chap. 5). They owed a certain amount of produce to the Spartiate to whom the kleros had been assigned at birth (see chap. 3). Spartan women were not assigned kleroi, but received the benefits of the system through male relatives. The system was unstable for one obvious reason: the population fluctuated. By the time of Demaratus, there were 8,000 Spartans (Herod. 7.234).

After the Spartan victory in the Peloponnesian War, the Lycurgan system regulating public property was abolished.[18] Thenceforth, a man could give his kleros and his house to anyone he wished, or bequeath them by testament. Furthermore, at the end of the Peloponnesian War a large amount of gold and silver entered Sparta.[19] Greed, which had been a vice attributed to Spartan men, was now seen in women as well. Expensive imported dresses were desired.[20] Xenophon reports that wives agreed to produce children for men in addition to their husbands so that they might control two oikoi.[21] These changes decisively undermined the ideal of economic equality, and eventually led to the concentration of great wealth in the hands of a minority and the creation of an impoverished majority who no longer met the property requirements necessary to enjoy full citizenship.

A parenthetical comparison with the evolution of the kleros system in Ptolemaic Egypt (which is better documented than the Spartan system) is illuminating.[22] Ptolemy I established the kleros system by distributing parcels of agricultural land in the Fayum to entice veterans of Alexander's campaigns to settle in Egypt. Tenure of a kleros was tied to military service in behalf of the Ptolemies and to the payment of certain taxes. The holder of the kleros could lease it out, but not sell it. The king could revoke the grant, and he repossessed the kleros upon the death of the beneficiary, giving it to another potential soldier.[23] A *stathmos* (billet or dwelling place) was included in the grant. In the second half of the third century, as the strong central government declined and natives entered

18. See further David Asheri, "Sulla legge di Epitadeo," *Athenaeum* n.s. 39 (1961), fasc. i–ii, 45–68.

19. Plut. *Agis* 5.1, Ps.-Pl. *Alcib.* 122E–123B, and see further Ephraim David, "The Influx of Money into Sparta at the End of the Fifth Century B.C.," *Scripta Classica Israelica* 5 (1979–80), 30–45, and S. Hodkinson, "Warfare, Wealth, and the Crisis of Spartiate Society," in *War and Society in the Greek World*, ed. J. Rich and G. Shipley (London, 1993), 146–76.

20. Plut. *Lys.* 2.7–8, *Mor.* 141d (26), 190e (1), 229a (1), and see further Ephraim David, "Dress in Spartan Society," *AncW* 19 (1989), 3–13, esp. 12.

21. Xen. *Lac. Pol.* 1.7–9, cf. Polyb. 12.6b.8, Plut. *Lyc.* 15.12–13, *Comp. Lyc. et Num.* 3.1–2, *Mor.* 242b(23), and see chap. 3.

22. See further Sarah B. Pomeroy, *Women in Hellenistic Egypt: From Alexander to Cleopatra* (New York, 1984), 151, and C. Préaux, *L'économie royale des Lagides* (Brussels, 1939), 463–80.

23. See further J. Modrzejewski, "Régime foncier et status social dans l'Égypte ptolémaïque," in *Terre et paysans dépendents dans les sociétés antiques* (Paris, 1979), 163–88, esp. 172, and see now P. Petrie², pp. 37–39.

the military, cleruchs (holders of kleroi) regularly bequeathed billets to wives, sons, and daughters, and the kleroi became hereditary in the male line.[24] Eventually, in the first century B.C.E., a brotherless girl inherited her father's kleros.[25] Despite obvious differences, in both Sparta and Ptolemaic Egypt the kleros system aimed at creating a hereditary army which would always be ready and willing to go out and fight, inasmuch as sustenance from the land was constantly available for the soldier's family and for himself. In both places, the interests of the private family triumphed over the goals of the central government. The documentary papyri record the gradual evolution of the house and the land from public to private tenure, and the change from the inheritance of land exclusively by male kin to inheritance by both sexes. It is also apparent that, doubtless for practical reasons, women could inherit dwelling places before they were able to inherit kleroi. At Sparta, there are no comparable records documenting change over time; consequently it is not possible to determine whether the decree attributed to Epitadeus accomplished or acknowledged the transformation by one radical piece of legislation.[26]

The aims of the state were at variance with the economic ambitions of individual families. Like other Greeks, Spartans practiced diverging devolution, but the Spartans alone attempted to counter the decline in economic status that large families would experience when the paternal estate was divided. Diverging devolution works well only in a capitalistic economy with ever-expanding resources. In a city like Athens, expansion was the result not only of intensification of agriculture,[27] but also of trade, colonization, banking, manufacturing, and services. Sparta's economy, however, was based on agriculture, and property consisted of a finite amount of land and a servile population not augmented by purchase.

The liberation of part of Messenia in 369 seriously undermined the Spartan economy as well. The Messenian helots and the income from the land they tilled were lost to the Spartans. Perhaps it was to some extent due to economic pressures that Spartans began to experiment with various unique methods of family planning (see chap. 3).

Aristotle criticized the Spartan system of land tenure, which permitted women to own land, manage their own property, and exercise authority in the family:

24. Around 60 B.C.E. Auletes recognized the right to dispose of the kleros by testament: *BGU* VI.1285.

25. *P. Berol.* Inv. no. 16 223 (Heracleopolis) = *SB* VIII.9790.

26. Also note the suggestion of Thomas J. Figueira, "Population Patterns in Late Archaic and Classical Sparta," *TAPA* 116 (1968), 186, that in order to stem the decline in population after the earthquake, the *arkhaia moira* (Arist. fr. 611.12, Plut. *Mor.* 218e) was intended to prevent the alienation of the original kleros.

27. See further Pomeroy, *Xenophon, Oeconomicus*, 46–50.

Again, the licence in the matter of their women is detrimental both to the chosen aim of the constitution and to the happiness of the state. For just as man and wife are part of a household, so clearly we should regard a state also as divided into two roughly equal bodies of people, one of men, one of women. So, in all constitutions in which the position of women is unsatisfactory, one half of the state must be regarded as unregulated by law. And that is just what has happened there. For the lawgiver, wishing the whole state to be hardy, makes his wish evident as far as the men are concerned, but has been wholly negligent in the case of the women. For being under no constraint whatever they live unconstrainedly, and in luxury.

An inevitable result under such a constitution is that esteem is given to wealth, particularly if they do in fact come to be female-dominated; and this is a common state of affairs in military and warlike races, though not among the Celts and any others who have openly accorded esteem to male homosexuality. Indeed, it seems that the first person to relate the myth did not lack some rational basis when he coupled Ares with Aphrodite; for all such people seem in thrall to sexual relations, either with males or with females. That is why this state of affairs prevailed among the Laconians, and in the days of their supremacy a great deal was managed by women. And yet what difference is there between women ruling and rulers ruled by women? The result is the same. Over-boldness is not useful for any routine business, but only, if at all, for war. Yet even to those purposes the Laconians' women were very harmful. This they demonstrated at the time of the invasion by the Thebans: they were not at all useful, as in other states, but caused more confusion than the enemy.

So it seems that from the earliest times licence in the matter of their women occurred among the Laconians, reasonably enough. For there were long periods when the men were absent from their own land because of the campaigns, when they were fighting the war against the Argives, or again the one against the Arcadians and Messenians. When they gained their leisure, they put themselves into the hands of their legislator in a state of preparedness brought about by the military life, which embraces many parts of virtue. People say that Lycurgus endeavoured to bring the women under the control of his laws, but that when they resisted he backed off. These then are the causes of what took place, and clearly, therefore, of this mistake as well. But the subject of our inquiry is not whom we ought to excuse and whom not, but what is correct and what is not.

The poorness of the arrangements concerning women seems, as was said earlier, not only to create a sort of unseemliness in the constitution in itself on its own, but also to contribute something to the greed for money; for after the points just made one could assail practice in respect of the uneven levels of property. For some of them have come to possess far too much, others very little indeed; and that is precisely why the land has fallen into the hands of a small number. This matter has been badly arranged through the laws too. For while he made it (and rightly made it) ignoble to buy and sell land already possessed, he left it open to anyone, if they wished, to give it away or bequeath it—and yet the same result follows inevitably, both in this case and in the other. Moreover, something like two-fifths of all the land is possessed by women, both because of the many heiresses that appear, and because of the giving of large dowries. Now it would have been better if it had been arranged that there should be no dowry, or a small or even a moderate one. But as it is one may give an heiress in marriage to any person one wishes; and if a man dies intestate, the person he leaves as heir gives her to whom he likes. As a result, although the land was sufficient to support 1,500 cavalry and 30,000 heavy infantry, their number was not even 1,000. The sheer facts have shown that the provisions of this system served them badly; the state withstood not a single blow, but collapsed owing to the shortage of men.[28]

Luxury

As we have seen, by Aristotle's time, women owned nearly two-fifths of the land of Laconia. Because the Spartan economy was based entirely upon agriculture, women controlled a significant portion of the means of production. The wealthiest women in mainland Greece were Spartans. They advertised their wealth flamboyantly by winning victories in horseraces at Olympia. One woman is named in a fragmentary inscription listing Spartans who had made monetary donations for the rebuilding of the temple of Apollo at Delphi. Philostratis is cited for giving three obols in 360. Only one man gave as little as she, and most gave at least twice that amount.[29] As time went on, Macedonian queens and royal women (like Amastris) on the fringes of the Greek world rivaled and surpassed Spartan women in wealth, for, like the Romans, the former had access to many sources of revenue in their various empires, while the Spartans were limited to incomes derived from a polis economy based on agriculture.[30]

Spartan society as a whole had become stratified, with the majority of male Spartiates so impoverished that they could not meet the requirements of membership in a syssition. They were no longer homoioi, but known as "inferiors" (Xen. Hell. 3.3.6). Moralists claimed that wealth, rather than the old Spartan virtues, had become the principle criterion for high social status. In any event, this social change gave women an opportunity to be members of the elite on the same terms as men. Some were even able to enrich themselves illegally, as men did. Theopompus reports that during the Third Social War (356–346), Archidamus III took some of the money at Delphi and that the Phocians bribed his wife Deinicha so that she would persuade her husband to support them (Paus. 3.10.3).

---

28. Arist. Pol. 1269b12–1270a34, trans. T. J. Saunders, Aristotle, Politics: Books I and II (Oxford, 1995), 42–43.

29. Gifts to the Naopoioi: CID II.4.1.55–6, table 3, and see further Hodkinson, Property and Wealth in Classical Sparta, 174–75, 439.

30. Pomeroy, Women in Hellenistic Egypt, 14–16.

Despite their vaunted austerity, Spartans apparently were tempted to keep some items of luxury in private at home. Xenophon (*Lac. Pol.* 7.6) reports that houses were inspected to ascertain whether anyone was hiding any gold or silver. This practice may have become more common in Xenophon's day, because that was the time when large amounts of precious metals were entering Sparta. Doubtless Aristotle associated women with greed and luxury, for these were features of private life.[31] A parallel from Roman history is of interest. In 195 B.C.E., during the debate over the repeal of the Oppian Law at Rome, a speaker argues that women should be granted the opportunity to display their wealth by wearing gold and purple and riding in carriages, for they had few other avenues by which to satisfy their ambitions.[32] The single item of conspicuous consumption that Spartan women were permitted was racehorses. It is no accident that a Spartan was the first woman whose horses were victorious at pan-Hellenic games, for such triumphs provided women with an approved avenue for the display of their wealth.[33] Entering such a competition was expensive, for the owner was obliged to pay for horses, trainers, charioteer, chariot, and—if victorious—a victory monument.

Dowry

Lycurgus had outlawed dowries, but by the end of the fifth century, if not earlier, women had them.[34] Perhaps the tradition that Spartan women did not have dowries was revived or invented in the Hellenistic period under the influence of Agis IV and Cleomenes III or some other utopian program (see below). In the Greek world various lawgivers, philosophers, and moralists disapproved of dowries, or believed they should be regulated. In Plato's *Republic* there is neither marriage nor private property, and therefore there are no dowries, and in *Laws* (742C), dowries are specifically outlawed. Justin (*Epit.* 3.3.8) states that girls marry without a dowry so that they will not be chosen for their wealth.

In an ideal Sparta, just as all the men are *homoioi* who enjoy equal status, so are all the girls equally endowed. It is reasonable to suppose that in a Sparta lacking precious metals, slaves, or other movable wealth, there would be little, except land and horses, to constitute a substantial and useful dowry. A theory about dowry supports the view that there was a time when dowries did not exist in Sparta. Dowries are found principally in parts of the Mediterranean where men

31. Plutarch (*Agis* 4) also associates women with luxury, for he writes that "even though he had been brought up by women," Agis IV was not self-indulgent. In the *Andromache*, Euripides portrays Hermione as having a large dowry when she marries Neoptolemus, who is less affluent.

32. Livy 34.7 and n. 41 below.

33. For an egregious example, see chap. 1 on Cynisca.

34. Plut. *Mor.* 227f15, cf. *Lyc.* 15, *Lys.* 30.5–6; Ael. *VH* 6.6; Athen.13.555b–c citing Hermippus = *FGrH* IV.3 1026 F 6 = F. Wehrli, *Die Schule des Aristoteles*, suppl. 1 (Basel, 1974), fr. 87; Justin *Epit.* 3.3.8.

cultivate land with a plow and own the instruments and beasts needed for production. In such societies, women's work is undervalued: a woman is viewed as a burden to her husband, and her father must contribute a dowry for her support.[35] This analysis is appropriate to a society like that of Athens, where women were barred from access to most economic resources and the means of production, and men performed agricultural labor. In Sparta, in contrast, women were not economic liabilities, for the kleros system ensured their basic sustenance.

Certainly by the end of the fifth century, if not earlier, along with the decline in the kleros system and the accumulation of precious metals and other valuable items in private hands, dowries were a conspicuous part of the economic regime and doubtless contributed to the impoverishment of some families and the accumulation of wealth by others. Aristotle (*Pol.* 1270a25–26) mentions dowries as a means by which women came to possess wealth. Lack of a dowry in Sparta, as elsewhere in Greece, threatened to make a girl an unwilling spinster. The fiancés of Lysander's daughters attempted to break their engagements when they discovered that their brides-to-be were poor (Plut. *Lys.* 30.5). Without giving any historical background by which the event may be dated, Plutarch (*Am. narr.* 775d) tells of a woman's attempted act of savage revenge on other women when her daughters could no longer have dowries after her husband's property was seized by his political enemies. Aelian (*VH* 6.6) reports that a man who had five sons could give his daughters in marriage without a dowry. This exception implies that such a father would be so highly honored that a man might marry his daughter just for the sake of becoming a son-in-law of such a man, but that in ordinary circumstances a dowry was necessary.

Heiresses

In terms of Greek law, an "heiress" was a fatherless, brotherless woman. The heiress at Athens was called *epikleros*; in Gortyn, she was known as *patroiokos*; in Sparta, as *patrouchos*. In the absence of a male descendent, such a woman could be the means by which her father's lineage was perpetuated. She also might transmit her father's property to her son (who thus became his grandfather's heir), or inherit it herself. In some cases there was no property, but the filial obligation to perpetuate the lineage remained. At Athens, the filial obligation was always foremost; at Sparta, the meager sources suggest that the emphasis in the role of the heiress changed over time, with concerns about her property eclipsing those of her father's lineage.[36]

The principal primary sources that help to define the position of the heiress at Sparta include Herodotus, Aristotle, and analogies with the Code of Gortyn. At

---

35. See further Pomeroy, *Xenophon, Oeconomicus*, 60.
36. See further Schaps, *The Economic Rights of Women in Ancient Greece*, 43–45.

Gortyn, the heiress (*patroiokos*) was permitted to keep part of her patrimony and marry outside her father's lineage.[37] According to Herodotus (6.57.4), the kings originally exercised the right to give an heiress (*patrouchos*) in marriage if she had not already been betrothed by her father. If her legal situation was similar to that in Gortyn, the heiress at Sparta was never subject to an inflexible rule that she marry her father's closest male next of kin. She may, however, have been under some moral and religious obligation to see that her father's lineage not be extinguished.[38] There was some concern for the continuity of oikoi at Sparta: for his suicide mission at Thermopylae, Leonidas selected men who had children (Herod. 7.205.2, 5.41.3). Furthermore, we may speculate that the prestige of the kings made it virtually impossible for the Spartan heiress to reject the bridegroom chosen for her.

The power of the state over the heiress and her property decreased as the power of the private family increased, for Aristotle's testimony differs markedly from that of Herodotus. Therefore the change probably occurred at the same time as the other changes increasing the individual's rights over private property that are associated with the reforms attributed to Epitadeus. According to Aristotle, however, the *kleronomos* (heir apparent: *Pol.* 1270a28) had the power to give the heiress (*epikleros*) as well as the property to whomever he pleased. The "heir apparent" was doubtless the nearest male kin of the heiress's father: he was the man who exercised authority over the heiress and her property.

The inheritance regime for Spartan males was the same as for Athenians, but the system was more favorable for Spartan women than for their Athenian counterparts, who did not inherit at all, and who were given dowries that were perhaps one-sixth of what their brothers received.[39] In contrast, the Spartan woman's share of the patrimony was half as much as her brother's. Girls who were fatherless and brotherless were better off at Sparta than at Athens, for the Spartans got to control their property, while the Athenians were simply conduits of the patrimony to their sons. Moreover, the brotherless, fatherless Athenian woman was required to marry her father's closest kinsman, usually her uncle or cousin, even if both were married at the time the woman's father died. On the other hand, in cases where the heiress was not wealthy, the inexorable obligation of the male next of kin to marry her themselves or to find her a husband assured her marriage at Athens, but could compromise her Spartan counterpart. The daughters of Lysander, who were brotherless, nearly lost their bridegrooms when the men

---

37. *Lex Gort.* = *Inscr. Creticae*, VIII.8–12.

38. Hodkinson, *Property and Wealth in Classical Sparta*, 95–98, argues against the majority of scholars—including most recently E. Karabélias, "L'epiclerat à Sparte," in *Studi in onore di Arnaldo Biscardi*, vol. 2 (Milan, 1982), 469–80; E. David, "Aristotle and Sparta," *Anc. Soc.* 13–14 (1982–83), 67–103, esp. 88–89; and Anne-Marie Vérilhac and Claude Vial, *Le mariage grec du VIe siècle av. J.-C. à l'époque d'Auguste, BCH* suppl. 32 (Paris, 1998), 111–12—that there never was a change in the rules governing heiresses in Sparta.

39. See further Schaps, *Economic Rights of Women in Ancient Greece*, 77–79.

learned that their finaceés were poor.[40] It is not certain, however, whether they were engaged to kinsmen.

Aristotle reports that at Sparta, heiresses were numerous (see above). This plethora of heiresses was exaggerated inasmuch as Sparta was always plagued by oliganthropia (sparse male citizen population). Aristotle and later writers drew attention to the connection between oliganthropia and women's ownership of property (see chap. 3). In addition, women of the property-owning classes may have outnumbered men at Sparta, as they did at Rome during and after the Second Punic War. Fearing that men would no longer fulfill the criteria necessary for their census classes and that the number of men eligible for military and governmental service would be diminished, the Romans passed legislation aimed at preventing women from owning great wealth.[41] As is apparent in the western world nowadays, women's survival and longevity is a significant factor in property ownership.

Change Over Time

At the end of the fifth century, private property triumphed at the expense of public property. The reforms attributed to Epitadeus that allowed women to inherit kleroi, the influx of precious metals, the use of dowries, and the laws affecting heiresses permitted women to possess a large portion of the total wealth of Sparta. The period of the Peloponnesian War was a watershed in the history of Athenian women as well. After the Spartans occupied Decelea and war was waged throughout the year rather than just in the summer, as had previously been customary, Athenian women had to assume more responsibility and exercise greater economic power. Like Spartans, in the absence of men Athenian women managed their affairs.[42] Defeat cost the Athenians their empire and produced an immediate, though temporary, decline in the city's economy. Some thirty years after the Peloponnesian War, Athens had returned to its traditional way of life: in contrast, the Spartan defeat at Leuctra and the loss of the rich agricultural land of Messenia dealt a lethal blow to the Spartan economy. A generation later, Sparta pointedly refused to support the campaigns of Alexander: consequently, Spartans missed the opportunity to share in plundering the wealth of Persia. By the third century, the economy was characterized by many mortgages and by large estates in the hands of a few. These few included royal women, who were among the wealthiest people in Sparta (see below). Only 700 old Spartan families remained, and of these only about 100 possessed land and kleros (Plut. *Agis* 5.4). Female members of these fortunate 100 families benefited from

---

40. See chap. 2 n. 33.
41. See above on the Lex Oppia, and see further Pomeroy, *Goddesses, Whores, Wives, and Slaves,* 162–63, 178, and Jane Gardner, *Women in Roman Law and Society* (London, 1986), 171–77.
42. See further Pomeroy, *Goddesses, Whores, Wives, and Slaves,* 71–73, 119.

the concentration of wealth. A brotherless woman could inherit all her father's land, as did Agiatis, who inherited from the extremely wealthy Gylippus (Plut. *Cleom.* 1.2). With such assets, she was claimed as wife by two kings, Agis IV and Cleomenes III.

Women and the Reforms of Agis and Cleomenes

In 244 B.C.E., when he was not quite twenty, Agis IV became the Eurypontid king of Sparta.[43] He had been raised by his mother Agesistrata and his grandmother Archidamia. The Agiad king, Leonidas (ca. 316–235), was older, had lived with the Seleucids in great luxury, was married to a daughter of one of them, and had two children by that wife.[44] Agis, in contrast, recreated himself as a Spartan of the old austere tradition, wearing the short cloak, for example, and following the laws attributed to Lycurgus. He proposed a program of reform, principally designed to increase the number of full-fledged citizens and restore Sparta to its former prestige. Redistribution of the wealth was essential to reinstate the 600 landless citizens as homoioi. Agis donated 600 talents and his own huge estate for redistribution (Plut. *Agis* 9). Women controlled most of the wealth in Sparta: therefore their support was essential for the success of the reforms. Agis was able to convince his mother and grandmother, who were not only the two wealthiest women, but who were the wealthiest of all Spartans, to contribute their property. They were both widows, and doubtless doted on the charismatic young king, but other wealthy women did not support his program. According to Plutarch (*Agis* 7), they were corrupted by their desire for luxury and were reluctant to give up the prestige and influence derived from their wealth. We also observe that the women exercised full control over their own property.

Leonidas led the opposition to Agis' program, and after much strife was deposed and replaced by Cleombrotus, his son-in-law, who supported the reforms (Plut. *Agis* 11.3–4). At this juncture, Leonidas' daughter Chilonis took her father's side and joined him in the temple of Athena of the Bronze House, where

43. Plut. *Agis* 4. See further Claude Mossé, "Women in the Spartan Revolutions," in *Women's History and Ancient History*, ed. Sarah B. Pomeroy (Chapel Hill, N.C., 1991), 138–53, and A. Powell, "Spartan Women Assertive in Politics? Plutarch's *Lives of Agis and Kleomenes*," in *Sparta: New Perspectives*, ed. S. Hodkinson and A. Powell (London, 1999), 393–419. Powell (esp. 414–15) argues that the support of women was crucial to the reforms and that some of the stories about heroic women were shaped by contemporary political factions in ways designed to influence women's opinion.

44. Plut. *Agis* 10. A. S. Bradford, *A Prosopography of Lacedaemonians from the Death of Alexander the Great, 323 B.C., to the Sack of Sparta by Alaric, A.D. 296* (Munich, 1977), 261, states only that he married the daughter of a Syrian ruler and had children. Probably her father was Seleucus Nicator: H. Bengtson, *Die Strategie in der hellenistischen Zeit*, Münchener Beiträge zur Papyrusforschung und antike Rechtsgeschichte 32, 3 vols. (Munich, 1964–67), vol. 2, 46.

he had sought asylum.[45] The favor she showed the dissolute old man was the best recommendation he had. He was eventually recalled. Chilonis was able to convince her father to spare her husband Cleombrotus, but Agis was summarily murdered in 241. Agesistrata and Archidamia were killed as well. One of the ephors had a particular reason for wanting to eliminate Agesistrata: he had borrowed some expensive cups and clothing from her and did not want to return them (Plut. *Agis* 18.4). Leonidas saw to it that Agiatis, the extremely wealthy widow of Agis IV, was given in marriage to his son Cleomenes III, though he was too young for marriage. Her young son by Agis was not heard from again. Pausanias (2.9.1) asserts that Cleomenes poisoned him, but this charge is difficult to accept, unless Agiatis was an unusually forgiving and stoical woman. She had at least one son by Cleomenes (Plut. *Cleom.* 22.8).

Royal women in the Hellenistic period were influential in politics as powers behind the throne. As we have seen, Agiatis was married first to Agis IV, and when widowed she was married to Cleomenes III. In Plutarch's descriptions, both marriages were paradigmatically harmonious and loving, typical of the ideals of the Hellenistic period.[46] Agiatis was able to instill in her second husband the revolutionary ideas of her first (Plut. *Cleom.* 1.2). Cleomenes also was influenced by his studies with Sphaerus, a Stoic who came to Sparta to lecture (Plut. *Cleom.* 2.2, 11.2). In 235, when Cleomenes became the sole king of Sparta, he attempted to revive Agis' program. His mother, Cratesicleia, who was extremely wealthy, supported his efforts and, in fact, remarried so that her husband Megistonous would use his influence on her son's behalf. Plutarch indicates that it was her own independent choice both to remarry and to select her new husband. Megistonous and his supporters contributed their property for redistribution (Plut. *Cleom.* 10–11.1). Abolition of debt and redistribution of land followed. The agoge and syssitia were revived. Sparta was restored to its former military eminence for a time, but with Macedonian forces threatening him, Cleomenes turned to Ptolemy III Euergetes for assistance. Megistonous had been killed in battle, and Agiatis had died around 224. Ptolemy promised to help, but only if Cleomenes sent Cratesicleia and his children to Egypt as hostages.

Eventually Cleomenes was defeated by an alliance of Macedonians and Achaeans and fled with three thousand soldiers to Egypt, where the degenerate Ptolemy IV, Philopator, was now ruler. Philopator ordered that Cleomenes be imprisoned.[47] and the Spartan women and children in Alexandria be killed. At

45. See chap. 3 n. 27.

46. See further Sarah B. Pomeroy, *Plutarch's Advice to the Bride and Groom and A Consolation to His Wife* (New York, 1999), passim.

47. Plut. *Cleom.* 37, Polyb. 5.37–39, and see further F. W. Walbank, *A Historical Commentary on Polybius*, 3 vols. (Oxford, 1957–79), vol. 1, 568–69.

first Cratesicleia panicked, but in the end they died stoically and bravely.[48] Plutarch (*Cleom.* 39.1) commented: "Sparta played out these events with the deeds of women rivaling those of men."

The Last Reformers: Apega and Nabis and Chaeron

Nabis reigned as sole king of Sparta from 207 to 192. He may have been a member of the Eurypontid dynasty, though he executed all members of the royal houses. His wife Apega is probably identical with Apia, daughter of Aristippus of Argos who, like Nabis, ruled as a tyrant.[49] By marrying one of their daughters to Apia's brother, Pythagoras of Argos, and by trying to arrange marriages for their adult sons with the daughters of Philip V of Macedon in 197, they mimicked the political endogamy of tyrants in the archaic period.[50] Polybius disliked both Nabis and Apega and portrays them in an unfavorable light. He indicates that Apega wielded a great deal of power, furthering her husband's ambitions and gratifying her greed. Like a Hellenistic queen, an Arsinoë or Cleopatra, she received men at court alongside her husband. She evidently wanted to be wealthy like her royal predecessors, and Nabis sent her to her native Argos to procure money. Her viciousness exceeded her husband's. A woman, she knew how to humiliate women, and also how to dishonor men by humiliating the women in their family. She subjected the Argive women to suffering and violence and stole nearly all their gold jewelry and valuable clothing (Polyb. 13.7). Inspired by his wife, Nabis invented a female robot as evil and deceptive as Pandora:

> He also had made for himself a machine, if one should call such a thing a machine. It was the image of a woman, dressed in expensive clothing, in appearance a well-executed likeness of the wife of Nabis. Whenever he sent for any of the citizens, wishing to exact money, he would begin by speaking gently. . . . If any refused and said they would not pay the sum, he said something like, "Perhaps I am not able to persuade you; however, I think this Apega will." This was the name of Nabis' wife. He said this, and soon the image I have described was present. When the man shook her hand, rising from his chair, he made the woman stand and embraced her with his hands and drew her little by little to his chest. Under her dress she had arms and hands and breasts covered with iron nails. Whenever Nabis placed his hands on his wife's back and by means of certain devices drew the man towards her and drove him against her

---

48. Plut. *Cleom.* 38, and see chap. 1. Graham Shipley, *The Greek World After Alexander, 323–30 B.C.* (London, 2000), 440, comments that Plutarch's use of vivid details indicates that "this may be a real episode, described for Plutarch by his sources."

49. See further Bradford, *A Prosopography of Lacedaemonians,* 39.

50. Livy 32.38.3, 34.25.5.

breasts very slowly; he forced the man who was being crushed to say anything. In this way he destroyed quite a few of those who refused to pay him. (Polyb. 13.7)[51]

Nabis was a reformer, like Cleomenes. His program included the redistribution of land, but unlike the reigns of Agis and Cleomenes, in Nabis' time the donations were not voluntary. His program, like that of the reformer kings, included abolition of debts and the restoration of the Lycurgan constitution (Livy 34.31.16–18). In 195, he executed eighty of the *principes iuventutis* (Livy 34.27.8). He also exiled the wealthiest and most prominent Spartiates who were his enemies, and gave their property as well as their wives and daughters (Livy 34.35.7 *liberos coniuges*) in marriage to newly freed helots.[52] We are not told if the helots were bachelors or what happened to their former wives, or how many women were involved. Doubtless the men were enthusiastic about marrying the wives of their former masters, at the very least because they would enjoy their estates.[53] Previously when helots were freed, they had not usually been made citizens, but Nabis conferred citizenship on them in large numbers (Livy 38.34.6). Polybius (16.13.1) refers to the men as *douloi* (slaves) and Livy (34.27.9) once uses the word *ilotae* (helots), but elsewhere (34.21.11) refers to *servi* (slaves). It seems more likely that the members of the lower class who married the wives and daughters of the Spartan exiles were helots and mercenaries rather than slaves.[54] The early Ptolemies had already demonstrated that mercenaries could be recruited as citizens by the offer of an oikos,[55] and Nabis certainly was interested in increasing the number of soldiers at Sparta. Furthermore, at least judging by the swashbuckling adventurers depicted in New Comedy, mercenaries often captivated the hearts of women. In any case, to force upper-class Greek women to marry purchased slaves, who were possibly foreign born, and to confer Spartan

51. Though Walbank, *A Historical Commentary on Polybius*, vol. 2, 420–21, and P. A. Cartledge and A. J. S. Spawforth, *Hellenistic and Roman Sparta: A Tale of Two Cities* (London, 1989), 72, disbelieve the story, the existence of other robots and automatic devices in the Hellenistic period helps to lend credence to this one. For example, at the front of his parade, Demetrius of Phalerum had a mechanical snail that spit saliva (Polyb. 12.13.11).

52. Livy 34.31.11,14, 38.34.6, Plut. *Philop.* 16.4. Polyb. 13.6.3 states they were married "to the most prominent of the rest and the mercenaries."

53. André Aymard, *Les premiers rapports de Rome et de la Confédération Achaienne (198–189 avant J.-C.)* (Bordeaux, 1938), 35, followed by J.-G. Texier, *Nabis* (Paris, 1975), 57, 75, argues that marriages with Spartan wives and daughters were profitable inasmuch as women controlled two-fifths of the wealth. The figures given by Aristotle for women landowners need not have been true for the time of Nabis, especially after the redistributions under Agis and Cleomenes, but it is likely that Spartan women in Nabis' time were still wealthy.

54. See further J.-G. Texier, "Nabis and the Helots," *DHA* 1 (1979), 189–205. John Briscoe, *A Commentary on Livy, Books XXXIV–XXXVII* (Oxford, 1991), 92–93, makes the reasonable suggestion that Livy will not have understood the precise status distinctions between helots and slaves.

55. See Pomeroy, *Women in Hellenistic Egypt*, 100–103.

citizenship on such people, would have been unthinkable. Marriage to a Spartan wife or daughter instantly supplied a helot with an oikos sufficient to maintain a citizen soldier. According to a treaty of 194 B.C.E. between Nabis and the Romans, the wives and daughters of the men exiled by Nabis were permitted to join their original husbands.[56] The treaty stated explicitly that the women would not be forced to join their previous husbands. We are not told whether any of them chose to do so.[57] Plutarch's use of the verb *metoikizo* (*Phil.* 16.4), with its connotations of transferring an oikos, to describe Philopoemen's eviction of the slaves and mercenaries whom tyrants had made Spartan citizens implies that they left with their Spartan wives and families. Furthermore, we may speculate that, considering the social hierarchies in force in antiquity, the older women wanted to continue to control and enjoy younger husbands who were clearly their social inferiors, and not exchange them for the original husbands, who were doubtless irate and displeased with what had transpired in their absence. The older women may also have stayed to support their daughters, who knew no other husbands. Moreover, the women wanted to keep their land, and were afraid that the children they had borne to the helots would suffer the same fate as those supposedly born to their ancestors during the Second Messenian War. It was said that when the Spartan husbands returned after the war they exiled these half-breed children to Italy, where they allegedly founded the colony of Tarentum (see chap. 2). In any case, in 188 after Nabis had been killed under Philopoemon, the Achaean commander who had restored Sparta as a member of the Achaean League, the exiles returned to Sparta and those who had been made citizens by "tyrants" were exiled to Achaea (Plut. *Phil.* 16.4, Livy 38.34). We are not told what happened to the women. We may speculate that their original husbands were willing to take them back, if for no other reason than the fact that they possessed substantial amounts of property.[58]

Nabis was killed in 192 by Aetolians, who were his putative allies. The Romans reluctantly settled affairs in Sparta for a time. The last radical leader of Sparta was Chaeron, who had been exiled from Sparta and had served as an envoy to Rome in 182–181. He seized the property of the sisters, wives, mothers, and children of men who had been exiled (by rulers from Cleomenes through Nabis), and distributed it at random to his most needy supporters (Polyb. 24.7.3). Finally, the Spartans invited Aristaenus, the commander of the Achaean League,

56. Livy 34.35.7, see also Plut. *Philop.* 16.3. Aymard, *Les premiers rapports de Rome et de la Confédération Achaienne*, 241 n. 50, argues that the Latin texts makes it abundantly clear that some of Spartan women willingly stayed with their new husbands. Linda Piper, "Spartan Helots in the Hellenistic Age," *Anc. Soc.* 15–17 (1984–86), 75–88, esp. 87 n. 77, states (without citing any evidence) that none of the women chose to join her original husband.

57. See the laconic remark of B. Shimron, *Late Sparta* (Buffalo, N.Y., 1972), 121, that the forced marriages enjoyed "at least partial success."

58. Thus Aymard, *Les premiers rapports de Rome et de la Confédération Achaienne*, 241–42, who stresses the lucrative aspect of marriage to Spartan women.

to put an end to Chaeron's tyranny, and returned the property to those from whom it had been seized.

Autonomy and Social Power

Individual women like Gorgo, Agiatis, Cratesicleia, and perhaps Deinicha exercised a significant influence on male members of their own family and on society at large. Moreover, women in groups were encouraged to uphold Spartan ideals by activities such as publicly praising brave men and reviling cowards and bachelors. No other Greek women are reported to have been involved in elections to the extent that Spartans were. When a member of the Gerousia was elected, he was followed by throngs of young men who praised him and many women who sang of his excellence and congratulated him on his good fortune in life. His syssition awarded an extra portion of food to the victor. After dinner, his female relatives congregated at the doors of the mess-hall. Thereupon, in public, a second selection took place, but the competitors were female. The victor summoned the woman whom he held in the highest esteem and gave her the food, saying that he had received it as an indication of his excellence and he gave it to her in the same way.[59] The rest of the women congratulated her and escorted her home (Plut. *Lyc.* 26.3–4).

Such reports do not indicate that women were fully active citizens in the sense that men were, that they could defend their polis, vote, or hold governmental office, for overt political power was not exercised by women anywhere in the Greek world before the advent of Hellenistic queens. But, as Aristotle remarked in his discussion of Sparta, in warlike societies men are dominated by their wives. Even if he is exaggerating, he did perceive that women had a voice in managing affairs at Sparta. Some scholars in the second half of the twentieth century have gone even further than Aristotle in detecting the power and influence of Spartan women.[60] Stephen Hodkinson paints the grandest picture of Spartan women in a plutocratic society. Hodkinson argues that the kleros system governing public lands that Plutarch describes was solely an invention of the Hellenistic period. Consequently, no category of land was ever restricted to ownership only by males. If Hodkinson were correct, the situation described by Aristotle would have had roots as early as the archaic period when women would have possessed

---

59. In the same way, the kings were given a double portion of food so that they could offer it as gifts of honor.

60. For a different view see Jean Ducat, "La femme de Sparte et la cité," Ktèma 23 (1998), 385–406, esp. 393, who criticizes Hodkinson's interpretation of female inheritance and property rights and postulates the existence of kyrioi for women at Sparta, because they are mentioned in the Lawcode of Gortyn. Using the same evidence, J. Christien, "La loi d'Epitadeus: Un aspect de l'histoire économique et sociale à Sparte," RD 52 (1974), 197–221, esp. 211, maintains that Spartan women enjoyed free disposition of their property.

and managed vast amounts of property.[61] The evidence from women's history, however, indicates that he is not correct, but rather that an additional source of great wealth was available to women at the end of the fifth century. Indeed, Hodkinson draws the bulk of his evidence for women's wealth from fourth-century evidence. Victories in pan-Hellenic chariot races were evidence of vast wealth. All twelve Olympic victories won by Spartans from 548 to 420 were won by men. In contrast, half of the six victories from 396 to 368 were won by women. The sudden appearance of female victors in chariot races at Olympia beginning in 396,[62] the new craving for expensive imported dresses, and even Agesilaus' scoffing remark about Cynisca seem suitable to the conspicuous consumption characteristic of the nouvelles riches.

G. E. M. de Ste Croix contrasts "the inferior position of women at Athens" with "the powerful position of women in the Spartan system of property owner-ship."[63] James Redfield points out that women were active in the system of mar-riage exchange and in motivating men to increase the economic status of the oikos.[64] According to Barton Kunstler, women made major decisions concerning the disposition of household and communal wealth, discussing financial matters with helots and perioikoi.[65]

Women's influence, however, was not restricted to the private sphere. Maria H. Dettenhofer argues that wives managed the kleroi, and were therefore respon-sible for their husbands' social status.[66] She claims that women wielded political influence through their economic power. As we have seen above, Plutarch's description (Agis 7) of women's participation in the reforms of Agis gives a clear picture of the direct relationship between wealth and public power. For elite women at Sparta at that time, wealth was probably the only secure basis of influence and autonomy. In each of the sagas of reform, royal women were directly involved because they were property owners and controlled their own wealth. Agesistrata, Archidamia, and Cratesicleia espoused the political beliefs of the men in their family, and like the men, paid for their involvement with their lives. That they were executed is testimony to their power.

---

61. Hodkinson, *Property and Wealth in Classical Sparta,* 99–103. On Plutarch and Hodkinson, see further Preface n. 11, and Appendix n. 90.

62. Hodkinson, *Property and Wealth in Classical Sparta,* 308, table 12.

63 "Some Observations on the Property Rights of Athenian Women," *CR* n.s. 20 (1970), 274–78, esp. 277.

64. "The Women of Sparta," *CJ* 73 (1977–78), 146–61, esp. 158–60.

65. "Women and the Development of the Spartan Polis: A Study of Sex Roles in Classical Antiquity" (Ph.D. diss., Boston University, 1983), 427.

66. "Die Frauen von Sparta," *Klio* 75 (1993), 61–75, esp. 71–75.

5

THE LOWER CLASSES

Lower-class inhabitants of Laconia and Messenia far outnumbered their Spartan rulers, but we know very little about them aside from their relationship to the Spartans. For Greek history in general, far more is known about the upper class. Furthermore, even among the upper class, there is less evidence for women than for men. Like women elsewhere in Greece, and like upper-class Spartan women, their status and reputation probably depended largely both upon the property they possessed and upon the men with whom they were associated. For example, as we have seen in the upper class, the mothers of brave men were respected and the mothers and sisters of cowards were dishonored and shunned like the cowards themselves (see chap. 3). Unfortunately, neither ancient sources nor modern studies have made gender a defining category in discussions of the lower classes at Sparta. Hence this chapter is the shortest in the book.

Helots

More is known about helots than about any other non-Spartiates. Helots were Greeks living in Laconia and Messenia whom the Spartans had reduced to servitude early in the archaic period. They performed the work that slaves (and free people) performed in the rest of the Greek world. Moreover, because Spartans, unlike free people in the rest of the Greek world, were not trained to farm or engage in manual labor, helots were more essential to the Spartan economy than slaves were elsewhere.

Helots belonged to the state and could not be sold away from Sparta.[1] Unlike the families of slaves, whose liaisons had no legal status and who did not own

1. Nino Luraghi, "Helotic Slavery Reconsidered" (paper delivered at the Celtic Conference in Classics, National University of Ireland, Maynooth, Sept. 8, 2000), argues that they could be sold or lent within Sparta.

their children, the families of helots were much less likely to be broken up by sale or testament, or by the caprice of an individual owner. They lived in family groups in houses designated for them.[2] More than one helot family was assigned to a *kleros* (country estate: Xen. *Hell.* 3.3.5). They farmed in Laconia and Messenia and were required to send a fixed portion of produce to the Spartan man to whom their kleros had been allocated.[3] Helotage was fundamental to the kleros system, but because the entire system of land tenure at Sparta is not well understood and changed over time (see chap. 4), the details of helotry are not clear. It is reasonable to assume, however, that since Spartan women were landowners, they supervised the work of helots on their property, riding or driving out to visit them as men did (Xen. *Hell.* 3.3.5).

Helots also supplied domestic labor for Spartan homes.[4] Xenophon's comment on domestic weaving (see chap. 1) and Plutarch's report on Timaea, wife of Agis II, indicate that female helots were included in this obligation.[5] Plutarch (*Ages.* 3.1 = Duris *FGrH* 76 F 69) represents Timaea not only conversing with her female helots, but also trusting them enough to tell them that the child she was bearing had been fathered by Alcibiades, not by her husband. Since Agis was unsure about the child's paternity, Timaea must have been having intercourse with both her husband and her lover in the same period of time. Because it is impossible to keep secrets from domestics, the helots must have known that she was having intercourse with both. Inasmuch as Timaea was the only person who actually knew who the child's father was, she was probably using contraception during intercourse with her husband.

By the fourth century, with the rise of private property in Sparta, helots were thought (at least by some non-Spartan commentators) to belong to individuals and in some respects to be the equivalent of slaves. Thus Xenophon (*Lac. Pol.* 6.3) speaks of Spartans lending helots to other Spartans who needed them. At this time, there were probably slaves of non-helot origin in Sparta as well (see below).

Free Noncitizens

There were several other categories of non-Spartiates living in Sparta. These included the *perioikoi* (dwellers about) who were free, but not citizens. They seem to have lived in poleis and had some sorts of civic organizations like other

---

2. Diod. Sic. 12.67.4; Strab. 8.5.4 (365); Xen. *Hell.* 3.3.5.

3. The amount apparently varied through the centuries from one-half, according to Tyrtaeus 5 (quoted by Paus. 4.14.4–5), to the fixed amount described by Plutarch (see chap. 3 n. 8).

4. E.g., Xen. *Hell.* 5.4.28 (attendants of Agesilaus); Xen. *Lac. Pol.* 7.5; Herod. 6.63 (attendants of King Ariston); Polyb. 4.81.7, 5.29.9 (attendants of King Lycurgus); and the mothakes who were raised in Spartan homes (see below).

5. For nurses, see below.

freeborn people in the Greek world beyond Sparta. Though some worked as farmers, the perioikoi as a whole shouldered a disproportionate share of craft and commercial endeavors, since Spartan men were trained to work only in the military and government,[6] though, as we have mentioned, they did supervise their country estates. Perioikic men worked as craftsmen and merchants and did the jobs that male Spartans were not permitted to do. Perioikic men also served in the army, some holding positions of command. Presumably most perioikic women lived like other Greek women (but not like upper-class Spartan women), raising children, managing their households, and performing domestic labor in their own homes. Some probably worked in service jobs like baby nursing and prostitution (see below).

There were other free people at Sparta distributed in a number of categories that exceeded anything we know about social distinctions in any other Greek polis. This mass of people included helots who had been freed for performing good service (*neodamodeis*); mixed-blood members of the lower class who had been through the agoge and were elevated above the class they had been born into (*mothakes*); bastards born of helot mothers and Spartan fathers (*nothoi*: Xen. *Hell.* 5.3.9); and, at the top of these inferior ranks, those who had been born into citizen status but had been demoted for non-payment of the dues owed to their syssition (*hypomeiones*).[7] The men in all these categories were free and (with the exception of the *neodamodeis*) had been educated in the agoge, so they were able to undertake military service and thus compensate for the ever-dwindling supply of Spartiate men. Because they were Greeks and not foreign born, it was doubtless easier to grant them some social mobility. Thus, for example, helots might be given their freedom by the state in return for military service. We do not know if their wives were simultaneously liberated at all such occasions, but Thucydides (1.103.3) notes that after the helot rebellion in the 460s, rebels were free to leave Spartan territory, taking their wives and children. Helots could own private property and could purchase their freedom when the state offered them an opportunity.

Especially at times when the state needed funds, helots were encouraged to purchase their freedom at a set price,[8] but we do not know if they had to pay for their wives as well, and whether the price was the same. Slaves in the rest of the Greek world also had opportunities to purchase their freedom, but they were not

6. See further P. A. Cartledge, *Sparta and Lakonia: A Regional History, 1300–326 B.C.* (London, 1979), 182–85.

7. For additional categories including *trophimoi* and offspring of foreigners, and discussion of the definition of each status, see J. Ducat, *Les hilotes, BCH* suppl. 20 (Athens, 1990), 166–68. The definitions remain controversial; e.g., S. Hodkinson, *Property and Wealth in Classical Sparta* (London 2000), 198, 355–56, considers mothakes as sons of poor or demoted citizens.

8. According to Plut. *Cleom.* 23.1–5, to fill his war chest in 223 Cleomenes raised 500 talents by selling freedom to about 6,000 helots, charging five Attic minas per man.

regarded as equals: the prices varied and had to be negotiated for each individual man, woman, or child.

Working Women

Prostitutes

Because precious metals and useful money did not circulate in archaic and classical Sparta, and because Lycurgus had imposed a strict moral regime, there was no prostitution (Plut. *Lyc.* 9.3). Non-Spartiates, however, were not subject to such a stringent discipline. Spartan women were forbidden to wear gold and cosmetics, but hetairai could adorn themselves.[9] Before the end of the fifth century, patrons might surreptitiously use foreign money, but when large amounts of gold and silver began to be available to private citizens, prostitutes became more accessible. A few were notorious and wealthy.[10] In 397, the ephors and some members of the Gerousia gave orders to Cinadon, who was suspected of fomenting a conspiracy, that he was to go to Aulon, a perioikic community in northwest Messenia on the border between Messenia and Elis, and bring back a particular woman reputed to be the most beautiful, for she had been corrupting Spartans of all ages who came there (Xen. *Hell.* 3.3.8). The Hellenistic geographer Polemon (fl. ca. 190) reports that he saw the bronze sculptures dedicated by the hetaira Cottina.[11]

After the death of his wife, Cleomenes took a freeborn woman of Megalopolis as his concubine (*paidiskē*: Plut. *Cleom.* 39.2) She may have borne him a child, for he had one son by Agiatis (Plut. *Cleom.* 22.8), but more than one of his children accompanied his mother to Egypt and died there.[12]

Nurses

Spartan nurses were highly praised. Plutarch (*Lyc.* 16.3), who was especially interested in the rearing and education of children, points out that Spartan nurses did not apply swaddling bands. They were famous for raising children to be happy, not discontented or finicky about their food or afraid of the dark or of being left alone. The devotion of a nurse who carried her ugly charge daily two miles uphill to the Menelaion so that Helen would make her beautiful is noteworthy (see Conclusion). For these reasons, foreigners sometimes acquired Spartan nurses

---

9. Xen. *Lac. Pol.* 5.8; Plut. *Lyc.* 1.4.4; Athen. 15.686–67; Clement of Alex., *Paid.* 2.10.105.

10. On foreign coinage: Plut. *Lys.* 17.1–4, Ephorus *FGrH* 70 F 193, and see further G. L. Cawkwell, "The Decline of Sparta," *CQ* 33 (1983), 385–400, esp. 395–96.

11. Athen. 574c–d and see chap. 6 n. 70.

12. Plut. *Cleom.* 38.3. See further G. Marasco, *Commento alle biografie Plutarchee di Agide e di Cleomene*, 2 vols. (Rome, 1981), vol. 2, 589, and chap. 4, above.

for their own children. Plutarch uses *oneomai* (purchase), which indicates that the nurses could not have been helots, since helots were not sold to foreigners.[13] Their status is not clear: the spotty evidence suggests that they were drawn from helots as well as from other groups of non-Spartiate women. In his comedy *Helots*, Eupolis mentions a special festival in which Spartan nurses participated.[14] He might have heard about such an occasion from a Spartan nurse living in Athens. Plutarch notes that non-Spartans purchased Spartan nurses because of their care and skill, and goes on to report that Amycla, who nursed (*tittheusasan*) Alcibiades, was said to be a Spartan (*Lyc.*16.5, see also Plut. *Alcib.* 1.2). The participle refers to wet-nursing. An Athenian inscription of the fourth century commemorates Malicha of Cytheria, nurse (*titthe*) of the children of Diogeitus, an extremely righteous woman who came from the Peloponnesus.[15]

Religion

Helots and other members of the lower classes shared the same religion with their masters. Shrines for the various gods have been found throughout Laconia and Messenia, presumably, for the most part, created for the use of the local inhabitants.[16] Archaeologists have verified the existence of many religious sites described by Pausanias and others. Some women dedicated altars. The humble nature of their offerings indicates that they were not wealthy.[17] A few religious occasions were directly connected with social status. Children's nurses participated in the festival called Tithenidia in honor of Artemis. They brought boy babies to a temple for Artemis Corythalia by a river (see chap. 6). The nurses enjoyed a varied and sumptuous feast. In addition to the regular celebration of "The Cleaver" (*kopis*), which included the sacrifice of goats, and eating cakes, cheese, sausage, figs, and beans, they also sacrificed suckling pigs and bread, and celebrated by dancing and wearing masks.[18]

13. On the status of Spartan nurses, see most recently Valerie French, "The Spartan Family and the Spartan Decline," in *Polis and Polemos*, ed. C. Hamilton and P. Krentz (Claremont, Calif., 1997), 241–73, esp. 260–61, where French suggests that though most Spartan nurses were slaves or helots, they may also have been freeborn women of lower status (*hypomeiones*).

14. See chap. 6 n. 15.

15. *IG* II³.3111. For the date: Kaibel, *Epigr. Graec.*, p. 17, no. 47.

16. On the continuity of religion in Messenia even after liberation from Spartan rule, see Thomas J. Figueira, "The Evolution of the Messenian Identity," in *Sparta: New Perspectives*, ed. S. Hodkinson and A. Powell (London, 1999), 211–44, esp. 229.

17. M. N. Tod and A. J. B. Wace, *Catalogue of the Sparta Museum* (Oxford, 1906), p. 21; p. 63, no. 427; p. 69, no. 528; pp. 70–71, no. 546; p. 74, no. 618.

18. Athen. 4.139a–b, citing Polemon (Preller, pp. 136–40, para. 56); Hesych. s.v. koruthalistriai 3689 and s.v. kurittoi 4684 (Latte); and see further M. Pettersson, *Cults of Apollo at Sparta: The Hyakinthia, the Gymnopaidiai, and the Karneia* (Stockholm, 1992), 14–17.

On the second day of the Hyacinthia, citizens offered dinner to everyone they knew, including helots.[19] Dining together was a rite of inclusion expressing the solidarity of the entire population.[20] Hierarchies were also temporarily dissolved, not only in dining, but also in the Spartan ceremonies of mourning for the king. When a king or other dignitary died, helots and their wives were obliged to mourn, and the women to wear black or suffer the death penalty Though the mourning was imposed, and may be the Spartans' equivalent of the paid professional mourners found in Athens, it may also show that the helots were conceived of as members of the large fictitious Lacedaimonian family.[21]

Doulai

The development of private property raises the question of the status of the *doulai* (slave women) whom Xenophon mentions in the *Spartan Constitution* (*Lac. Pol.* 1.4). Xenophon reports that Lycurgus thought that doulai were capable enough of producing clothing so that freeborn women could devote their energies to motherhood. In the archaic period, these doulai were doubtless helots; by the fourth century, they may also have been slaves whom Spartans purchased with their newly acquired wealth and who catered to their taste for luxury goods and conspicuous consumption. Helots belonged to the state, whereas slaves constituted part of the private property of the oikoi. Xenophon uses the word *heilotes* in other contexts,[22] but he does not carefully distinguish between the two statuses when describing the women to whom the weaving was delegated in his time. Elsewhere in the *Spartan Constitution* (*Lac. Pol.* 6.3), Xenophon speaks of private property as including hounds, horses, chariots, and *oiketai* (household slaves). He died long after the battle of Leuctra and may have continued to work on the *Spartan Constitution* until after the emancipation of the Messenian helots.[23] After the loss of part of Messenia, when the need for purchased slaves would have increased and there was money to buy them, there is a strong possibility that many of the women who worked in the Spartan household were slaves, though Laconian helots continued to be available.[24] Accordingly, both statuses are

19. Polycrates (before 1st cent. B.C.E.) = *FGrH* 588 3B F 1 = Athen. 4.139f, who mentions *douloi* (slaves) not helots; but this was an old custom and probably included helots. In Plut. *Am. narr.* 775d–e, Spartan women dine with *oikeioi* (see chap. 6).

20. See further Pettersson, *Cults of Apollo*, 18.

21. Tyrtaeus fr. 5; Herod. 6.58.2 (perioikoi and helots). See further Sarah B. Pomeroy, *Families in Classical and Hellenistic Greece* (Oxford, 1997), 51.

22. F. W. Sturz, *Lexicon Xenophonteum*, 4 vols. (1801, repr. Hildesheim, 1964), vol. 2, s.v.

23. Chap. 14, which is critical of Sparta and seems to undermine much of the treatise, may have been written after Leuctra.

24. Ducat does not discuss *Lac. Pol.* 1.4, but in *Les hilotes*, 21 n. 9 and 46, he argues that Xenophon uses *douloi* and *oiketai* indiscriminately of slaves and helots.

possible in the fourth century and the Hellenistic period, at least until the helots were liberated in the time of Augustus.

Reproduction

Helots seem to have had no problem with reproduction, though there were constant forces depleting their number: Spartiates could kill them individually and en masse with impunity, and Athens offered asylum to those who rebelled. At any rate, they continually outnumbered their masters. Although there are no census figures for the helot population, there is some basis on which to compare the number of helots to Spartiates in three successive centuries. Among those who served at the battle of Plataea, helots outnumbered Spartans by at least seven to one (Herod. 9.28–29). Early in the fourth century, approximately 80 Spartiates and 4,000 others milled about in the Spartan agora (Xen. *Hell.* 3.3.5). In other words, the Spartans were outnumbered 50 to 1. The helot population at this time has been estimated at 170,000–224,000, including women.[25] Around 240 B.C.E., some Spartans considered the helots too numerous (Plut. *Cleom.* 18.3).

As we have mentioned, helots lived on farms with their families, though we know little about them. In any case, there was no need to have single-sex dormitories with a bolt on the women's door, as Xenophon describes for the slaves in the *Oeconomicus* (9.5), to prevent the males from gaining access to the females. Unlike slaves, whose numbers could be increased by purchase or conquest, helots themselves were the only source of the helot population and of other segments of the lower classes as well. It was essential for the Spartan economy that helots reproduce.[26] Both men and women helots had a strong incentive to have as many children as possible, although they were constrained by their limited access to arable land. Since the men were constantly vulnerable to murder by the *cryptoi* (secret hunters [of helots]), and to being killed when they served in the Spartan army, for them there was strength in numbers. David Hume astutely observed that helots were the only ancient servile group to reproduce, and argues that this success was the result of their living apart and being public slaves rather than the property of individuals.[27]

Helots were subjected to what amounted to a kind of eugenics, or better, dysgenics, which the Spartans probably learned from breeding animals, and also understood in terms of the Greek belief in the inheritance of acquired

25. P. A. Cartledge, *Agesilaos and the Crisis of Sparta* (London, 1994), 174, and personal communication Oct. 16, 1999.

26. See further M. Whitby, "Two Shadows: Images of Spartans and Helots," in *The Shadow of Sparta*, ed. A. Powell and S. Hodkinson (London, 1994), 87–125, esp. 110.

27. "Of the Populousness of Ancient Nations" (1742), in *Essays, Moral, Political, and Literary* (Oxford, 1963), 381–451, esp. 393.

characteristics. The crypteia was instructed to kill the strongest men (Thuc. 4.80.3–4) so that those who were more servile and might be more easily domesticated would survive to reproduce. Nevertheless, helots served in the military. The wives and children they left behind doubtless were hostages for their good behavior.

Helots not only did work that was normally done by citizens in other Greek states, but they also were forced to become parents of half-Spartan children. Women were regularly used for this purpose: men perhaps only once. The Spartans exploited the reproductive capacity of helots to produce mixed-breed offspring who filled the lower niches of Spartan manpower. The story about the founding of Tarentum by children born of Spartiate women and helots is relevant here.[28] More credible is the evidence for the inclusion of mothakes in Spartan manpower. The definition of *mothakes* is controversial, but they seem to have been children of Spartan fathers and helot mothers who were not reckoned as Spartiates but were free. Apparently, practical considerations outweighed theoretical eugenics in these arrangements. Xenophon (*Hell.* 5.3.9) reports that the bastards (*nothoi*) of Spartan men had experienced the benefits of the state and were fine-looking. This remark lends credence to the view that the helots and Spartans were not originally ethnically distinct, but that their statuses evolved as a result of political and economic developments. In any case, wealthy Spartan men reared mothakes alongside their legitimate sons, and they passed through the agoge together. The mothakes seem to have been given some modified form of citizenship if they completed the agoge.[29] Indeed, the generals Lysander and Gylippus were said to have been mothakes. The Lawcode of Gortyn, Crete, offers some examples of free children born of intercourse between serfs and free men and women.[30] Therefore it is appropriate to ask whether Spartan women had liaisons with lower-class men, although, considering the sex ratio in the Hellenistic period and Greek reluctance to submit women to hypergamy, it is unlikely that Spartiate women were given in marriage to lower-class men (aside from the incident concerning the founding of Tarentum and the outrages perpetrated by Nabis [see chap. 4]). Lower-class female infants may have been subject to infanticide, since the deliberate production of babies of mixed parentage served primarily to create more soldiers to fill the Spartan ranks.[31] Otherwise such women probably bore additional generations of children of mixed parentage.[32] In any case, the use of helot women for the production of mothakes must

28. See chap. 2 n. 44.

29. Phylarchus, *FGrH* 81 F 43 = Athen. 6.271e–f.

30. R. F. Willetts, *The Law Code of Gortyn*, *Kadmos* supp. 1 (Berlin, 1967), p. 15 and cols. VI.55–VII.2.

31. Thus C. J. Tregaro, "Les bâtards spartiates," in *Mélanges Pierre Lévêque*, ed. M.-M. Mactoux and E. Geny (Paris, 1993), esp. 37–38.

32. Thus D. Ogden, *Greek Bastardy* (Oxford, 1996), 223.

have increased the rebelliousness of helot men, especially if the liaisons were the result of individual choice and longlasting, rather than brief encounters (like those in Spartiate husband-doubling) encouraged by the state.

There is no evidence for slave breeding in other parts of the Greek world.[33] Hesiod (*WD* 602–3) advised the novice farmer to get a slave woman without a baby to nurse. Xenophon (*Oec.* 9.5–6) allows slaves to reproduce only as a reward for good behavior. Slave reproduction compromised productivity. Pregnancy and childbirth jeopardized the slave's health or even her life, and the baby might not survive anyway. The Spartans were unique and innovative in exploiting the reproductive potential of servile women.

In sum, the Spartans, who were notorious for their innocence of business matters, had devised a reproductive calculus as early as the constitution attributed to Lycurgus. Even if several of the practices reviewed above and in chapter 3 were temporary, or not widespread, or invented in the Hellenistic period and attributed to Lycurgus, or part of the mirage, it is clear that Sparta served as a kind of laboratory for demographic ideas or actual experiments in which the state and private individuals made investments in order to reap dividends in the form of human capital.

---

33. See further Sarah B. Pomeroy, *Xenophon, Oeconomicus: A Social and Historical Commentary* (Oxford, 1994), 297–300.

6

WOMEN AND RELIGION

This chapter is devoted to the religious experiences of Spartan women. It is not an attempt to cover every aspect of each cult or divinity mentioned, nor to report all the textual and archaeological evidence unless a connection with women's activities can be detected. The evidence is often obscure and fragmentary. In many cases, the sole source of information is a single brief definition in a Byzantine dictionary. Furthermore, the reader must be cautioned that the great majority of votives and small objects that have been excavated—disproportionately those that would illuminate women's history—have not yet received proper scholarly attention (see Appendix). Since the ancient sources are often specific about the ages of the female participants in the cults and whether they are virgins, in this chapter we will also draw as much attention as possible to age groupings or marital status. Athletics, including nude athletics, were often connected with religion; these activities have been discussed in chapter 1.

Greeks everywhere worshipped the same gods and generally in the same ways, but the emphases varied from place to place. Thus in Athens, domestic cults were important and women were particularly involved in mourning the dead. Owing to the the Spartan emphasis on the public sphere, private cults are unknown. In contrast, Spartan cults for women reflected the society's emphasis on female beauty, health, and, most of all, fertility.[1] Furthermore, the shrine of a historical woman, Cynisca, who had been heroized for her equestrian victories, was centrally located in Sparta (see chap. 1). As elsewhere in Greece, there were some cultic activities exclusively for women, others exclusively for men, and some for both. For example, at Sparta women were prominent in the cults of Dionysus, Eileithyia (goddess of childbirth), and Helen (a local heroine), were

---

1. D. Musti and M. Torelli, *Pausania: Guida della Grecia*, vol. 3, *La Laconia* (Milan, 1997), 249, see a direct connection between the connotations of the cult of Helen as divine, rather than merely heroic, and Spartan society where "la donna occupa una posizione di primo piano per la conservazione delle strutture socio-economiche."

excluded from a festival of Ares (Paus. 5.22.7), but participated along with men in the Hyacinthia. As part of their religious experience, women sang, danced, raced, feasted, dedicated votive offerings, drove chariots in processions, and wove clothing for cult images of the gods. In comparison with the cultic activities of their counterparts in Athens, the activities of Spartan women included substantially more opportunities for racing and far less weaving. Since Spartans were always allowed to drink wine, their festivals were probably quite jolly. For example, the festival celebrated in Alcman, *Partheneion* 1, included a sumptuous banquet.[2] The modern reader is free to imagine the behavior of a group of adolescent girls who know each other intimately at an all-night festival. At such banquets women drank unmixed wine as usual, and ate cakes that were fashioned in the shape of breasts.[3] Influenced by Alcman's choral lyrics for maidens, scholars have drawn attention to the communal aspects of religious experience at Sparta that was restricted to women.[4] Even when the rituals were enacted by women only, however, they were considered an essential part of the religious life of all citizens.[5] Sundry votive offerings by individual women are evidence of a variety of personal relationships with divinities, as well.

Artemis Orthia

Artemis was worshipped throughout Greece as a divinity who brought fertility to human beings and animals and protected mothers and children. According to myth, her cult was imported from the East. Pausanias (3.16.7,9) states that the archaic image of the goddess he saw at Sparta was the original that Iphigenia and Orestes had brought from Taurus in the Chersonese. At Sparta, Artemis was associated with Orthia, who, like Artemis, was a nature goddess concerned with both plant and animal life. She was probably the focus of the festival commemorated in Alcman, *Partheneion* 1, where she is referred to as "Orthria," (line 61) and Aotis (goddess of the dawn, line 87). The actual connotations of the word "Orthia" (straightness or uprightness) have puzzled interpreters from antiquity to the present.[6] Pausanias (3.16.11) offers a practical explanation for the title "Orthia": the statue itself stood upright because it was placed in a thicket of willows that supported it. Other interpretations are also possible. The goddess raises children

---

2. Line 81: *Thosteria. LSJ* s.v.: *thosterion* refers to *euoxeterion* "a sumptuous feast" or "a banquet."

3. Sosibius *FGrH* 595 F 6 in his work "On Alcman," bk. 3 = Athen. 14.646a.

4. E.g., Claude Calame, *Les chœurs de jeunes filles en Grèce archaïque* (Rome, 1977).

5. If Eva Stehle, *Performance in Ancient Greece* (Princeton, 1997), 30–41, 74, and passim, is correct, the girls will have performed before the entire Spartan community.

6. *Parthenion* 1.61, and see O. Höfer, "Orthia and Orthosia," in *Ausführlicher Lexikon der griechischen und römischen Mythologie*, ed. W. H. Roscher, 6 vols. (1884–1937), vol.3.1, 1210–13, H. J. Rose, "The Cult of Artemis Orthia," in Dawkins, *AO*, 399–407, esp. 403.

up or she directs them to safety. Or she sets them on a straight path through the cycles of their lives; thus she presides over various rites of passage as boys and girls reach puberty and adulthood. The centrality of the cult of Artemis reflects Sparta's interest and investment in nurturing and educating the young. These concerns are echoed at Sparta in the cult of Artemis Corythalia at the festival of the Tithenidia (see chap. 5). The sanctuary of Orthia was situated on flat ground alongside the Eurotas, conveniently located near the children's exercise grounds. When Theseus as an old man raped Helen, who was just a young girl, he found her dancing at the sanctuary (Plut. *Thes.* 31.2, Hyginus *Fab.* 79).

As Alcman indicates, maidens sang and danced as part of the cult.[7] Sometimes men participated along with the girls. Their choirmasters might be male poets such as Alcman. Lead figurines dated to the seventh and sixth century found at the Orthia sanctuary depict women and men playing flutes and lyres, and one shows a woman playing cymbals.[8] Castor and Pollux were reputed to have taught the Spartans a special dance that the maidens performed annually at Caryae near the northeast border of Spartan territory in historical times in honor of Artemis, whose image stood there out of doors.[9] The girls must have danced in a secluded place without men present. At one performance early in the eighth century, at a time when both Messenians and Lacedaemonians shared the sanctuary, Messenian men supposedly raped the Spartan girls.[10] At another performance during the Second Messenian War, Aristomenes of Messenia seized the daughters of wealthy, noble fathers and carried them off to a village in Messenia awaiting ransom.[11] If the story is true and not only meant to stimulate outrage against the perpetrators, the lack of effective male protectors at this particular performance may be attributable to the war which demanded their full attention: Aristomenes and his force probably had expected to find the girls alone. As these stories and that of Helen and Theseus related just above demonstrate, girls dancing out of doors in secluded places were vulnerable to rape.[12] These stories may also be interpreted in the context of myths about abduction, as a metaphor for marriage, where the girl is plucked from a protected group and from a

7. See further S. Constantinidou, "Spartan Cult Dances," *Phoenix* 52 (1998), 15–30, and Musti and Torelli, *Pausania: Guida della Grecia*, vol. 3, *La Laconia*, 227.

8. Lead, 7th cent. to ca. 560: see W. G. Cavanagh and R. R. Laxton, "Lead Figurines from the Menelaion and Seriation," *ABSA* 79 (1984), 34–36; other materials: Dawkins, *AO*, 262, 269, 276, pls. 180.19 (a lyre),183,189,191,195–96.

9. Lucian, *De salt.* 10; Paus. 3.10.7; Pollux 4.104; Statius, *Theb.* 4.225; Diomede, bk. III, p. 486 (H. Keil, *Gramm. Lat.* 1). Clearchus gave Tissaphernes a ring showing the maidens dancing at Caryae (Plut. *Artax.* 18).

10. Paus. 4.4.2, and see Poralla², pp. 117–18, no. 690 s.v. Teleklos. A king may have been present in his capacity as priest. We need not deduce from his presence that men generally attended this festival.

11. Paus. 4.16.9–10, and see chap. 1.

12. See further Deborah D. Boedeker, *Aphrodite's Entrance into Greek Epic* (Leiden, 1974), 47–49, and Susan Guettel Cole, "Landscapes of Artemis," *CW* 93 (2000), 471–81, esp. 472.

circumscribed, choreographed existence and must begin to fend for herself as a bride and an adult.[13] The theme is reiterated in the story surrounding the rape and marriage of the Leucippides (see below).

The site of the most famous cult of Artemis Limnatis ("of the lake") was on the border of Messenia and Laconia. An epigram commemorates the dedication Timareta made to the goddess before marriage. Despite the brevity of the poem, it is clear that Artemis is a goddess who presides over the important rite of passage from girlhood to marriage, and that appropriately enough she is worshipped in a liminal area, safe on the Laconian side, dangerous on the Messenian:

> Timareta, before marriage, dedicated cymbals,
> her lovely ball, the snood that held her hair,
> her maiden-dolls, she a maiden, to the maiden Goddess of the Lake,
>   as is suitable,
> and the dolls' clothes too, to Artemis.
> Daughter of Leto, holding a hand over the child Timareta
> Keep her pure.[14]

Girls and women also performed lewd dances in honor of Artemis, celebrating her as a fertility goddess. These dances, which are known only through brief citations in late lexicographers, included the *kallabides* or *kallabidia*. The *kyrittoi* wore masks and phalli at the festival of Artemis Corythalia and at the Tithenidia.[15] The *baryllika* was a comic or indecent dance in honor of Artemis and Apollo. According to Pollux (4.104), it was danced by women; according to Hesychius, it was performed by men who put on ugly female masks and sung hymns.[16] Perhaps both men and women cross-dressed and danced.[17] The orgiastic nature of the Orthia cult at Sparta may be somewhat surprising to those familiar with the austere Artemis of Athenian myth. A vase from the Orthia sanctuary,

---

13. See further Christiane Sourvinou-Inwood, "Erotic Pursuits: Images and Meanings," *JHS* 107 (1987), 131–45, esp. 144–45, and Steven H. Lonsdale, *Ritual Play in Greek Religion* (Baltimore, Md., 1993), 229–30. W. Burkert, *Structure and History in Greek Mythology and Ritual*, Sather Classical Lectures, 47 (Berkeley, 1979), 74, sees the rape of virgins as part of a mythological pattern justifying revenge and the defeat of the army of the rapists.

14. *Anth. Pal.* 6.280 Anonymous = A. S. F. Gow and D. L. Page, *The Greek Anthology. Hellenistic Epigrams*, 2 vols. (Cambridge, 1965), vol. 1, 208, no. 41.

15. Hesych. s.v. lombai states that women who begin the sacrifices to Artemis wear phalli. See further M. P. Nilsson, *Griechische Feste von religiöser Bedeutung* (Leipzig, 1906), 184, 187. For other lewd dances performed by Spartan women, see chap. 1.

16. S.v. Brudalicha 1343 (Latte): see R. C. Bosanquet, "The Cult of Orthia as Illustrated by the Finds," *ABSA* 12 (1905–6), 331–43, esp. 338–43, for the masks; G. Dickens, "Terracotta Masks," in Dawkins, *AO*, 163–86, esp. 179–80, and pls. 47–49; and see now Jane Burr Carter, "The Masks of Ortheia," *AJA* 91 (1987), 355–83, esp. 356.

17. Thus Margaret C. Miller, "Reexamining Transvestism in Archaic and Classical Athens," *AJA* 103 (1999), 223–53, esp. 242, following A. W. Pickard-Cambridge, *Dithyramb, Tragedy, and Comedy*, 2d edn. revised by T. B. L. Webster (Oxford, 1927), 164–65, who suggests that the women wore phalli.

dated 580 to 575, shows a *komos* (revel) or orgiastic dancing in progress.[18] The vase is fragmentary and the restoration of the figures uncertain. It does, however, appear to show men and women dancing and having intercourse in the presence of a hairy, ithyphallic, satyr-like figure.[19]

A Laconian vase also of the archaic period depicts women and men together at a symposium (fig. 6).[20] Because the woman reclines with the man and doubtless drinks wine as he does, some viewers, perhaps because they are more familiar with the iconography of Athenian vase painting, may deduce that she is a hetaira.[21] Lycurgus, however, was reputed to have prohibited Spartiate women from practicing prostitution, and this prohibition may well have been in effect in the sixth century (Plut. *Lyc.* 9.3, and see chap. 5). Furthermore, the chorus of girls in Alcman, *Parthenion* 1 (67–68), mention that they wear Lydian mitres, and Spartan girls and women regularly drank wine. This vase does not depict a secular banquet: rather, the winged daemon, the altar on the right, and the fruit and vegetation suggest that the cup was used at a festival of a fertility divinity.[22] The divinity was most probably Artemis Orthia, or perhaps Apollo Hyacinthius.

Artemis Orthia in the Hellenistic and Roman Periods

Artemis and her priestess were also involved in cultic activities for youths. The priestess controlled the intensity of the ritual whipping of youths which is attested for the Roman period.[23] In fact, Plutarch (*Lyc.* 18.1) asserts that he saw many youths die because of this flagellation:

> The priestess, holding the xoanon, stands by [the ephebes]. It is usually light because it is very small; but if those who administer the whipping ever decrease

---

18. Sparta Museum from Orthia sanctuary, manner of Naucratis Painter. C. M. Stibbe, *Lakonische Vasenmaler des sechsten Jahrhunderts v. Chr.* (Amsterdam, 1972), no. 64 = Maria Pipili, *Laconian Iconography of the Sixth Century B.C.*, Oxford University Committee for Archaeology Monograph, no. 12 (Oxford, 1987), no. 179 = E. A. Lane, "Lakonian Vase-Painting," *ABSA* 34 (1933–34), 99–189, esp. pls. 39a and 40.

19. According to Lane, "Lakonian Vase-Painting," 160, there are four women and two men. Lane points out that since allusions to wine are absent, the vase was connected to the worship of Artemis, not Dionysus.

20. Stibbe, *Lakonische Vasenmaler des sechsten Jahrhunderts v. Chr.*, no. 191, pl. 58 = Pipili, *Laconian Iconography*, no. 196. My interpretation follows Pipili, *Laconian Iconography*, 71–74. Uta Kron, "Kultmahle im Heraeon von Samos archaischer Zeit," in *Early Greek Cult Practice: Proceedings of the Fifth International Symposium at the Swedish Institute at Athens 26–29 June, 1986*, ed. R. Hägg, N. Marinatos, and G. C. Nordquist (Stockholm, 1988), 136–48, draws attention to the cultic nature of the scene, arguing that it depicts a meal in the sanctuary of Hera at Samos.

21. Thus, e.g., Kron, "Kultmahle im Heraeon von Samos archaischer Zeit," 141.

22. See further Pipili, *Laconian Iconography*, 71–75.

23. On the xoanon see above and chap. 1, and Irene Bald Romano, "Early Greek Cult Images," Ph.D. diss., University of Pennsylvania, 1980), 115–27.

Fig. 6. Symposium with women.

Fragments of a cup depicting a symposium with women on the ground playing flutes and men reclining on couches on the ground. The right-hand fragment showing trees and building base signifies that the location is out of doors. The winged daemon (perhaps Eros) hovering above the woman indicates that the scene is sacred rather than secular. The woman wears a Lydian mitre on her head. Border of pomegranates above. Arcesilas Painter, ca. 565. Fragments Samos (from the Heraion) K 1203, K 1541, K 2402, and Berlin Charlottenburg, Staatliche Museum Inv. Nos. 478x, 460x. Photo, Deutsches Archäologisches Institut, Athens. Drawings courtesy of Maria Pipili.

the whipping because of the beauty or high status of the ephebe, then the xoanon becomes heavy for the woman and no longer easy to carry. She blames those who administer the whipping and says she is being weighed down because of them. (Paus. 3.16.10–11)

It was rare for a Greek woman functioning regularly in a religious capacity and independently of male authority to exercise as much control over men as did the priestess of Artemis Orthia.[24] Like the Pythia, she transmitted superhuman directives.

Dedications to Orthia continue from the archaic period through the third century c.e. Among those from the Hellenistic period worthy of note is a set of black-glazed bowls inscribed from Chilonis to Orthia.[25] Chilonis is a common name, but this Chilonis may have been royal.

Eileithyia

The cult of Orthia served as the model for cults of lesser goddesses including those of Eileithyia and Helen. Like Orthia, Eileithyia was a goddess of fertility. Her special realm was childbirth. Her cult was closely connected to cults of Artemis, and their sanctuaries located near each other in both the area of the Dromus where Spartan youths raced and on the banks of the Eurotas (Paus. 3.17.1, 3.14.6). The exact sites of Eileithyia's sanctuaries have not been determined, but her name was discovered inside Orthia's sanctuary inscribed on the head of a bronze pin,[26] on rooftiles,[27] and on an unusual large six-sided votive gaming die.[28] The die, dated seventh or sixth century, is of bronze, with six faces and lion heads at the ends. The faces are inscribed with one to six concentric circles, marking the values for the game. The dedication, which is distributed among the faces, is: "to Artemis Orthia of Eileithyia." This elegant piece seems to the modern observer the perfect objective correlative for the fortunes of childbirth, for it

24. A. Spawforth, "Spartan Cults Under the Roman Empire," in *Philolakon: Lakonian Studies in Honour of Hector Catling.* ed. Jan Motyka Sanders (London, 1992), 227–38, esp. 232, notes that she is the only sacerdotal official in Roman Greece to be named in a Greek text.

25. J. Hondius and A. Woodward, "Laconia: Inscriptions: Votive Inscriptions from Sparta," *ABSA* 24 (1919–21), 88–117, esp. 110–12, nos. 61–65, fig. 2, and 116 = *IG* V.i.1573. She may have been: (1) daughter of Leotychidas and wife of Cleonymus; or (2) daughter of Leonidas II, granddaughter of Cleonymus and Cratesiclea (see chap. 4 n. 6); or yet another woman: A. S. Bradford, *A Prosopography of Lacedaemonians from the Death of Alexander the Great, 323 b.c., to the sack of Sparta by Alaric, a.d. 296* (Munich, 1977), 452–53.

26. See further I. Kilian, "Weihungen an Eileithyia und Artemis Orthia," *ZPE* 31 (1978), 219–22, esp. 221.

27. Dawkins, *AO*, tiles 31, figs. D and E, 51, 143, and see also 402.

28. Dawkins, *AO*, bronze dies: pp. 201–2 and 370, no. 169.23 inscribed to Orthia, end of 7th cent.; no. 169.24 a larger but similar die inscribed to Eileithyia, 7th or 6th cent. = Sparta Museum inv. 2147.

Fig. 7. Nude, kneeling, pregnant female in labor.

Perhaps Eileithyia or Hera or Helen, or a mortal woman who is helped by the presence of the goddess. She is flanked by two small male figures. The figure on the right was probably playing a double flute. Marble group found at Magoula near Sparta. Height 48 cm. Sparta Museum 364 = M. N. Tod and A. J. B. Wace, *A Catalogue of the Sparta Museum* (Oxford, 1906), 171–72, no. 364, figs. 50–51 = M. Pipili, *Laconian Iconography of the Sixth Century B.C.*, Oxord University Committee for Archaeology Monograph, no. 12 (Oxford 1987), cat. no. 156, pp. 58–60, fig. 86. Photo, Deutsches Archäologisches Institut, Athens.

evokes such questions as: How will the mother fare? Will the child be a girl or a boy? Who is really the father?[29]

Crude terracotta statuettes of Eileithyia dating to the eigth or seventh century were discovered in the first year of the excavation at the sanctuary of Artemis Orthia.[30] One shows a stocky woman holding an infant, the other shows a pair of birth spirits supporting a mother and child. In addition to the inscribed die mentioned above, spindle whorls and pins of the seventh to sixth century (typical dedications by Greek women), and other offerings to Eileithyia, were found in the Orthia sanctuary.[31]

Hera

Although the ancient sources discuss women's racing at Sparta predominantly as an athletic activity, they do consider a few races in the context of religion (see chap. 1). Modern scholars have interpreted the latter type as initiatory rites for girls preceding marriage, and argue that races in honor of Hera, Helen, and the Leucippides, and choruses of Physcoa and Hippodamia constituted a premarital ritual.[32] What the association is between racing and marriage and why the ritual should take the form of seeming to run away from marriage is not immediately obvious to the modern observer, unless it was an ordeal or a qualifying test. In any case, the college of sixteen women at Elis that was in charge of the races at the Heraea also arranged choruses of women in honor of Hippodamia and Physcoa.[33] These choruses may have been restricted to maidens, and thus have

29. Pace J. Hondius and A. Woodward, "Laconia, Inscriptions," 103, who do not understand the appropriateness of offering dice to Eileithyia.

30. J. Farrell, "Excavations at Sparta, 1908: Archaic Terracottas from the Sanctuary of Orthia," *ABSA* 14 (1908), 48–73, esp. 53, fig. 2.1; R. M. Dawkins, "Excavations at Sparta, 1909," *ABSA* 15 (1909), 1–22, esp. 21; R. M. Dawkins, "Excavations at Sparta, 1910. Artemis Orthia: The History of the Sanctuary," *ABSA* 16 (1910), 18–53, esp. 52, fig. 18, 53; and see H. J. Rose, "The Cult of Artemis Orthia," in Dawkins, *AO*, 399–407, esp. 402. For associations between Eileithyia and Artemis, see Semeli Pingiatoglou, *Eileithyia* (Würzburg, 1981), 54–55, 59, 99.

31. For associations between Eileithyia and Helen see M. N. Tod and A. J. B. Wace, *Catalogue of the Sparta Museum* (Oxford, 1906), 116–18. For connections between Eileithyia at Sparta and in the Greek east, see José Dörig, "Eleuthía," in *Sculpture from Arcadia and Laconia*, ed. Olga Palagia and William Coulson (Oxford, 1993), 145–51. R. Olmos, s.v. Eileithuia in *Lexicon Iconographicum*, vol. 3.1 (Zurich, 1986), 685–99, esp. 695, argues that some sculptures of fertility goddesses (including Sparta Museum 364) have been incorrectly identified as Eileithyia.

32. E.g. Calame, *Les choeurs de jeunes filles*, vol. 1, 213–14, and passim, and see Appendix n. 17; Thomas Scanlon, "The Footrace of the Heraia at Olympia," *AncW* 9 (1984), 85; and most recently N. Serwint, "The Female Athletic Costume at the *Heraia* and Prenuptial Initiation Rites," *AJA* 97 (1993), 403–22.

33. Paus. 5.16.6, Plut. *Mor.* 251e–f, and see further, Calame, *Les choeurs de jeunes filles*, vol. 1, 212, 326, who interprets the choruses for Hippodamia, who married Pelops, in connection with the married woman.

also constituted a prematrimonial rite.[34] That the choruses were two in number suggests that they competed against one another. Racing, of course, was competitive, too. At the Heraea, running was a cult activity limited to *parthenoi*. Girls wore the short peplos exposing one breast only to race at the Heraea. This costume seems to be a version of the exomis, a tunic worn regularly by men (see chap. 1). Transvestism may constitute part of an initiation rite preceding marriage, and on her wedding night the Spartan bride was dressed as a man.[35]

Helen

The Menelaion, the principal shrine of Helen, Menelaus, and Helen's brothers Castor and Pollux, was at Therapne on a mountain top where they were all said to be buried (Paus. 3.19.9, Pind. *Nem.* 10.56, *Pyth.* 11.62–63). There were also additional shrines for Helen and her brothers around Sparta, and Phylonoë, another daughter of Tyndareus, also had a cult.[36] The urban sanctuary of Helen was located near the Platanistas and quite close to Alcman's tomb (Paus. 3.15.2–3). Although the principal shrine is usually called "the Menelaion," Herodotus (6.61) referred to it as Helen's temple. Moreover, the archaeological finds testify to a cult of Helen who is not subordinate to a husband: sometimes she is worshipped along with her brothers, at other times she seems independent of men.[37] Offerings were made to Helen and Menelaus alone, and each may have had an altar. The Menelaion is the most important hero shrine in Greece, and probably the earliest, for it was founded ca. 700.[38] The datable offerings specifically inscribed to Helen precede those to Menelaus.[39] These were a bronze aryballos (perfume vase) dated to ca. 675–650 and a bronze harpax (hook) dated to ca. 575–550. Around three hundred terracotta figurines were found, including some depicting human figures on horseback; most of these show female figures riding astride or side-saddle. In enjoying both independence from men and partnership with them, Helen as a religious figure reflects the lives of mortal Spartan women.

---

34. Jan Bremmer, "Greek Maenadism Reconsidered," *ZPE* 55 (1984), 267–86, esp. 283.

35. See chap. 2. Serwint, "The Female Athletic Costume at the *Heraia*," 79–81, 83, considers the dress an Amazon costume—contra Scanlon, "The Footrace of the Heraia at Olympia."

36. Apollod. 3.10.6. According to Athenagoras *Leg.* 1.1, Phylonoë was worshipped as Enodia, an epithet of Hecate.

37. H. W. Catling, "Archaeology in Greece, 1975–76," *AR* 22 (1975–76), 3–33, esp. 14, and "Excavations at the Menelaion, Sparta, 1973–76," *AR* 23 (1976–77), 24–42, esp. 36–37, on dedications to Helen alone.

38. P. Cartledge, "Early Lacedaimon: The Making of a Conquest-State," in *Philolakon: Lakonian Studies in Honour of Hector Catling*, ed. J. M. Sanders (London, 1992), 49–55, esp. 55.

39. See Carla M. Antonaccio, *An Archaeology of Ancestors: Tomb Cult and Hero Cult in Early Greece* (Boston, 1995), 155, 158, 160, and chap. 1 n. 65, above.

The cults of Helen and Artemis Orthia were similar in many ways. Both were concerned with nature and fertility. Helen's name means "reed" or "shoot."[40] Helen and Artemis in her guise of Orthia were local divinities. Outside Sparta, Artemis was worshipped in various manifestations, but Helen was considered a mythological or literary figure as well as divine.[41] The finds from the Menelaion are a microcosm of the Orthia material. These two major shrines were close enough to be visited in a single day. The shrine dedicated to Helen alone at the Platanistas was in close proximity to the Orthia sanctuary and the exercise grounds of girls and boys.[42] Music and dancing was part of the cult of Helen, as it was part of the cult of Artemis.[43] As we have mentioned above, Helen was dancing in the Orthia sanctuary when Theseus and Perithoos abducted her. Some of the anecdotes told about the divine Helen suggest that she was especially concerned with the welfare of marriageable girls, for example, endowing ugly ones with beauty (see Conclusion). Theocritus' *Epithalamium for Helen* depicts her as a paradigmatic figure for the most important rite of passage of a woman: Helen was the first of a large group of Spartan maidens to become a bride. At the springtime festival of the Heleneia, maidens anointed a plane tree with olive oil.[44] Theocritus (18.1–4, 43–46) gives the aetiology of this practice:

> Once in Sparta at the house of yellow-haired Menelaus
> Maidens wearing hyacinth blossoms in their hair
> Organized a choral dance in front of the freshly-painted bridal
>   chamber.
> They were twelve girls, the foremost in the city, a large crowd of
>   Spartan girls.
> . . . .
> "For you first [Helen], we will weave a wreath of the lotus growing
>   close to the ground,
> And place it on a shady plane tree.
> And first we will pour liquid oil from a silver flask
> And let it drip beneath the shady plane tree.
> And on its bark shall be inscribed in Dorian so that a passerby may
>   read
> 'Revere me. I am Helen's tree.'"

40. Linda Lee Clader, *Helen: The Evolution from Divine to Heroic in Greek Epic Tradition* (Leiden, 1976), 79–80.

41. E.g., Eur. *Hel.* 1667, Isocr. *Hel.* 61, M. L. West, *Immortal Helen* (London, 1975), and see Appendix, below.

42. Calame, *Les choeurs de jeunes filles*, vol. 1, 333–50, argues that the cult of Helen at Therapne emphasized her role as a wife, while the cult at Platanistas was initiatory and celebrated Helen before marriage. However, distinctions between the two cults are difficult to detect. Furthermore, the story in Herodotus (6.61) refers to an infant who was taken to Helen at Therapne.

43. On connections between the cults of Artemis Orthia and Helen, see Clader, *Helen*, 74–77.

(a)

Fig. 8. Helen and Menelaus.

Sparta, 1, from Magoula (?). Stone pyramid stele with relief, ca. 600–570. Man hugs veiled woman with left arm. She raises her right arm, probably to embrace him. In her left hand and probably in his right, they hold a wreath, symbolizing love. Their eyes meet in an intimate gaze.

(b)

On the reverse a man, who here is considerably taller than the woman and whose hair has grown longer (after ten years of bivouacking in Troy), threatens her with his sword. Though the reliefs are not inscribed, they probably both depict Helen and Menelaus. Sparta Museum, 1 = Tod and Wace, *Catalogue*, 132–33, no. 1, figs. 26–27 = Pipili, *Laconian Iconography*, cat. no. 87, pp. 30–31, fig. 45 = L. B. Ghali-Kahil, *Les enlèvements et le retour d'Hélène dans les textes et les documents figurés* (Paris, 1955), 71, no. 24, pl. 42.1 = *LIMC* s.v. Hélène, p. 539, no. 230. Photos, Deutsches Archäologisches Institut, Athens.

There is evidence for the cult of Helen and the Dioscuri (Castor and Pollux) in Hellenistic Sparta. Rules for members of a society who sacrificed and held communal feasts in their honor are extant. Mention of a *gynaikonomos* (regulator of women) in the inscription indicates that women certainly were included in the festivities.[45] Such communal co-ed feasts were common in the Greek world in the Hellenistic period, but they were not entirely new at Sparta. As we have mentioned, there were co-ed symposia in honor of Orthia in the archaic period (see fig. 6).

Dionysus

Hilaeira and Phoebe ("bright" and "shining"), daughters of Leucippus ("white horse"), fled from the Spartan heroes Castor and Pollux, but were captured and married their pursuers. Their rape and marriage were therefore a mythical archetype for the Spartan wedding ritual in which the husband seized the bride.[46] Their cult, unlike that of Helen, was confined to Sparta, where a shrine to their sister Arsinoë was also located (Paus. 3.12.8). The namesakes of the mythical brides, the Leucippides, were priestesses who were responsible for weaving a garment for the cult image and who also organized a race for Dionysus. As is appropriate for virgins and for those involved in racing, the priestesses were also called *poloi* (fillies).[47] Eleven Dionysiades (daughters of Dionysus), probably unmarried girls, ran in the race.[48] The race was held near the place where the suitors of Penelope were said to have begun the race which was part of their prenuptial contest.[49] Also close by was a sanctuary of Hera Hypercheiria ("whose hand is

44. She was also worshipped at Rhodes as a vegetation goddess connected with trees: Paus. 3.19.10. See further Otto Skutsch, "Helen: Her Name and Nature," *JHS* 107 (1987), 188–93, esp. 189.

45. *IG* V.i.1390.27, 32 (92/91 B.C.E. Andania) = *LSCG* 65. The Andanian cult in Messenia is perhaps derived from a Spartan cult. A. M. Woodward, "Excavations at Sparta, 1908: Inscriptions from the Sanctuary of Orthia," 74–141, esp. 125, distinguished the gynaikonomos in the Andania inscription as an official pro tempore from those who held state office as in *IG* V.i.170.3–4, 209.10, and 1390.27. More recently, however, Spawforth, "Spartan Cults Under the Roman Empire," 229 n. 17, argues that they were state officials. For other gynaikonomoi (whose existence is conjectured based on the expansion of abbreviations in *IG* V.1.1314 and 1315), see Spawforth 230 n.21, and see *SEG* (1950), XI.626–29 "Catalogi gynaeconomorum."

46. Xen. *Lac. Pol.* 1.6, Plut. *Lyc.* 15.4, and see chap. 2 n. 26. Deborah Larson, *Greek Heroine Cults* (Madison, Wis.,1995), 20, 68, suggests that originally the cult of the Leucippides emphasized their virginity rather than marriage.

47. Hesych. s.v. polia. For additional references to virgins as colts (with sexual implications), see chap. 1 n. 66, and Sarah B. Pomeroy, *Plutarch's Advice to the Bride and Groom and A Consolation to His Wife* (New York, 1999), 47–48.

48. Paus. 3.16.1: see further Calame, *Les choeurs de jeunes filles*, vol. 1, 323–33.

49. See further M. L. Napolitano, "Donne spartane e teknopoiia," *AION (archeol.)* 7 (1985), 19–50, esp. 28, and Musti and Torelli, *Pausania: Guida della Grecia*, vol. 3, *La Laconia*, 208–9.

above"), a goddess of marriage, and the image of Aphrodite Hera to which mothers of brides sacrificed (see below).[50]

Women were conspicuous in the Spartan worship of Dionysus. Vergil describes Mount Taygetus "virginibus bacchata lacaenis" ("celebrated in Bacchic revels by Laconian virgins": *Georgics* 2.487–88). Near Taygetus was a temple of Dionysus with images both outside and inside the building. Only women could view the image within and perform the secret sacrifical rites. Similar rules of exclusivity applied to young women: the rites of Dionysus of the Hill (Colonatas) could be performed only by virgins.[51] Interestingly enough, however, near the temple of Dionysus there was a brothel named for a notorious courtesan, Cottina. This business was probably established in the Hellenistic period (Athen. XIII.574c–d, Strabo 8.363, and see chap. 5).

Demeter

Demeter was a goddess of agriculture and of women's life cycle. The Spartan Eleusinion was discovered at Kalyvia tes Sochas just south of the city. The site has not been fully excavated, but it apparently was quite large and included areas for sitting and feasting.[52] Finds from the fourth century B.C.E.—a period of increasing visible wealth—are noteworthy. All the archaeological evidence and the inscriptions concern women, though inscriptions from the Roman period indicate that the majority of statues erected in honor of women were dedicated and paid for by men, or groups of family members including men (see below). Nevertheless, women acting alone alone paid for some. Thus, for example, the mother of Pomponia Callistonice dedicated a statue in honor of her daughter, who served as hereditary priestess of Artemis Orthia and other divinities.[53] Nicippia, honored her great granddaughter Agesippia with a statue.[54] There are at least thirty inscriptions from the Roman period, the majority from the second and third centuries C.E.[55] Women were numerous among cult officials, but their

50. Paus. 3.13.8–9, and see further Musti and Torelli, *Pausania: Guida della Grecia*, vol. 3, *La Laconia*, 209–10.

51. Paus. 3.13.7. On Artemis, Dionysus, and virgins: Hesych. s.vv. Dionysiades and Leukippides; Nilsson, *Griechische Feste*, 184–85, 297–99; Calame, *Les choeurs de jeunes filles*, vol. 1, 271–76, 323–33, and *Alcman* (Rome, 1983), 520–21; Bremmer, "Greek Maenadism Reconsidered," 282–84; and Ziehen, *RE* II.6 (Stuttgart, 1929), s.v. Sparta (Kulte), 1452–1525, esp. 1495–96, and n. 21 above.

52. See further Susan Walker, "Two Spartan Women and the Eleusinion," in *The Greek Renaissance in the Roman Empire*, ed. S. Walker and A. Cameron, *ICS Bull.* suppl. 55 (1989), 130–41 and pls. 51–52, esp. 131.

53. *IG* V.i.602. For her name, see A. J. S. Spawforth, "Families at Roman Sparta and Epidaurus: Some Prosopographical Notes," *ABSA* 80 (1985), 239.

54. *SEG* XI.677, 1st cent. C.E., *LGPN* 3A, s.v. Agesippia, 2nd cent. C.E. See also J. M. Cook, "Laconia: Kalyvia Sochas," *ABSA* 45 (1950), 261–81, esp. 270, 277, and chap. 4 n. 9, above.

55. Spawforth, "Families at Roman Sparta and Epidaurus," 206.

activities were subject to male approval.[56] Beginning in the third century B.C.E., dedications by women who were worshippers or who held sacred office in the cult were inscribed on parts of the building.[57] Later, their kinsmen or the state dedicated statues of them.[58] The Roman emphasis on increasing fertility among the upper class stimulated interest in the cult of Ceres. Portraits of imperial women on coins with the paraphernalia of the goddess probably encouraged Spartan involvement in the cult of Demeter. Like Rome, Sparta was concerned about the fertility of the upper class. One relief that was dedicated by a priestess in the Roman period depicts paraphernalia used by women in the cults for themselves or for the cult image. These include toilet items such as cosmetic boxes, sandals, a mortar and pestle, a spatula, a strigil, an unguentarium, a pin with a pick (?), a sponge, a snood, a mirror, a comb, a spindle and distaff, bowls, and, most unusually, a loincloth (resembling a very skimpy bikini bottom) that was worn only by menstruating women.[59]

Apollo

Women played an important role at the Hyacinthia, the great communal festival of Sparta.[60] They wove Apollo's chiton (Xen. *Hell.* 4.5.11; Paus. 3.16.2). This garment was probably presented during the festival.[61] In the Roman period, at least two women were the leaders of the Hyacinthia. Presumably they presided over the contests that were held at the festival.[62] Two women are also known to have officiated at the contests in honor of the Dioscuri.[63] Presiding over festivals in

56. See further Susan Cole, "*Gynaiki ou Themis*: Gender Difference in the Greek *Leges Sacrae*," *Helios* 19 (1992), 104–22, esp. 114.

57. Robert Parker, "Demeter, Dionysus and the Spartan Pantheon," in *Early Greek Cult Practice: Proceedings of the Fifth International Symposium at the Swedish Institute at Athens 26–29 June, 1986*, ed. R. Hägg, N. Marinatos, and G. C.Nordquist (Stockholm, 1988), 99–103, esp. 102.

58. Cook, "Laconia: Kalyvia Sochas," *ABSA* 45 (1950), 261–81, esp. 265–67.

59. One of the "Aberdeen reliefs" (*IG* V.i.248), 1st or 2d cent. C.E.: Walker, "Two Spartan Women and the Eleusinion," 135–38 and pl. 51.

60. C. N. Edmonson, "A Graffito from Amyklai," *Hesperia* 28 (1959), 162–64, suggests a connection between the festival and a list of women's names. See further Appendix.

61. But probably, originally, not every year: see chap. 1 n. 122.

62. *IG* V.i.586.7, Memmia Xenocratia: Bradford, *A Prosopography of Lacedaemonians*, 276, and *IG* V.i.587.5–6; Pompeia Polla, early 2d cent.: Bradford, *A Prosopography of Lacedaemonians*, 352, and Spawforth, "Families at Roman Sparta and Epidaurus," 244. Riet van Bremen, *The Limits of Participation: Women and Civic Life in the Greek East in the Hellenistic and Roman Periods* (Amsterdam, 1996), 88 n. 21, has overemphasized the isolation of the woman in the role of theoros at the Hyacinthia. This festival was open to all, and girls participated actively (see chap. 1).

63. *IG* V.i.602.12–15: Pomponeia Callistonice, see below n. 90. *IG* V.i.168 + 608.1–2 refers to another woman who officiated at an agonistic festival. Neither her name nor the name of the festival is extant: see further A. J. S. Spawforth, "Notes on the Third Century A.D. in Spartan Epigraphy," *ABSA* 79 (1984), 263–88, esp. 285–86.

which men competed is a noteworthy honor granted to elite women in the Roman period.

The Hyacinthia was celebrated at Amyclae, a numinous site from which the Eurotas, the ancient city of Sparta, and many of its shrines are visible. The celebration lasted for three days and included a period of mourning followed by the singing of songs to the gods.[64] Boys sang and performed on citharas and flutes and rode on horseback. In the procession in view of the whole city, some girls rode in elaborately decorated wicker carts, others in chariots ran races. Their chariots, fashioned like goats and stags, may have been connected to an attribute of Artemis, goddess of wild animals (see chap. 1). The festival included feasting and women's nocturnal dancing and choral singing.[65]

Athena

We may be certain that Spartan women did not fail to pay due homage to other divinities in the Greek pantheon, even those who, though important—at least judging from the paucity of anecdotes, and of published votives and inscriptions—were not their top favorites. Athena Poliouchos was the protector of the polis (Paus. 3.17.2). Athena was also titled Chalkioikos ("of the Bronze House"), for her sanctuary that was on the acropolis. A statue of the Olympic victor Euryleonis stood near the temple (Paus. 3.17.6). The original temple and altar, begun probably in the eighth century, have now been obscured by monumental Roman and Byzantine buildings.[66] A few stories and votives attest to women's concerns. When the traitor Pausanias sought asylum in the temple of Athena, and the ephors were in a quandary, Theano, his mother, did not plead for her son's life. Instead, she placed a brick at the door of the temple and left (ca. 470; see chap. 3).

Four of ten bronze bells inscribed with the donor's name were dedicated by women to Athena. For example, in the late fifth or early fourth century, a certain Eirana dedicated a bell.[67] It is interesting that the woman's name means "peace" and that she made her offering at a critical time in Spartan military history. In addition, over forty bells made of bronze and eighty made of terracotta without

64. Athen. 4.139d–f; Paus. 3.19.1–5; and see further Michael Pettersson, *Cults of Apollo at Sparta: The Hyakinthia, the Gymnopaidiai, and the Karneia* (Stockholm, 1992), 10, 38, etc., who follows Calame, *Les choeurs de jeunes filles*, vol. 1, 305–19, in interpreting the activities as rites of initiation preparing girls for marriage. However, since the ages of the girls are not specified, one would have to conclude that just about anything they did until the age of marriage at eighteen was preparatory for marriage.

65. Eur. *Hel.* 1465–75, Hieronymus, *Adv. Iovinianum* 1, 308, and see chap. 1.

66. See further Cartledge, "Early Lacedaimon," 55.

67. Hondius and Woodward, "Laconia: Inscriptions," 117–18, no. 66. Callicrateia dedicated a bell: *ABSA* 30 (1928–30), 252, no. 5.

inscriptions have also been found associated with Athena's sanctuary on the acropolis. Though bronze bells are usually used for military purposes, these bells may have been used for musical performances for the cult, and in that case women may have been among the dedicants.[68] Euonyma dedicated a more traditional gift for a woman: a bronze mirror.[69] Polemon, a geographer of the second century B.C.E., reports that beyond the statue of Athena of the Bronze House, he saw an offering given by the hetaira Cottina consisting of a small image of herself or perhaps of the goddess and a small bronze cow.[70]

Aphrodite

At Sparta, Aphrodite was worshipped in several guises of relevance to women. Mothers of brides sacrificed to Aphrodite Hera, an unusual hybrid.[71] Another complex version of Aphrodite was a warrior.[72] The archaic temple of the Armed Aphrodite who was called "Morpho" drew attention to her double nature: it was the only two-storey temple known to Pausanias (3.15.10). It housed a statue of the goddess veiled, with chains on her feet.[73] Pausanias explains that Tyndareus had put chains on the statue to demonstrate that wives were faithful to their husbands.[74] Lactantius' interpretation of the origin of the Armed Aphrodite, in contrast, is based on a view of Spartan women as more feisty.[75] When the Spartan army was away during one of the wars against the Messenians, some of the Messenians invaded Sparta. The women donned armor and managed to defeat

68. S. Hodkinson, *Property and Wealth in Classical Sparta* (London, 2000), 293 and 301 n. 39, quoting unpublished work of Alexandra Villing.

69. *LGPN* 3 s.v., 6th?/5th cent.; M. L. Lazzarini, *Le formule delle dediche votive nella Grecia arcaica*, Atti dell' Accademia Nazionale dei Lincei. Memorie. Classe di Scienze Morali, Stor., e Filol., ser. 8, 19 (Rome, 1976), p. 102, no. 91, middle of the 5th cent.

70. Athen. 13.574d. Nothing more is known about her: L. Preller, *Polemonis Periegetae Fragmenta* (Leipzig, 1838), 48–49, para. 18.

71. Paus. 3.13.9. For connections between the cults of Aphrodite and Hera, see M. Torelli, "Il santuario greco di Gravisca," *PP* 32 (1977), 398–458, esp. 437.

72. Paus. 17.5 also mentions the temple of Aphrodite Areia (Warrior) on the citadel near the temple of Athena.

73. The Armed Aphrodite attracted a great deal of attention from non-Spartans, and was the subject of epigrams and rhetorical exercises: Gow and Page, *The Greek Anthology: Hellenistic Epigrams*, vol. 2, 334–35.

74. Paus. 3.15.11. According to Hesiod (fr. 176 Merkelbach and West), Tyndareus had ignored Aphrodite in his sacrifices. In revenge, the goddess had made his three daughters adulterous. The chains were probably a compensatory gift.

75. *Div. Inst.* 1.20, 29–32. Fritz Graf, "Women, War, and Warlike Divinities," *ZPE* 55 (1984), 250, sees the Armed Aphrodite as reversing gender roles. This interpretation may be true in most parts of the Greek world: however, as an exception note Spartan women's bravery at the invasion of Pyrrhus: Plut. *Pyrr.* 27.4, and see chap. 4.

the invaders.[76] Meanwhile, some Spartan soldiers returned, and seeing people in armor, deduced that they were the enemy, and attacked the Spartan women. The women undressed, the Spartan men recognized them, and an orgy ensued. For this reason the Spartans built a temple and dedicated a statue of the Armed Aphrodite (Enoplios or Hoplismene). This story in some ways echoes the tale Herodotus relates (4.146) about the Spartan wives of the Minyae, who were descendants of the Argonauts. When the women's fathers imprisoned their husbands, intending to kill them, the wives entered the prison and exchanged their clothing with their husbands. Thus dressed as women, the husbands escaped. The sanctuary of the Armed Aphrodite was grouped with others that were particularly meaningful for women. Pausanias (3.16.1–3) next describes the sanctuary of the Leucippides, Hilaeira and Phoebe, daughters of Leucippus whose pursuit and rape, as we have suggested above, were mythical analogues of the Spartan marriage ceremony. The egg of Leda from which Helen was born hung from the roof of their sanctuary.[77] Then Pausanias mentions the chamber where women wove a chiton for Apollo at Amyclae. Nearby was the house of Tyndareus, whose marriage to Leda was a husband-doubling or wife-sharing arrangement, with Zeus as the uninvited impregnator.[78]

Roman Period

Priestesses

As a result of the prohibition on commemorating women except those who had died in childbirth, and the general paucity of data about women, there is little information about Spartan priestesses until the late Hellenistic and Roman periods. Because there are more inscriptions about specific priestesses and festivals for the Roman period, this epigraphic data should not lead us to overexaggerate its importance in its own time. The material is, however, of great value to the historian; for example, providing some evidence that naming patterns for Spartan women show a tendency to alternate names with granddaughters named for their grandmothers just as they had been in classical Athens.[79] Interest in horses

76. Cf. the story of the poet Telesilla who armed the women of Argos and defeated Spartan invaders: Paus. 2.20.8–10, Plut. Mul. Virt. 245c–e, see also Herod. 6.77.2.

77. They were probably also associated with Helen in a cult at the Phoebaeum near Therapne: Paus. 3.20.2, and see further Musti and Torelli, Pausania: Guida della Grecia, vol. 3, La Laconia, 253–54.

78. A red figure vase of the late 5th cent. manufactured in the Peloponnese depicts Helen's birth. Her upper torso and arms rise from the egg. The eagle of Zeus flies over her head and Leda flies toward the left. Unlike scenes of Helen's birth in Attic vase painting, Tyndareus is not shown at all. See S. Karouzou, "He Helene tes Spartes," AE 1985 (1987), 33–44, esp. 37, and pl. 6.

79. See further Sarah B. Pomeroy, Families in Classical and Hellenistic Greece (Oxford, 1997), 73–75, and n. 90 below, for references to seven illustrious women of the 2d–3d centuries named Callistonice.

is reflected in names of Roman Sparta, as it had been in the classical period: thus Nicippia is the great-grandmother of Archippia.[80] The emperor Augustus had led the way by reviving the woman-oriented cults of the early and middle Republic at Rome,[81] and Hadrian and the Pax Romana had created an atmosphere in which Greek cities like Sparta could revive and reenact their past. The relative abundance of epigraphic evidence at Sparta, however, is not only indicative of the increased interest in reviving old religions, but is also a reflection of the increase in inscriptions and commemoration in the late Hellenistic world (see Appendix). Furthermore, Xenophon, one of our major sources on Spartan women in the classical period, does not report on their religious activities, In contrast, Plutarch (who was himself a priest at Delphi) does endeavor to include such information. Inscriptions, however, are the best source for women's cults in Roman Greece.[82] Once again, the intrepid historian must consider whether archaizing tendencies, good research on the part of Plutarch and other officials, and tradition will have caused previously existing cults and practices to be revived as far as possible in a fair semblance of their original form in the radically new political context. Some of the religious powers that had been exercised by the king in the days of the monarchy were distributed among high-ranking commoners, both male and female.[83] Because we do not know whether royal women had played any special role in religion, for example analogous to the role of the wife of the king archon in Athens, we do not know whether the powers exercised by Spartan women in the post-monarchical period derived ultimately from women. Thus, that women in the Roman period served as officials in the Hyacinthia may indicate that Sparta was hard up to find citizens wishing to take on such responsibilities and opened the position to women in order to double their pool of candidates, or it may indicate that, inasmuch as the entire city participated in the Hyancinthia, women had held such positions in earlier periods, but merely happened not to be mentioned in any historical record. Those who are more skeptical must nevertheless admit that at least some elements of the earlier cult activities were revived—though sometimes in an exaggerated form designed to attract the interest of tourists and to swell the hearts of Greeks with pride in their past.[84] Certainly the archaeological finds at the Eleusinion

80. See above, n. 54, Hipparchia (*IG* V.i.611, 1st cent. B.C.E.), etc., and chap. 1 nn. 75–76.

81. See further Robert Palmer, "Roman Shrines of Female Chastity from the Caste Struggle to the Papacy of Innocent I," *RSA* 4 (1974), 113–59.

82. For prosopographical studies of these inscriptions, see Bradford, *A Prosopography of Lacedaemonians*; Spawforth, "Notes on the Third Century A.D. in Spartan Epigraphy"; Spawforth, "Families at Roman Sparta and Epidaurus"; and Spawforth, "Spartan Cults Under the Roman Empire."

83. P. A. Cartledge and A. J. S. Spawforth, *Hellenistic and Roman Sparta: A Tale of Two Cities* (London, 1989), 99.

84. See the warning against reading religion from the Roman period back to the archaic and classical periods in Robert Parker, "Spartan Religion," in *Classical Sparta*, ed. A. Powell (Norman, Okla., 1989), 142–72, esp. 163 n. 1.

demonstrate that women's religious activities honoring Demeter in the fourth century B.C.E. were similar to those in the Roman period.[85] Therefore the later evidence may be used with caution to shed some light on earlier practices.

Feasting was a traditional part of Greek festivals. Practices varied and changed over time. Some feasts were held for the entire community. A painting on a cup by a Spartan artist depicts men and women at a symposium together perhaps at such an occasion (see fig. 6, above). In cults that were restricted to women, priestesses presided and women often were in charge of organizing the activities.

There was a resurgence of women-oriented cults in Roman Greece in the second century C.E.[86] Some of these cults had existed in the past, others were created in the Roman period. In Sparta, civic-minded women of high status served as *thoinarmostria* (mistress of the banquet), often simultaneously holding other sacred offices and titles such as "Hestia Poleos" (Hestia of the City).[87] These women probably filled a post analogous to that of the Vestals at Rome and were responsible for seeing that the fire in the city's official hearth burned eternally. This hearth was in the very center of the agora, the public space frequented by Spartan men.[88] The woman who served as Hestia of the City may have been present sometimes when the Boule (Assembly) was convened, for one such woman is attested in an inscription from the mid-second century listing members.[89] *IG* V.i.602 records the dedication of a statue around the third century C.E. in honor of Pomponia Callistonice, who was not only a hereditary priestess of Artemis Orthia but also priestess of other divinities including those sharing the precinct of Orthia, the Fates, Armed Aphrodite, Asclepius Schoinatas, Artemis Patriotis, the Dioscuri, and the contest of the most august Dioscuri. Her statue may have stood at the sanctuary of Orthia.[90] Since the population of Sparta was small, it must have been difficult to find many women with the funds, leisure, and interest necessary to fill all the priestesshoods, and thus an eligible woman like Pomponia Callistonice served in many capacities. In at least one case, a foreign-born woman filled the post of *hypostatria* (dresser of the cult image) at the Eleusinion.[91]

---

85. Walker, "Two Spartan Women and the Eleusinion," 132.

86. I owe this suggestion to Lucia Nixon, and see n. 81, above.

87. E.g., *IG* V.i.229, 589, *SEG* XI (1950), Add. et Corr. 812a.

88. N. Kennell, "Where was Sparta's Prytaneion?" *AJA* 91 (1987), 421–22.

89. Preucletia: *IG* V.i.116, late 2d cent. C.E., and see further N. Kennell, "The Elite Women of Sparta," paper delivered at the Annual Meeting of the American Philological Association, Dec. 28, 1998; abstract published in *American Philological Association 130th Annual Meeting: Abstracts*, 84.

90. *LGPN* 3A s.v. Kallistonike (6), 3d cent. C.E. A. M. Woodward, "Inscriptions," 285–377, in Dawkins, *AO*, 295, and see n. 63 above and Appendix n. 70.

91. Anthousa, daughter of Damainetus (*IG* V.i.248), 1st or 2d cent. C.E.: Walker, "Two Spartan Women and the Eleusinion," 132.

As in earlier periods, many of the religious posts were hereditary, or at least dominated by members of the same families. Because the elite families were highly endogamous, the hereditary priesthoods devolved on fewer and fewer people who were kinsmen.[92] Endogamy also simultaneously accelerated a concentration of wealth that made the expenses associated with the posts tolerable.[93] Thus father and daughter, sister and brother, and cousins are attested in priesthoods that are related such as those of the Dioscuri and Helen.[94] Sons and daughters of the sacerdotal officials also served religious functions.[95] The priesthoods were transmitted through both the male and female lines.[96]

In the Roman period, titles such as "Mother of the Demos and the Boule," "Daughter of the City," and "Hestia of the City" were awarded to some women of the highest elite status, with some women bearing two or three of these titles.[97] Such official acts incorporated these women into the public family that was otherwise exclusively male.[98] These edicts may be compared with public decrees and grants of citizenship honoring outstanding female benefactors in other cities in Hellenistic and Roman Greece[99] and with the the the designation of Julia Domna and other empresses as "Mater Senatus" (Mother of the Senate) and "Mater Castrorum" (Mother of Military Camps).[1000] The honor was not gratuitous. In return for these adoptions the city expected to be treated with the respect due a member of the family, including a willingness to offer financial support.[101]

Most of the honorary inscriptions of the Roman period honor priestesses and other women not only for their piety and specific religious activities, but they also praise them for conventional female virtues including modesty (*sophrosyne*), dignity (*semnotes*), piety (*eusebeia*), and orderliness (*kosmiotes*). Such virtues were likely to be attributed to people of lesser status including

---

92. Spawforth, "Families at Roman Sparta and Epidaurus," 200.

93. Freedmen of both Eurybanassa (50 B.C.E.–20 C.E.) and Tyndares are attested in *IG* V.i.212.57–58.

94. P. Memmius Deximachus IV and Memmia Xenocratia; Eurybanassa and Tyndares; and P. Memmius Pratolaus III and Volusene Olympiche (3d cent.): see further Spawforth, "Spartan Cults Under the Roman Empire," 231, and "Families at Roman Sparta and Epidaurus," 197, 235.

95. For examples of children (*paidia*), see *IG* V.i.141, and see further Spawforth, "Spartan Cults Under the Roman Empire," 229 n. 1.

96. Spawforth, "Spartan Cults Under the Roman Empire," 231.

97. Claudia Damosthenia: *IG* V.i.589, 2d–3d cent. C.E.; name not extant: *IG* V.i.608; Julia Etearchis: *IG* V.i.593, ca. 250–60 C.E.; Preucletia: *IG* V.i.116, ca. 170 C.E.; Claudia Tyrannis: *SEG* XXXV (1985), 337; and see further Van Bremen, *The Limits of Participation*, 167, 348, 350.

98. See chap. 2 n. 27, and Pomeroy, *Families*, 48–50.

99. E.g., Aristodama: see Sarah B. Pomeroy, *Goddesses, Whores, Wives, and Slaves: Women in Classical Antiquity* (New York, 1995), 126, and Van Bremen, *The Limits of Participation*, passim.

100. E.g., *BMC* V.clxxvi and cxcv; *CIL* VIII.26598; Dio 72.5; and *HA, Marcus* 26.8.

101. L. Robert, "Laodicée du Lycos: Les inscriptions," in *Laodicée du Lycos: Le Nymphée, campagnes 1961–1963*, ed. J. des Gagniers et al. (Paris, 1969), 247–387, esp. 316–22.

youths and boys, rather than to adult men.[102] A dedication of the first century
B.C.E. in honor of Alcibia, daughter of Tisamenus, praises her virtue (*arete*), the
good works of her ancestors, and her irreproachable sixty-year marriage (*IG*
V.i.578.2). *IG* V.i.599, third century, records the dedication by the polis of a statue
in honor of Aurelia Heraclea, daughter of Marcus Aurelius Teisamenus, at the
Orthia sanctuary. The inscription does not state why the statue was erected, but
it does praise her dignity, love of philosophy, nobility, good sense, modesty, and
possession of every virtue.[103] The identity of a woman being commemorated was
probably defined by the donor who gained prestige from the reflected glory of
the honorand. One woman donor, however, praised herself extravagantly in a
dedication honoring her father.[104] In a brief inscription of ten lines, Charision
managed to refer to herself as first among Spartan maidens, and a new Penelope,
thus combining the praise associated with virgins with that due to the most
chaste and loyal wife. In this hyperbole, one senses the old competitive spirit of
Spartan maidens displayed in the new arena of personal virtue in the later period
when Spartan women no longer boasted of the gods' favor by commemorating
their athletic victories. *Sophrosyne* (chastity, self-restraint) was the virtue most
often ascribed to women throughout antiquity and it is the most common on
the inscriptions, including those from the Roman period honoring Spartan
women.[105] The city heroized some women solely because of their sophrosyne.[106]
One would not immediately think of it in connection with Spartan women of an
earlier period. In fact, Xenophon (*Lac. Pol.* 3.4) reports that Spartan boys surpassed girls in modesty. The inscriptions from the Roman period add some new
notions: generosity (*IG* V.i.595.3–4); love of wisdom (*IG* V.i.598.2, 4); love of husband (or philanthropy: IG V.i.600.6–7, 601.10, 605.4); and reverence toward the
city and the Boule (*IG* V.i.589.14, 608.8–9).

References to gynaikonomoi in inscriptions concerning religion indicate
state surveillance of women's activities. Indeed, one imagines that some participants might have over-indulged in feasting, drinking, singing, and dancing in the
guise of religious activity. Furthermore, in some cults priestesses exercised
authority over men, and it is unlikely that women would be granted such power
without masculine surveillance. Gynaikonomoi in other poleis not only supervised women, but imposed sumptuary restrictions. Presumably they refrained
from censuring women such as Xenaria who spent lavishly in behalf of other

102. Kennell, "The Elite Women of Sparta."

103. Poralla², 416, Teisamenos (4), and Dawkins, *AO*, 295–96.

104. *IG* V.i.540 (*SEG* XI.797), ca. 225–50 C.E., and see further Spawforth, "Notes on the Third
Century A.D. in Spartan Epigraphy," 276–77.

105. E.g., *IG* V.i.587.6, and see further Helen North, *Sophrosyne: Self-Knowledge and Self-
Restraint in Greek Literature* (Ithaca, N.Y., 1966), esp. 252–53, and Sarah B. Pomeroy, *Xenophon,
Oeconomicus: A Social and Historical Commentary* (Oxford, 1994), 275, 279, 344.

106. E.g., Leonis: *IG* V.i.610, and Hipparchia: *IG* V.i.611, 1st cent. B.C.E.

citizens (see above). The earliest reference to a gynaikonomos in a Spartan source is ca. 110 C.E., but there is no reason to believe that the man mentioned is the first to hold that office.[107] Nevertheless, it is important to remember that in archaic and classical Sparta, older women had supervised girls: in the Roman period, Spartan practices more closely approximated those of other Greek cities.

The Visit of Julia Balbilla, the Pious

Female members of the royal family of Commagene and their descendants were present in Sparta beginning with the reign of Vespasian. When King Antiochus IV was deposed by the Romans and confined in Sparta with his wife and daughters, one of the daughters married a member of one of the leading families (Joseph. BJ 7.234). C. Iulius Eurycles Herculanus L. Vibullius Pius was born of this union.[108] The king and the rest of the family then were permitted to move to Rome. Julia Balbilla was a granddaughter of Antiochus IV, born to the king's son C. Antiochus Epiphanes. She was named for her maternal grandfather Ti. Claudius Balbillus, who had served as prefect of Egypt in 55–59 C.E. He was a learned man from whom she may have acquired her intellectual interests and special knowledge of Egyptian religion.[109] As an old woman, Balbilla came to Sparta to attend personally to the construction of a heroon honoring her cousin Herculanus. Presumably she was his heir. Though this edifice is no longer extant, it is the most impressive funerary monument known to have stood in Roman Sparta. She evidently invested her time well in making certain that it was properly built.

Balbilla wrote elegiac poetry in the archaic Aeolic dialect that Sappho had used almost a thousand years before. When she accompanied Hadrian and Sabina on a trip to Egypt in 130, like some other wealthy travellers she probably paid the native priests in the neighborhood to have her words inscribed on the Colossus of Memnon, where her poetry is still visible. Her poetry refers to Egyptian deities, and was complimentary of the imperial couple as well as of herself, whom she identifies as the descendant of Balbillus the wise, granddaughter of King Antiochus, Balbilla the pious. Piety, as we have seen, was a cliché in honorary inscriptions for elite women in Roman Sparta. Doubtless as they became older and closer to death they became more pious and their interest in leaving monuments that would survive after death increased. Piety was also a much-vaunted virtue attributed to Hellenistic kings. Balbilla's claim to piety may

---

107. SEG XI.626.1–2.

108. See further A. J. S. Spawforth, "Balbilla, the Euryclids, and Memorials for a Greek Magnate," ABSA 73 (1978), 249–60 and pls. 34–35, esp. 254.

109. Seneca, QN 4.2.13, and see further T. C. Brennan, "The Poets Julia Balbilla and Damo at the Colossus of Memnon," CW 91 (1998), 215–34, esp. 218.

have deliberately alluded to her royal descent.[110] If this hypothesis is true, then the epigraphic claims of elite Spartan women to piety are even more grandiose than is immediately apparent. The majority of extant inscriptions in their honor were dedicated after Balbilla's visit and may reflect her influence.

A woman of tremendous wealth, Balbilla not only paid for the heroon and the inscription, but it has been suggested that she was responsible for the monument of her brother Philopappus in Athens from whom she may have inherited as well.[111] No husband or child is known for Balbilla. Her independence may have been largely a result of her unmarried state, either throughout life or at least when she was older, as a divorcée or widow.

One may speculate about the effect on elite women exercised by an illustrious woman of Greco-Macedonian ancestry who was a member of the sophisticated international set at Rome and an intimate friend of Hadrian and Sabina. Balbilla embodied a glamorous mixture of dilettantism, piety, antiquarian learning, and self-importance. Her presence, that of her aunt, and the visits of other women tourists cannot but have caused a stir in the small quiet city of Sparta. If Balbilla's relationship with Sabina was modelled on Hadrian's with Antinous, she may have also lent some support to lesbian relationships— which were a tradition at Sparta in any case.[112] When she departed, she left a conspicuous monument so that the Spartans would not forget either her or her cousin.

As had been true throughout Athenian history, in Hellenistic Sparta religion offered the only acceptable milieu in which respectable women could play a public role. A female official who was expert at divination would influence political decisions.[113] As we have seen, the priestess of Artemis Orthia policed erotic relationshps between men and youths. The reknown probably attracted women to religious activities. A survey of the history of upper-class women in the west will reveal that many women whom etiquette prohibited from working as men did outside the home worked without wages as volunteers in religious contexts that allowed them to exercise some authority and social and economic independence. The expenditure of funds for charitable and civic purposes was praiseworthy. Nevertheless, repeated references in inscriptions honoring women for domestic virtues such as modesty and love of husband, and alluding to their fertility as advertised by naming their descendants, seem to seek to compensate for or undermine the playing of such public roles. As microcosmic historical

110. Thus Brennan, "The Poets Julia Balbilla and Damo at the Colossus of Memnon," 227.

111. Diana Kleiner, *The Monument of Philopappos in Athens* (Rome, 1883), esp. 52, 95.

112. E. L. Bowie, "Greek Poetry in the Antonine Age," in *Antonine Literature*, ed. D. A. Russell (Oxford, 1990), 53–90, esp. 62, suggests she was the equivalent of Hadrian's Antinous; and see chap. 1, above.

113. E.g., *manteis* in *IG* V.i.142.5, 7, *IG* V.i.599.17–18, and see further Spawforth, "Spartan Cults Under the Roman Empire," 228, 234.

documents, the inscriptions indicate that in the imperial period some Spartan women were integrated into the Roman world and had accepted its values, but they continued to cherish their peculiarly Spartan traditions and were encouraged to do so. A modern reader can sense the pride that inspires these inscriptions and continue to wonder whether Sparta's women were the same as or different from other Greek women.

CONCLUSION

GENDER AND ETHNICITY

Of all the earth, Pelasgic Argos is best, and Thessalian horses,
and Lacedaemonian women, and men who drink the water
of beautiful Arethusa.

Parke and Wormell, *The Delphic Oracle*, no. 1

Gender and Ethnicity

Do knowledge and consideration of Spartan women change our overall view of
Spartan society and institutions? In what ways were Spartans different from
other Greek women, and how does this difference contribute to our ideas about
Sparta as a whole? Studies of Spartan ethnicity have not heretofore used gender
as a defining category, except in a negative way so as to exclude women.[1] In this
brief epilogue, I will attempt to remind the reader of some of the points made in
the book and draw some conclusions. I will not review change over time, nor
repeat the details, arguments, and citations of ancient sources that can be found
in the preceding chapters.

The First Spartan Woman

Everyone in ancient Greece and every educated person in the western world even
nowadays knows the name of at least one Spartan woman: Helen. Legends
about Helen have helped shape the image of Spartan women. She was the most

---

1. E.g., Jonathan Hall, *Ethnic Identity in Greek Antiquity* (Cambridge, 1997), and J.-P. Vernant,
"Entre la honte et la gloire: L'identité du jeune spartiate," *Métis* 2 (1987) 269–99, repr. in *L'individu, la
mort, l'amour* (Paris, 1989), 173–209, the latter a study of the development of self-identity in the young
Spartan male, and see Preface n. 5, above.

beautiful woman in the world. She was also wealthy, and she dominated men. Guilty of flagrant adultery, she nevertheless was able to subjugate her infuriated warrior husband. Although Aristotle does not mention Helen, he repeats most of these attributes in his denunciation of Spartan women and their effect on the community. He considered that gender relations in Sparta were the reverse of what they should be in a normal Greek society like that of Athens.

Beauty

From earliest times, Sparta was known as a land of beautiful women—in Homer's words, *Sparte kalligynaika* (*Od.* 13.412). Spending time out of doors in the nude meant that women were exposed to public scrutiny from the time when they were very young. They competed with their peers not only in formal athletic events, but also in the eyes of their beholders and in their own judgment. Young girls learned to evaluate the beauty of other girls, and to compare their own appearance with that of their peers. In Alcman, *Partheneion* 1 (57–58), the chorus decide that Agido is first in beauty, and Hagesichora is second. Three hundred years later, Theocritus captured the sentiment. The 240 girls who race in honor of Helen declare that when they compare themselves to Helen not one of them is faultless (*Idyll* 18.25). Lycurgus had outlawed cosmetics, but Spartan women had mirrors, proving there can be artifice in nature. Ancient mirrors that have been identified as Laconian had a convex disk which displayed the face, hair, neck, and cleavage (see Appendix). The user would have been able to dress her hair, care for her skin, and adjust her facial expression and posture. In *Partheneion* 1 (6, 21), the girls refer to Agido's radiance and to Hagesichora's silver face. When the color of a woman's hair is mentioned, it is blonde, like Helen's. The girls in Alcman's *Partheneia* and the poet Megalostrata whom Alcman was said to love were all blonde.

Men also prized beautiful women and sought them as brides, even breaking some of society's rules to win them. Unlike men in Athens where girls were secluded and veiled, Spartans will have had many opportunities to look over potential brides who were completely nude. Herodotus (6.61) tells the story of a young girl who was afflicted with *dysmorphia* (misshapenness). More than ugly, she may have been deformed, for her parents had forbidden her nurse to show her to anyone. The nurse was concerned that the daughter of fortunate parents was so disfigured: she carried her every day to the shrine of Helen at Therapne and prayed to the goddess to free the child from her ugliness. Helen appeared, and touched the child. Thereupon the ugliest girl grew up to be the most beautiful of all Spartan women. Helen's magic had made her lovely (Paus. 3.7.7, Herod. 6.61). When the girl grew up her beauty, like Helen's, became a curse and a cause for a bitter quarrel between men who had been the best of friends. Although she was married, the Spartan king Ariston, who had two wives already, conceived a desperate passion for her. Tricking his friend, he won the woman, who became his third wife. The competitive phrase "most beautiful woman" occurs in the story of the prostitute whom Cinadon was ordered to bring back to Sparta (see chap. 5). At the other end of the social scale, the wealthy Agiatis was lovelier than other Greek women (Plut. *Cleom.* 1.2, 22.1–2). "More beautiful than all the other women in the Peloponnese" also appears in the story of Xenopeithia, mother of Lysandridas, who had commanded Spartan forces at Thebes in the time of Agesilaus II.[2]

Lysander, who was famous for bending the rules of proper Spartan behavior, rejected the bride he had acquired at a "lottery," and planned to marry a more beautiful one.[3] Perhaps he married the homely woman after all, and his daughters took after their mother. They were unable to find husbands not only because their father was poor, but because, as their father said, they were "ugly" (*aischrai*: Plut. *Lys.* 2.5, 30.5).

In Sparta, beautiful people were highly esteemed: the best looking man and woman were most admired (Heraclides Lembus in Athen. XIII.566a = *FHG* III.168). Since Homer (*Od.* 6.102–7) described Nausicaa as towering over her handmaidens like a palm tree, and in the visual arts gods were depicted as taller than mortals, Greeks considered height an attribute of beautiful, noble women.[4] Timasimbrota, who is mentioned in a fragment of archaic poetry, was as tall as a man, for she is described as resembling the golden-haired son of Polydorus in her noble stature.[5] The Ephors fined King Archidamus for choosing a short woman, because it was expected that the children produced by the couple would look like their mother.[6] Plutarch (*Cleom.* 38.5) described the heroic wife of Panteus, who accompanied Cleomenes' family to Egypt, as tall and robust.

Nutrition

Diet reflected ethnic difference. The height of Spartan women probably resulted not only from heredity and eugenics, but also from their generous food rations. Spartans were the only Greek women who were well fed and drank wine. Aristophanes alludes to Cleitagora, a Spartan woman poet whose name was

---

2. He was also called Lysanoridas. See Theopompus in Athen. 13.609b = *FGrH* 115 F 240.

3. Hermippus of Smyrna = Athen. 13.555b–c = *FGrH* IV.3 1026 F 6 = fr. 87 (Wehrli). C. Meillier, "Une coutume hiérogamique à Sparte?" *REG* 97 (1984), 381–402, esp. 388–89, suggests that this story was invented to discredit Lysander. See further chap. 2 n.32.

4. See further Sarah B. Pomeroy, *Xenophon, Oeconomicus: A Social and Historical Commentary* (Oxford, 1994), 306.

5. *PMGF* 5, fr. 2, col. ii.17–18. For other interpretations of these fragmentary lines, see M. L. West, "Alcmanica," *CQ* 15 (1965), 188–202, esp. 189–90.

6. Athen. 13.566a–b; Theophrastus in Plut. *Ages.* 2.3, *De educ. puer.* 1d.

associated with a skolion, or drinking song. A Laconian vase depicts women at at a mixed symposium. Dionysus was a god of women in Sparta.[7]

Since wine drinking by women was not approved of elsewhere in Greece, the practice took on a negative connotation among critics of Spartan women. In Plato, *Laws* (637C), the Athenian Old Man talking to the Spartan criticizes Spartan women for licentiousness. This gratuitous and stereotypical criticism follows praise of moderate drinking by Spartan men at symposia and may allude to women's intoxication.[8] It was known that Spartan women drank wine as part of their regular diet, but there is no evidence that they were less temperate than Spartan men.[9]

Dress

Women's style of dress was used to characterize Dorians in general. *Doriazein* means "to dress like a Spartan girl" and connotes nudity or semi-nudity. The standard Greek-English dictionary gives the meaning "dress like a Dorian girl, i.e. in a single garment open at the side," and gives *doriazo* as an equivalent of *dorizo* "imitate the Dorians in life."[10]

Clothing, as well as the lack of it, marked differences between Spartans and other Greek women. Because Spartans spent time out of doors, they needed warm garments in some kinds of weather. The Dorian peplos was a heavier woollen dress than the Ionian, and had to be fastened on the shoulders by fibulae. This heavy dress had been worn by all Greek women in the archaic period. Spartan fashion was conservative. The light gauzy dresses of the Ionian style were new fashions. Herodotus explains that the change came about when a sole survivor of a battle returned to Athens and told the women that all their men had died.[11] They killed the bearer of this devastating news with their pins, which were subsequently associated with aggression on the part of women.[12] Thereafter the women were forbidden to wear fibulae. Indeed, some of the jewelry dedicated at

---

7. Robert Parker, "Spartan Religion," in *Classical Sparta: Techniques Behind Her Success*, ed. A. Powell (Norman, Okla., 1988), 142–72, esp. 151.

8. Thus N. R. E. Fisher, "Drink, Hybris and the Promotion of Harmony in Sparta," in *Classical Sparta: Techniques Behind Her Success*, ed. A. Powell (Norman, Okla., 1988), 26–50, esp. 29–30.

9. For Spartan temperance: Critias fr. 6 (Diels-Kranz) = Athen. 10.432d, and Plut. *Lyc.* 12.7.

10. *LSJ* s.v. Doriazo.

11. Herod. 5.87. On the fictitious nature of this aetiology, which emphasizes the cruelty of Athenian women, see Thomas J. Figueira, "Herodotus on the Early Hostilities Between Aegina and Athens," *AJP* 106 (1985), 49–74, esp. 50, 56–57 = *Excursions in Epichoric History: Aeginetan Essays* (Lanham, Md., 1999), 35–60, esp. 36, 41–42.

12. See further I. Jenkins, "Dressed to Kill," *Omnibus* 5 (1983), 29–32.

the sanctuary of Artemis Orthia resembles nails with very long spikes.[13] Wearing a Doric peplos meant always having a weapon to hand. Only when she was dressed in a man's costume as a bride was a woman disarmed.

Definition of Ethnicity by Women

As we have mentioned in chapter 3, Gorgo is the first Spartan woman who is reputed to have drawn attention to the special identity of Spartan women. When she was asked by a woman from Attica, "Why is it that you Spartans are the only women who can rule men?" she replied, "That is because we are the only ones who give birth to men."[14] In this story, the interlocutor assumes the special identity before Gorgo replies. About a century later, another royal woman, Cynisca, emphasized her uniqueness by declaring, "I am the only woman in all of Greece to have won this [Olympic] crown."[15] We have also mentioned the anonymous Spartan woman who was equally conscious of her ethnic distinctiveness: When an Ionian woman was proud of something she had woven (which was very valuable), a Spartan woman showed off her four well-behaved sons and said these should be the work of a noble and honorable woman, and she should swell with pride and boast of them (Plut. *Sayings of Spartan Women* 241.9). We observe, in passing, the competitive nature of the Spartan's retort.

That Spartan women were taught to speak and were encouraged to do so distinguishes them from Spartan men, who did not debate in law courts or in their General Assembly, and from Athenians and other Greek women, who were expected to remain silent and by no means to speak to men. In the *Oeconomicus*, Xenophon describes a young wife who was brought up so that she might see and hear and speak as little as possible.[16] Having an enlightened view of marriage, her husband describes how he taught his wife to converse with him. More than five hundred years later, Plutarch cautions: "the words of a modest woman must never be public property. She should be shy with her speech as with her body, and guard it against strangers. Feelings, character, and disposition can all be seen in a woman's talk. . . . A wife should speak only to her husband or through her husband."[17]

13. Dawkins, *AO*, 382–83 and pl. CCII. Dawkins published another bronze fibula in "Artemis Orthia: Some Additions and a Correction," *JHS* 50 (1930), 298–99 and pl. XI.1.

14. Plut. *Sayings of Spartan Women* = *Mor.* 240e5; cf. Plut. *Lyc.* 14, and *Sayings of Spartans*, 7e13.

15. See chap. 1.

16. Xen. *Oec.* 7.6, 10, and see further Pomeroy, *Xenophon, Oeconomicus*, ad loc. Laura McClure, *Spoken like a Woman* (Princeton,1999), 164–68, discusses the negative reflections of Spartan's women's outspokenness in Athenian literature and in Aristotle.

17. *Advice to the Bride and Groom*, 31–32, and see further Sarah B. Pomeroy, ed., *Plutarch's Advice to the Bride and Groom and A Consolation to His Wife* (New York, 1999), 38, 41, 42, 53, 104, 106, 119–20, 126, 151, 160.

Status, Autonomy, and Moral Authority

According to several criteria that may be applied to assess the status of women, Spartans were distinctive.

Health

Spartans must have been among the healthiest of Greek women. There are no reports that they suffered infanticide, as did some male babies. We have seen that a baby girl who was distressingly ugly or even malformed was reared. The nutrition of Spartan women was superior and their reproductive health was a matter of public concern. Prohibition of the use of cosmetics eliminated exposure to toxic substances. Marriage at a mature age produced healthy children for healthy mothers.

Education

Consistent with the concern for women's health, of all Greek women only Spartans were given physical training as were men. They also studied *mousike* (music, dancing, poetry).

Sexual Expression

The nudity of girls for athletics had sexual consequences, and girls and women alike were free to engage in homosexual relationships. Xenophon and Plutarch depict heterosexual intercourse as also desirable and pleasurable for both partners, and declare that constraints on the frequency of intercourse are beneficial for husband and wife alike.

Control over Reproduction

Women exercised some control over their own reproduction. According to Plutarch, Timaea thought she knew whether her child was fathered by her lover Alcibiades or by her husband. According to Xenophon, women took the initiative in husband-doubling arrangements for the sake of producing children who would inherit from more than one father. According to Cicero, Spartan women were in charge of their own fertility.

Control over Property

Property at Sparta was real property. It is impossible to discuss the Spartan economy and to exclude women. Women controlled real property including immovables, for Xenophon declares unambiguously that the wife who duplicates husbands wants to get possession of two oikoi (*gynaikes . . . boulontai katechein*). By the fourth century and the Hellenistic period, some of the wealthiest Spartans were women.

Influence in Society

Spartan women are rarely depicted as passive. Plutarch reports marriage by capture, but this ritual was an enactment of a previous arrangement and came as no surprise to the bride. She was carefully prepared ahead of time. In his description of the wedding, Xenophon draws attention to the wife as an active partner. The phrase *epei . . . gyne elthoi* ("after the woman goes": *Lac. Pol.* 1.5) appears in his first sentence about marriage. In contrast, in descriptions of the marriage ceremony in Athens, where the father or guardian gives the bride to the groom, who takes her, the verb commonly used is *lambano* (take, seize).[18] Furthermore, as we have noted, Xenophon mentions the personal ambitions of the woman who wants to control two oikoi.

Women also understood and enforced societal norms. They not only spoke, but jeered at cowards and bachelors. In some cases they wielded the power of life and death over their adult sons. Women also tested newborn male babies, and female babies were simply turned over to them. Though we cannot generalize from the activities of priestesses, some of them regulated the behavior of men. At least by the Hellenistic period, the Priestess of Orthia controlled the intensity with which the boys were whipped, especially when she saw that a man wielding the whip was showing favor to a particular boy. Plutarch's *Sayings of Spartan Women* give many examples of women's leadership and control over men throughout Spartan history.

Because of their influence and authority in society as a whole, to study Spartan women is not only to learn women's history, but also to have a more complete knowledge of Spartan history.

18. On the ekdosis in the Greek world, see most recently A.-M. Vérilhac and C. Vial, *Le mariage grec du VIe siècle av. J.-C. à l'epoque d'Auguste, BCH* suppl. 32 (Paris, 1998), 254–58.

APPENDIX

SOURCES FOR THE HISTORY OF SPARTAN WOMEN

In this survey I will discuss important works of literature and material remains that shed light on Spartan women. My purpose is not to include everything that could be said about a specific author or work of art, nor to raise formal literary, philological, or esthetic questions, but rather to focus on the ways in which the work in question can be exploited in the quest for the history of Spartan women. I will also try to draw attention to the limitations of the genre of the work, the bias of the author or craftsman, and the potential problems of modern interpretation. The amount of space devoted to the various sources discussed in this chapter is commensurate with their importance in constructing the history of Spartan women, rather than their general place in the hierarchy of great works of classical literature and art. Nor will this survey be exhaustive: not every primary source cited in the book will be discussed in this chapter. The sources will be examined, as far as possible, in chronological order: first, written texts; second, art and archaeological evidence. The sources range in date from the archaic through the Hellenistic and Roman periods. The chronological picture, however, is not straightforward, because some of the literature was performed again and the artifacts reused many years after their creation. The record is uneven, with certain kinds of evidence plentiful in one period, but rare or absent in another. The Spartans were xenophobic and did not use precious metals (at least openly) from the late archaic period until about the fourth century B.C.E. Consequently, for a long period in their history they could not pay foreign poets or artisans for their work, and there is a dearth of artistic material from this time. Furthermore, although statistical corroboration is lacking, the number of inscriptions dealing with women from the Roman period seems disproportionate to the size of the population.[1] As is true for major archaeological monuments, the remains of

1. P. A. Cartledge and A. J. S. Spawforth, *Hellenistic and Roman Sparta: A Tale of Two Cities* (London, 1989), 133, estimate a population of no more than 12,000.

inscriptions from the Roman period are more likely to have survived than earlier artifacts.

WRITTEN SOURCES

Almost all our major sources on Spartan women are the work of authors who were not Spartans, and who lived much later than the time periods they discuss. With the exception of a few poems by Alcman, Plutarch's *Sayings of Spartan Women*, and some brief inscriptions, none of the works focus on women; rather remarks about women usually constitute a small fraction of a text devoted to another subject. Furthermore, there are few inscriptions concerning private matters in pre-Hellenistic Sparta, for, in addition to the kings, only men who had died in battle, or women who had died in childbirth were permitted to have inscribed epitaphs (see chap. 3). Most important, in Sparta there are no counter-parts to the private orations that supply so much information about Athenian women and gender relationships. The orations are also a crucial source for Athenian law. In contrast, Spartan law and any debate over it were not written down, though there are occasional remarks scattered in other sources. For exam-ple, Herodotus (6.57.4–5) reports that the kings had jurisdiction over the mar-riage of an heiress; Philo (*De spec. leg.* 3.4.22) supplies the odd bit of information that at Sparta children by the same mother were permitted to marry, while at Athens only children by the same father could do so; and Aelian in *Various Histories* lists customs and laws including those relieving fathers of three or more children from various taxes and obligations (6.6 and see chap. 3). Xenophon's *Spartan Constitution*[2] and Plutarch's *Life of Lycurgus* give substantial accounts of the legislation attributed to Lycurgus. The use of such sources for legal history, however, poses many problems. Most of this information is reported without chronological reference. Aelian neglects to state when some of the practices he records were in force. Thus Aelian (6.6) and other sources tell us that women married without dowries, while different sources report that they had dowries and often quite large ones (see chap. 4). Even Xenophon (*Lac. Pol.* 14.1) is uncer-tain whether the laws of Lycurgus were unchanged in his own day. Nevertheless, scholars have deduced some features of Spartan law. Analogies with the laws of Gortyn, in Crete, a Dorian polis whose laws are extant in a lengthy inscription written in the fifth century, but recording archaic law, have been useful.[3] Women at Gortyn could inherit, control, and bequeath property. Laws governing real property and inheritance have also been inferred from descriptions of results: thus Aristotle's information on heiresses and land tenure has been used to deter-mine women's economic position (see chap. 4). As is the case in general for Greek

---

2. Herein referred to in brief citations as *Lac. Pol.*
3. See further R. F. Willetts, *The Law Code of Gortyn*, *Kadmos*, suppl. 1 (Berlin, 1967).

history, almost all our evidence concerns the upper class: little is known about female perioeci or helots (but see chap. 5). In any case, because the upper-class (Spartiates) constituted a ruling aristocracy, they were not a mere political minority as they would be in a democratic city.

How Unique Was Sparta?

Almost all extant ancient literature about Spartan women was written by non-Spartans who never lived in or even visited Sparta.[4] The Greeks tended to organize their thoughts in polarized categories; for example, Greek/barbarian, male/female, and Athenian/Spartan. This way of thinking exaggerated differences between the categories being compared. As a consequence, differences between Spartan and Athenian women were emphasized. Following ancient precedent, throughout this book, where relevant, I too have compared Spartan women to Athenian. It must be admitted that two highly unusual Greek cities are being compared: neither one might be described "average" or "ordinary." This comparison, however, is the only one possible, for we do not have abundant information on women in other Greek cities from the archaic through the Roman periods. For these reasons, the works of Alcman, Xenophon, and Plutarch are particularly important. Alcman may have been a Spartan. Certainly he was able to write the Doric dialect. According to another tradition, he was born in Lydia, perhaps as a slave, and came to work in Sparta. This tradition links him by birth with the luxuries of Lydia. In either case, he was certainly familiar with Spartan society, and the state authorized him to be one of its most influential poets. Xenophon, as well, lived in Sparta. Plutarch visited Sparta, but, of course, as an antiquarian, not as a direct observer of the archaic, classical, and Hellenistic society that interested him.

Women's Voices

All the extant literature about Sparta was written by men. Nevertheless, unlike Athenian women, whose voices were silenced, Spartans may perhaps be heard through several literary sources. For example, in the poetry of Alcman, girls who are named make statements about their current situation (see below). They are not dramatizing a myth, but rather talking about themselves and other girls like them. It would have seemed most peculiar to the speakers as well as to any observer if what they said was completely unnatural or unlike statements that could be made in such a situation. Another text where a woman's voice may be heard is the epigram composed in honor of Cynisca's chariot victories (see chap. 1). Cynisca is depicted as speaking in the first person. If she did not write the epigram herself, she may well have commissioned the poet and given orders about

---

4. T. Boring, *Literacy in Ancient Sparta* (Leiden, 1979), chap. 3, surveys Spartan authors.

the content. A final source for women's words is Plutarch's *Sayings of Spartan Women*. Spartan women were anything but laconic (see chap. 1). Moreover, they were not separated from their mothers and grandmothers, for they married men from their own polis. It is quite conceivable that through the oral tradition they passed down the *bons mots* of their female ancestors. Furthermore, male descendents as well could have remembered the pithy statements of their mothers and grandmothers. The *Sayings* show the wit, grace, and brevity characteristic of the Spartan style (*Lyc.*19.2, 21.1). Even in the modern world, where people often live in places remote from those of their ancestors, such oral traditions constitute a vital part of family histories. Thus it is quite credible that eventually some Hellenistic anthologizer compiled a collection of actual words once uttered by Spartan women and that Plutarch used this work as his source. That the statements are quoted out of their original context enhances their exaggerated and dramatic qualities.

Archaic

Alcman lived in Sparta in the archaic period, probably after the Second Messenian War, but before the ensuing militaristic reforms had profoundly transformed society.[5] As we have mentioned above, his origin and exact dates are disputed. He was variously said to be Laconian and the descendant of slaves, or Lydian.[6] Textual evidence points to the late seventh century.[7] Archaeological evidence indicates that he died no later than 570.[8] His tomb was near Helen's in Platanistas.[9] Whether an autobiographical interpretation of Alcman's oeuvre is appropriate has been debated.[10] Be that as it may, even if the poems may not provide completely reliable testimony about the life of the poet, nevertheless they constitute some of the most valuable evidence for the lives of Spartan women.

5. All references to Alcman's poetry are to M. Davies, *Poetarum Melicorum Graecorum Fragmenta* (*PMGF*), vol. 1 (Oxford, 1991). Except where noted, the translations of Alcman in the present book are from Davies's Greek text. I am grateful to Dr. Davies for his comments on my translation of *Partheneion* 1. For a text of Alcman with brief apparatus criticus (but in general more restorations than Davies), commentary, and translation, see D. A. Campbell, *Greek Lyric*, vol. 2 (Cambridge, Mass., 1988). Campbell also provides useful indexes. For full commentary with text, see C. Calame, *Alcman: Fragmenta* (Rome, 1983). Biographical testimonia are cited from Davies.

6. See *PMGF*, T A1a–9, 11a.

7. See F. D. Harvey, "Oxyrhynchus Papyrus 2390 and Early Spartan History," *JHS* 87 (1967), 62–73, esp. 69. Poralla², p. 18, no. 65, dates Alcman to the second half of the seventh century.

8. W. G. Cavanagh and R. R. Laxton, "Lead Figurines from the Menelaion and Seriation," *ABSA* 79 (1984), 23–36, esp. 35.

9. Paus. 3.15.1. F. Bölte, s.v. Platanistas, *RE* 20.2 (Stuttgart, 1950), cols. 2333–34.

10. M. Davies, review of *Alcman: Fragmenta*, by Claude Calame, *Gnomon*, 58 (1986), 385–89, esp. 387 n. 2, questions Calame's dogmatic rejection of such an interpretation.

Choral songs like those of Alcman were passed down through the generations at Sparta and probably elsewhere, forming a stable element in the educational curriculum. In 370/369, after the battle of Leuctra, the victors asked the helots to sing songs of Terpander, Alcman, and Spendon (Plut. *Lyc.* 28.5). They refused, not because as helots in the fourth century they did not know these songs, but on the grounds that if they sang them they would anger their Spartan masters. Athenaeus (14.632f–633a), who lived in the late second or early third century c.e., reports that even in his day the Spartans took painstaking care of their ancient songs and were well taught in them. The fragmentary nature of the poems of Alcman that are now extant is due to several reasons in addition to the obvious one that they were written more than 2,500 years ago. First, many brief quotations were preserved only in the works of later authors, especially grammarians and compilers of anecdotes such as Athenaeus. The grammarians were primarily interested in the unusual Doric dialect and in the use of meters, and do not always quote a full sentence or thought. These tantalizing tidbits of Alcman were all that were known to the modern world until the great papyrological discoveries of the nineteenth century. *Partheneion* 1, the oldest long fragment of archaic Greek lyric poetry, happens to be preserved because in the first century c.e. someone made a copy of the text on papyrus. Sometime later the manuscript probably became worn, bits of papyrus flaked off, and its owner or his or her heirs discarded it. The papyrus was then reused to wrap a crocodile mummy. In the course of excavating at Saqqara, the Egyptologist Auguste F. F. Mariette discovered the mummy and sent the papyrus to Paris, where it is now stored in the Louvre. The first edition was edited by the Greek scholar Émile Egger in 1863.[11] The papyrus must have belonged at first and some time later to a scholar or student. It includes a large number of marginal comments (scholia); most of these are in the same handwriting as the text. This papyrus provides a glimpse of a long tradition of scholarship on the text of Alcman. Some of the most erudite explanations are attributed to the great text editors of the third and second centuries, Aristophanes of Byzantium and Aristarchus, who worked in the library established by Ptolemy I and II in Alexandria. These scholia attempt to explicate the text, and usually include citations to other ancient authors and scholars. Their existence does not indicate that Alcman's poetry was more obscure and difficult than other archaic lyrics, but rather that the Alexandrians had deemed his work, like that of many archaic and classical authors, worthy of painstaking editorial attention.

Papyri published in the twentieth century have brought to light additional fragments of Alcman's poetry. Among these, most significant for the history of women is *Partheneion* 3, first published in 1957.[12] The fragmentary text of this

---

11. "Un fragment inédit du poëte Alcman," in *Memoires d'histoire ancienne et de philologie* (Paris, 1863), 159–75.

12. *PMGF* 3.3 = *P.Oxy.* xxiv.2387. See further E. G. Turner, *Greek Manuscripts of the Ancient World* (Princeton, 1971), pp. 42–43, no. 15.

Fig. 9. Alcman, *Partheneion* 3, fr. 3 (*P.Oxy.* xxiv.2387).

Photo courtesy of the Ashmolean Museum, Oxford.

poem was discovered on a papyrus from Oxyrhynchus dated to the second cent-ury C.E. Like the Louvre papyrus, the Oxyrhynchus text has scholia written in the margins, as is apparent in the upper left corner of the fragment illustrated in fig. 9. Translations of *Partheneia* 1 and 3 are printed in chapter 1, pages 6–7.

Performance and Preservation of Alcman. The poems contain highly specif-ic references to girls who are named and whose appearance, emotions, behavior, and effect upon other girls are described. Consequently, scholars have debated whether each poem was composed to be sung by identifiable girls at a particular occasion or whether the *Partheneia* were originally composed to be performed repeatedly at ritual occasions. The two hypotheses are not exclusive. The poems could have been composed to be sung by the girls who are named and described the first time, and then, because of their sheer excellence as well as the lack of sub-sequent poetic composition, repeatedly performed at rituals by other girls who played the roles of their predecessors.[13] Because of their use in ritual and Sparta's

13. See further J. Herington, *Poetry into Drama: Early Tragedy and the Greek Poetic Tradition* (Berkeley, 1985), 22–26, 48, 54–55, 207. The ancient evidence for reperformance of Alcman concerns male choruses, not *Partheneia*. Herington (25) argues that Sosibius was an eyewitness to a perfor-mance of Alcman: see below on Sosibius.

general conservatism, the poems will not have been changed or updated. In other words, the poems could have been an accurate reflection of erotic feelings and behavior in the days of Alcman, and have become more of a theatrical reenactment in later times. Another possibility is that they were originally written for performers who impersonated the characters named. A corollary to this theory is that Hagesichora and Agido were simply generic names for choir leaders, and that the rest of the girls were fictitious as well.[14] This theory seems less plausible to me because of the specificity of the descriptions of the individual girls and the fact that some of the names are real names and recur in Spartan prosopography.[15]

The poet gained circulation for his poetry by travelling to populated areas including pan-Hellenic sanctuaries and festivals. He claimed that his work was known far and wide (Ael. Arist. Or. 28.54 [II.159 Keil] = PMGF 148 [i]). Although this Appendix is not the place to discuss the complex issues concerning the preservation of archaic poetry through oral and written traditions, it seems likely that Alcman's poetry circulated by both means.

There is evidence for the performance of Alcman's poems more than a hundred years after his lifetime.[16] The circumstances of the performance may have changed over time.[17] Originally the Partheneia may have been performed before an audience comprised mostly of women, with the poet and perhaps a few officials as the only men present. In later times, when the poems had become part of Sparta's great heritage, men as well may have been welcome to witness the performances.[18] It has been suggested that terracotta masks from the sanctuary of

14. See further Denys L. Page, Alcman: The Partheneion (Oxford, 1951), 64, and Herington, Poetry into Drama, 238 n. 38.

15. LGPN 3A s.vv. cites the names in the Partheneia, and see below.

16. Sosibius, On the Sacrifices in Lacedaemon, FGrH 595 F 5 = Athen. 15.678b–c for a choral performance of Alcman celebrating a Spartan victory ca. 546. See further E. Stehle, Performance in Ancient Greece (Princeton, 1997), 55, and G. Nagy, Pindar's Homer: The Lyric Possession of an Epic Past (Baltimore, Md., 1990), 349. On the transmission of Alcman beyond Sparta, see P. A. Cartledge, "Literacy in the Spartan Oligarchy," JHS 98 (1978), 28.

17. Excluding the editions of the texts, probably the most influential full-length study of the Partheneia to be published in the later part of the twentieth century is Claude Calame, Les chœurs de jeunes filles en Grèce archaïque, vol. 1, Morphologie, fonction religieuse et sociale; vol. 2, Alcman (Rome, 1977). In his first volume, Calame gives a lengthy survey of the composition and formal structure of the lyric choir not only in archaic Greece, but in later periods. In volume 2, he examines the work of Alcman, especially Partheneia 1 and 3, which he understands to have been performed at pubertal rites of initiation for girls that paralleled those for boys. Calame reiterates this view in "Iniziazioni femminili spartane: Stupro, danza, ratto, metamorfosi e morte iniziatica," in Le donne in Grecia, ed. G. Arrigoni (Bari, 1985), 33–54. Calame's interpretation has been widely adopted by many scholars who write about Alcman's poems, Spartan girls, and religion. Nevertheless, there is nothing inherent in the texts that makes Calame's view more than an attractive suggestion.

18. Christina A. Clark, "The Gendering of the Body in Alcman's Partheneion 1: Narrative, Sex, and Social Order in Archaic Sparta," Helios 23 (1996), 143–72, assumes that men were in the audience and interprets the poetry as produced ultimately in order to make women conform to "their culture's male-structured gender codes" (169).

Ortheia beginning in the second half of the seventh century were used for enactments of *Partheneion* 1 as a ritual marriage.[19] Gold and silver were outlawed in Sparta, evidently some time after Alcman composed *Parthenion* 1 in which they are mentioned. If the performers in later times were actually wearing the luxurious apparel described in the poem, it must have been part of a costume, distributed solely on the occasions of the performance and then returned to storage until the next performance.

Herodotus of Halicarnassus was born a little before the Persian War and lived until the Peloponnesian War. He wrote the history of the Persian War, with many digressions. Spartan women are mentioned in the tales about Helen; in some of the descriptions of the royal succession (e.g., 5.39: the two wives of Anaxandrides; 6.61–66: Ariston's three wives and the parentage of Demaratus), the judicial duties of the kings, and in a variety of anecdotes. Herodotus imparts this information straightforwardly, without approval or criticism. Scholars differ greatly in their assessment of the historical veracity of Herodotus. In my view, not all anecdotes are necessarily false. The fact that Herodotus heard stories like those about Gorgo suggests that there was at least a kernel of historical truth behind them. From Herodotus' various brief remarks, it can be surmised that the ideal Spartan woman was clever, witty, tall, and beautiful.[20] (See esp. chap. 1 and Conclusion.)

Classical

Dramatic Poetry

In Athenian drama, Spartans may play the role of "Other" to the Athenians:[21] they fill the conceptual space usually occupied by barbarians, and provoke questions about the assumed superiority of Greeks over barbarians.[22] Female characters are used to exaggerate the distinctiveness of both ways of life. Thus in Euripides, *Andromache* (e.g., 29, 194, 889), Hermione, daughter of Helen and

---

19. Jane B. Carter, "Masks and Poetry in Early Sparta," in *Early Greek Cult Practice: Proceedings of the Fifth International Symposium at the Swedish Institute at Athens, 26–29 June 1986*, ed. R. Hägg, N. Marinatos, and G. C. Nordquist (Stockholm, 1988), 89–98, esp. 89, 98.

20. Herod. 5.51, 6.61, 7.239, and see further Carolyn Dewald, "Women and Culture in Herodotus' *Histories*," in *Reflections of Women in Antiquity*, ed. Helene P. Foley (New York, 1981), 91–125.

21. See further E. N. Tigerstedt, *The Legend of Sparta in Classical Antiquity*, 2 vols. (Stockholm, 1965–74), vol. 1, 114–27; Ellen Greenstein Millender, "Athenian Ideology and the Empowered Spartan Female," in *Sparta: New Perspectives*, ed. S. Hodkinson and A. Powell (London, 1999), 355–91, esp. 357–62, 373; and most recently Helene P. Foley, *Female Acts in Greek Tragedy* (Princeton, 2001), 99–102, 318–31.

22. See further Edith Hall, *Inventing the Barbarian* (Oxford, 1989), 214–15. Hall does not discuss gender issues.

Menelaus, is often referred to as a "Laconian" or "Spartan" woman, and herself criticizes Spartans as deceivers (445–53).

Tragic and comic dramatists alike draw attention to the semi-nudity and the physical development that was connected with the education of Spartan women. The Spartans were xenophobic in the fifth century and no Athenian poet is likely to have ever seen a Spartan woman. Perhaps the rumors spread when an embassy came from Athens, or when some ambassador from Corinth, for example, traveled to Sparta for a meeting of the Peloponnesian League and drove his chariot past a group of women exercising out of doors. Works of art that circulated beyond the frontiers of Laconia, including mass-produced bronze figurines in the shape of Spartan female athletes, and some vases that showed women engaged in activities that may have seemed scandalous (see below), probably also inspired ideas that foreigners held about Spartan women.

Euripides' portrait of Hermione as vicious and self-centered in *Andromache*, produced in the early years of the Peloponnesian War (427–426 B.C.E.), reflects the anti-Spartan bias of contemporary Athens:

> No Spartan girl could ever be modest
> even if she wanted to be,
> They go outside their houses with the boys
> with naked thighs and open dresses
> and they race and wrestle with the boys. Insufferable!
> It's not surprising that you don't train women to be chaste.
> (*Andromache*, 595–601)

Similarly Sophocles:

> And that young woman, whose tunic is still unbelted
> around her thigh, revealingly.
> (fr. 872 Lloyd-Jones)

Sophocles also wrote a tragedy titled *Lakainai* ("Laconian Women," frs. 367–68 Lloyd-Jones).

In contrast to Euripides and Sophocles, Aristophanes in *Lysistrata* (411 B.C.E.), also produced during the Peloponnesian War, portrays his representative Spartan woman favorably, for such a portrayal suits his story of reconciliation. Lampito is physically fit, and confident in her ability to carry out the sex strike. Aristophanes' plays are the only complete comedies from the classical period now extant. Spartan women occur in other Athenian comedies in brief fragments or mere titles. Eupolis, a contemporary of Aristophanes, wrote a play titled *Heilotes* ("Helots") in which he mocks them as lascivious (fr. 148, see also 385 Kassel-Austin). He also wrote a comedy titled *Spartans* or *Leda* (frs. 60–62 Kassel-Austin). The tradition continued in Middle and New Comedy. Alexis (ca. 372–270) wrote four comedies based on myths about Helen (frs. 70–76) and Apollodorus Carystius (third century) or Apollodorus Gelous (fourth or third century) wrote a *Lakaina* ("The Spartan Woman," Kassel-Austin II.508–9, frs. 7, 8).

Prose

Critias, an Athenian aristocrat related to Plato, lived ca. 460–403 and was one of the most ruthless of the Thirty Tyrants who ruled Athens at the end of the Peloponnesian War with the backing of the Spartans. He wrote poetry and prose, including a treatise on the Spartan Constitution. This work, known only through a few fragments, began with the statement: "I start, as you see, from a man's birth. How might he become physically best and strongest? [He could,] if the man who plants his seed would exercise and eat wholesome food and harden his body, and if the mother of the child-to-be would strengthen her body and exercise."[23] Critias was an associate of Socrates and a Sophist. Plato and Xenophon probably read his work, and Xenophon may have been influenced by Critias' views about the importance of the mother.

Plato lived ca. 429–347, a turbulent period in Athenian history. Sparta had defeated Athens in the Peloponnesian War, and the restored democracy at Athens condemned Socrates to death. Like other disciples of Socrates, he found much to admire in Spartan society. His utopian works, especially the *Republic* and *Laws*, prescribe features of women's life that in many cases correspond to the Spartan reality, or at least to the Spartan ideal.[24] In the *Republic* these include, for example, a full program of education for women administered by the state; physical exercise; late marriage; prohibition of money and private property (hence of dowries); wife-sharing; and marriage "lotteries." The *Laws* are less radical: Spartan lawgivers are criticized for permitting women (who are half the society) to indulge in a luxurious, expensive, and disorderly way of life (*Laws* 7.806C). It is perhaps more accurate to state that Plato is not so much a source for Spartan women; rather, Spartan women were an inspiration for Plato's ideas about the roles of women in utopia.

Xenophon, who lived ca. 430–356, was Plato's contemporary and a student of Socrates as well. His *Spartan Constitution* (*Lacedaimonion Politeia*) is our best source on Spartan women in the classical period.[25] Xenophon spent twenty years on an estate granted to him by the Spartans near Elis. His sons were probably educated in the agoge, for in the fourth century this education was made available to a few youths who were not full-fledged Spartan citizens.[26] Thus he writes

---

23. Diels-Kranz II (1969), 88, fr. 32.
24. *Republic* 5, passim, *Laws* 5.742C, 6.774C, 784–85, 7.814, 8.833D–834D.
25. I presented this material first in "Xenophon's Spartan Women," paper delivered at The World of Xenophon conference, University of Liverpool, July 8, 1999.
26. D.L. 2.54 and see further Nigel M. Kennell, *The Gymnasium of Virtue: Education and Culture in Ancient Sparta* (Chapel Hill, N.C., 1995), 16. E. Badian, "Xenophon the Athenian," paper

about Sparta from the unique perspective of a first-hand witness. Xenophon admired some aspects of Spartan society, though he was critical of others.[27] When he wrote the *Spartan Constitution* is unclear. Most recently it has been dated to after 371.[28] According to an alternative theory, if the treatise was written earlier, chapter 14, in which he laments the abandonment of the way of life established by Lycurgus, may have been written later than the rest of the work. There is a contemporaneous parallel to Xenophon's change in attitude. We may compare Plato's optimism about the Spartan way of life that may be detected in the *Republic* with the disillusionment he expresses in the *Laws* (see above). In any case, the viewpoint of Xenophon, like that of any writer, should be considered a lens through which we view his narrative. Nor did Xenophon come to Sparta as a *tabula rasa*. His ideas about Spartan women were doubtless shaped by prior influences and experiences. To start with the most obvious: he would have been in the audience at the production of *Lysistrata* and have seen the robust and aggressive Lampito, so different from the Athenian women whom he knew.[29] He also will have seen tragedies in which mythological Spartan women were portrayed in an unfavorable light (see above). In Athens he will have known the bright young Laconizers[30] of his day in a group associated with Socrates, and may have read what Critias wrote about women in his treatise on Sparta.[31] Furthermore, he will have learned much about Spartan society from Clearchus, Cheirisophus, Agesilaus, and the numerous Spartans who were engaged with him in military service in Asia over the years. It is universally acknowledged that soldiers gossip about sex and women.

Xenophon gives the theme of the *Spartan Constitution* in his opening sentence, by asking how it is possible for Sparta to be the most powerful and renowned of the Greek poleis when it has such a small population (*oliganthropotaton* [a translation of this passage is given in chap. 3]). He goes on to answer this rhetorical question. In brief, according to Xenophon, Lycurgus had designed social, political, and military institutions that created superb hoplites. As we have mentioned above, he states that he does not know whether the laws of Lycurgus were still unchanged in his day, because they were often disobeyed; nevertheless he describes them.

---

delivered at The World of Xenophon conference, University of Liverpool, July 10, 1999, questions whether the sons participated in the agoge.

26. See further C. Tuplin, "Xenophon, Sparta, and the *Cyropaedia*," in *The Shadow of Sparta*, ed. A. Powell and S. Hodgkinson (London, 1994), 127–81, esp. 132.

28. Badian, "Xenophon the Athenian."

29. Lampito had been the name of a historical woman, daughter of Leutychides II (a Spartan king), and was the mother of Agis II who was reigning in 411: Herod. 6.71 and Poralla², no. 474.

30. *Lac. Pol.* 1.4. According to Aristoph. *Birds*, 1281, all Athenians were Laconizers.

31. See n. 23, above.

Following a brief eulogy of Lycurgus, Xenophon resumes his discussion of reproduction with a detailed description of the rearing of girls. That Xenophon begins the *Spartan Constitution* with the upbringing of girls underlines his view of the importance of women in Spartan society.

Stating that he is beginning at the *arche* (beginning), Xenophon highlights women's role in child production. He points out that only in Sparta were girls well fed and given undiluted wine.[32] In fact, women had easy access to quantities of wine, for they used it in bathing newborns. Xenophon criticizes the rest of the Greeks for not providing adequate nourishment for girls who are destined to become mothers of citizens.[33] Xenophon approves of the generous food allocation of Spartan girls. As he stated in the *Oeconomicus* (10.11), if a woman exercises she will have a better appetite and a vibrant complexion. Comparisons between Spartan women and women elsewhere in Greece may well have fostered Xenophon's admiration of Sparta.

Ephorus of Cyme (ca. 405–330, *FGrH* II.70) read works by the Spartans Pausanias and Lysander. Though Ephorus is extant only in fragments, he was the main source for Diodorus, who wrote in the last quarter of the first century B.C.E. Diodorus (11.45, 12.74) probably found his stories about the mothers of Pausanias (the traitor) and Brasidas in Ephorus.

Aristotle lived from 384 to 322 B.C.E. Although he was born at Stagira in the Chalcidice, he spent much of his life studying and teaching in Athens and adopted the Athenian model as the standard against which he measured Greek family life and gender relations.[34] Aristotle doubtless discussed women in his treatise *The Constitution of the Spartans* which is no longer extant. That Aristotle disapproved of the Spartan way of life is apparent from passages in other works. In the *Politics* (1333b5), he criticizes other authors including a certain Thibron, a Spartan who had written in the first quarter of the fourth century in praise of the Lycurgan system.[35] Of course, Thibron wrote just after his polis had won the Peloponnesian War, and Aristotle wrote after the defeat at Leuctra. A lengthy critique of gender relations at Sparta appears in the *Politics* (1269b–1270a6 [a translation of this passage is given in chap. 4]). Aristotle believed that the basic

---

32. In Athens, small children participated in the Anthesteria, and drank the new wine from small choes (pitchers). That many more choes with designs appropriate for boys than for girls have been excavated suggests that more boys were brought to the festival. See further Sarah B. Pomeroy, *Families in Classical and Hellenistic Greece* (Oxford, 1997), 69, 118–19.

33. Arist. *HA* 608b observes that the female eats less. Doubtless this was both the effect and cause of systematically allocating less food to women.

34. See further Pomeroy, *Families*, 42–45, 61–66.

35. *FGrH* 581. Jacoby ad loc. suggests that by writing favorably about his polis, Thibron was trying to curry favor with potentates in Asia or with the Spartan authorities, or to denigrate (as not following the Spartan ethic) the ephors who had exiled him. On Spartan authors of the fifth and fourth centuries, including Thibron, Pausanias, and Lysander, see also T. Boring, *Literacy in Ancient Sparta* (Leiden, 1979), 50–55.

oikos (family, household, estate) consisted of an adult male, who played the roles of husband, master, and father; an adult female, who played the role of wife and mother; a child; and a slave. The master of the house was the dominant figure in all his three relationships. This hierarchy existed by nature and any perversion of it was monstrous. That Spartan women enjoyed authority in the oikos and owned and managed property appeared to him outrageous. He echoes Plato in the Laws (7.806C, see above) when he angrily declares that the women indulged in all sorts of luxury and licentiousness (Pol. 1270a1: anesis, see also Arist. Rhet. 1361a) because they would not accept the laws Lycurgus had designed for them and he decided not to continue the attempt. Plutarch (Lyc. 9), however, rejected Aristotle's view (see below).

Hellenistic

With the important exception of Polybius, all the Hellenistic historians surveyed below are extant not in complete or nearly complete works, but only through one or at most a few fragments cited by later authors, chiefly Plutarch.

Phylarchus of Athens (?) lived in the third century B.C.E. and gives the history of Sparta from the death of Pyrrhus (272) to the death of Cleomenes III (220/219). He admired Agis and Cleomenes and dramatizes the importance of women in furthering their revolutionary program.[36] Phylarchus was a principle source for Plutarch's Lives of Agis, Cleomenes, and Pyrrhus, and for his favorable desciptions in these Lives of the behavior of royal women including Archidamia, Agesistrata, Agiatis, Chilonis, Cratesicleia, and Cratesicleia's companion, the wife of Panteus, whose name Plutarch does not report. All the women, even Chilonis, wife of Cleonymus, who fell in love with her stepson Acrotatus, are presented favorably. Phylarchus was also Plutarch's source for his description of the bravery of Spartan women when Pyrrhus besieged Sparta (Plut. Pyrr. 27–30). In the Hellenistic period, the exaltation of heroines was a feature of the history of other ethnic groups as well. For example, among the Ptolemies, Arsinoë II (ca. 316–270) and Berenice II (ca. 273–221), and among the Jews, Judith and Esther (fictitious heroines, though with some historical features), were prominent.[37]

---

36. See further FGrH II.81; T. W. Africa, Phylarchus and the Spartan Revolution (Berkeley, 1961, repr. Millwood, N.Y., 1980), 43–47, 61; and cf. K. Chrimes, Ancient Sparta (Manchester, 1949), 6, who asserts that Phylarchus was ill-informed about Sparta in the days of Agis IV.

37. See Deborah Gera, Warrior Women: The Anonymous Tractatus de Mulieribus (Leiden, 1997), for paragraph-long descriptions of fourteen women (including the Spartan Argeia), written in the first century B.C.E. or later; and most recently Stanley M. Burstein, "Cleitarchus in Jerusalem," in The Eye Expanded, ed. F. B. Titchener and R. F. Moorton, Jr. (Berkeley, 1999), 105–12, esp. 107. See further chap. 4.

Sosibius of Lacedaemon, a historian, who worked in Alexandria during the reign of Ptolemy II,[38] wrote a treatise or commentary *On Alcman* in at least three books, and other works about Sparta including *On the Sacrifices in Lacedaemon* and *On Mimes in Laconia.*

Teles of Megara was a Cynic philosopher (fl. ca. 235 B.C.E.) whose work is preserved in fragments in Stobaeus. Some of Plutarch's *Sayings of Spartan Women* echo Teles' anecdotes about Spartan mothers.[39] Either Plutarch read Teles or they used a common source.

Polybius (ca. 200–118 B.C.E.) was aristocratic and anti-Spartan. He attributes to the Spartans behavior including polyandry (12.6b.8) that other Greeks would consider bizarre. He is a hostile source for the reports about Nabis (d. 192 B.C.E.), his cruel wife Apega, and the iron maiden, and for the ways in which both Nabis and his wife humiliated women (13.6–7, 18.17, and see chap. 4).

Hellenistic Epigrams: Dioscorides, Nicander, Tymnes, and perhaps Asclepiades of Samos wrote epigrams about Spartan mothers that were later incorporated into Plutarch's, *Sayings of Spartan Women.*[40] Dioscorides commemorates a mother who lost eight sons in one battle, Nicander a mother of seven who lost six, and Tymnes a mother who slew her cowardly son.

Polycrates was probably Hellenistic, since he predated Didymus (fl. ca. 40 B.C.E.), who quotes him. Polycrates wrote a work titled *Lakonika.*[41] One paragraph is extant: a vivid description of the Hyacinthia (see chaps. 1 and 5).

Nicolaus of Damascus, who was born ca. 64 B.C.E., wrote an immense universal history in the Peripatetic encyclopedic style. He gives odd bits of information about Spartan women: for example, husbands compel their wives to have children by well-built Spartiates and foreigners.[42] Yet, according to Xenophon, who must have have had more accurate knowledge than Nicolaus, women were not compelled, but rather were willing to bear children by Spartan men other than their husbands. Xenophon does not mention foreigners (see chap. 3).

---

38. According to *OCD³*, he was a Spartan who worked in Egypt probably in the mid-third century. Jacoby, *FGrH* III b, no. 595, is more doubtful about Sosibius' date and Spartan origin. Boring, *Literacy in Ancient Sparta*, 56, places him between 250 and 150, with the lower date more likely.

39. Edward O'Neil (ed.), *Teles, the Cynic Teacher* (Missoula, Mont., 1977), "On Freedom from Passion," pp. 65–66, ll. 53–76 (= *Teletis: Reliquiae,* ed. O Hense, 2d edn. [1909] 57.11–58.12), is very close to Plut. *Sayings of Spartan Women,* 241a3, b4, c8, and cf. *Virtues in Women* 246a. See further Tigerstedt, *The Legend of Sparta in Classical Antiquity,* vol. 2, 27, 38.

40. *Anth. Pal.* 7.433–35. = A. S. F. Gow and D. L. Page, *The Greek Anthology: Hellenistic Epigrams,* 2 vols. (Cambridge, 1965), vol. 1, Dioscurides, 32; Nicander, 1; Tymnes, 6; and Ascleipiades, 47. A Spartan mother who kills her son appears also in Erycius, *Anth. Pal.* 7.230 and Antipater Thess. *Anth. Pal.* 7.531 (Augustan). See further, Tigerstedt, *The Legend of Sparta in Classical Antiquity,* vol. 2, 27, 86.

41. *FGrH* III b F 588 quoted from Didymus by Athenaeus 4.139d–f. See further L. R. Farnell, *Cults of the Greek States* (Oxford, 1896–1909), vol. 4, 265–6.

42. Stobaeus iv.2.25 (p. 160 Hense) = *FGrH* 90 F 103 (144) and see further Tigerstedt, *The Legend of Sparta in Classical Antiquity,* vol. 2, 92.

Roman Period

Greek Authors

Plutarch lived 46–ca. 120 C.E., when Greece was a province of the Roman Empire. He is the author of the largest portion of extant ancient writing on Spartan women and has also had more influence than any other ancient author in shaping ideas about Sparta held by later generations to the present.[43]

Plutarch's writing about Spartan women is concentrated in several of the *Lives* and in one work of the *Moralia*: the *Life of Lycurgus;* the *Lives* of Agis and Cleomenes; and the *Sayings of Spartan Women.*[44] There are also brief remarks scattered among his other works. The most important of these texts, the *Life of Lycurgus*, was probably written between 97 and 110 C.E., nearly one thousand years after the date generally attributed to the legendary Spartan lawgiver.[45] Plutarch visited Sparta and was an eyewitness at the whipping ceremonies held in honor of Artemis Orthia (*Lyc.* 18.1); he reports that he saw many young men die. There, he also conducted research in the official Spartan archives which must have included records of oracles, official documents, victor lists, names of priests and magistrates, and the like.[46] In the Roman period there were officials in charge of preserving and interpreting Lycurgan customs and laws. Some of the cult organizations kept their own records, and we can assume that, inspired by his profound interest in religion, Plutarch consulted these.

Plutarch must also have had a huge library of his own as well as an excellent memory and in his writing on Spartan women, he cites many philosophers, poets, and ancient historians from the archaic through the Hellenistic period as his sources. These include Ibycus, Herodotus, Sophocles, Euripides, Plato, and Aristotle. Although he does not repeat Xenophon's name explicitly in the context of his discussions of women, Plutarch's views are generally consistent with those of Xenophon.[47] Like Xenophon, Plutarch was optimistic about the human

43. Elizabeth Rawson, *The Spartan Tradition in European Thought* (Oxford, 1969), 112.

44. *Sayings of Spartan Women* is now generally agreed to be the work of Plutarch: Donald Russell, in a personal communication. See also Tigerstedt, *The Legend of Sparta in Classical Antiquity,* vol. 2, 16–30.

45. For the dating, see Luigi Piccirilli and Mario Manfredini, *Plutarco: Le vite di Licurgo e di Numa²* (Milan, 1990), xl. For the five *Lives* (including *Lysander* and *Agesilaus*) as a unified cycle, see D. R. Shipley, *A Commentary on Plutarch's* Life of Agesilaos (Oxford, 1997), 3–4. Shipley (3) judges that Plutarch gives "a valid account of Agesilaos' character and reign."

46. *Ages.* 19.10 = *FGrH* 596 F 5. See further L. Piccirilli, "Cronologia relative e fonti delle *Vitae Lycurgi et Numae* di Plutarco," in *Philias Charin: Miscellanea di studi classici in onore di Eugenio Manni* (Rome, 1980), vol. 5, 1754–64, esp. 1762; Manfredini and Picciirilli, *Plutarco: Le vite di Licurgo e di Numa²*, xl–xlii; and Boring, *Literacy in Ancient Sparta*, 88–93.

47. See further Sarah B. Pomeroy, "Reflections on Plutarch, *Advice to the Bride and Groom:* Something Old, Something New, Something Borrowed," 33–42 passim, and Cynthia Patterson, "Plutarch's Advice to the Bride and Groom: Traditional Wisdom through a Philosophic Lens," 128–37,

potential for moral improvement, especially through education (*Advice to the Bride and Groom*, 145c). Both believed that virtue is the same in women and men.[48] Both felt that the goal of human existence was to live the good life in a way that would prove beneficial to oneself, one's family, and one's state. Both thought that child production was not the only purpose of marriage.[49] Plutarch (*Comp. Lyc. Num.* 4.1) believed that Spartan marriage customs were conducive to a relationship characterized by goodwill rather than hatred. Moreover, he asserted that the educational system designed by Lycurgus was ennobling for women inasmuch as it gave them a share in the arena of virtue and ambition (*Lyc.* 14.4). Plutarch appears somewhat ambivalent, if not self-contradictory, since he also prefers the Roman practice of marrying girls at twelve or younger, for it enabled the husband to mold the wife's character. Spartan marriage practices were better for child production, but Roman practices were better for marital harmony. Though in the *Life of Lycurgus* (14) Plutarch seems to approve of the physical and moral educational program designed for women by Lycurgus and to reject Aristotle's critical analysis, in the *Comparison of Lycurgus and Numa* (3.3–5) he declares that Spartan women were too bold and masculine and offered opportunities for poets to criticize them. He quotes Ibycus, Euripides, and Sophocles on the girls' uncovered thighs (see above). In any case, his views of women and marriage are not a direct reflection of gender relations as they existed in Roman Greece in his day, where women certainly enjoyed more authority and independence from men than readers confined to Plutarch's works would surmise.[50] For example, he tells the story of the Spartan girl who was asked whether she made overtures to her husband, and replied, "No, but he has come to me" (*Advice to the Bride and Groom*, 140c, *Sayings of Spartan Women*, 242c). Plutarch endorses the wife's reluctance to take the initiative, preferring her husband to make the advances. On the other hand, he does approve of the Spartan women who goad their men to virtuous and brave actions or who set a good example themselves when the men appear to waver.[51] In fact, Plutarch's Greek heroines are good

---

passim, both in *Plutarch's Advice to the Bride and Groom and A Consolation to His Wife*, ed. Sarah B. Pomeroy (New York, 1999).

48. Xen. *Oec.* 7.14–15, 9.14–15, 10.1, Plut. *Virtues of Women* 249f , and see further Sarah B. Pomeroy, "Reflections on Plutarch," in *Xenophon, Oeconomicus: A Social and Historical Commentary* (Oxford, 1994), ad loc., and chap. 4, above.

49. Xen. *Oec.* 7.11–12. See further Pomeroy, *Xenophon, Oeconomicus*, ad loc.; Plut. *Comp. Lyc. Num.* 4; and L. Goessler, "Plutarchs Gedanken über die Ehe" (diss. Zurich, 1962), trans. by David and Hazel Harvey as "Advice to the Bride and Groom: Plutarch Gives a Detailed Account of His Views on Marriage," in *Plutarch's Advice to the Bride and Groom and A Consolation to His Wife*, ed. Sarah B. Pomeroy (New York, 1999), 97–115, esp. 106–7.

50. See further Lin Foxhall, "Foreign Powers: Plutarch and Discourses of Domination in Roman Greece," in *Plutarch's Advice to the Bride and Groom and A Consolation to His Wife*, ed. Sarah B. Pomeroy (New York, 1999), 138–50.

51. Foxhall, "Foreign Powers," 148.

competition for some of Rome; for example, the mother and sister of Coriolanus (Livy 2.40) and Arria (Pliny the Younger, *Epistles*, 3.16; Martial, *Epigrams*, 1.13), whose Stoic deaths resembled those of Cratesicleia and Panteus' wife.[52]

Plutarch was not a historian; rather, he wrote philosophical and biographical works. Doubtless because Hellenistic writers were interested in women and personal details, in writing about Spartan women Plutarch refers most frequently to Hellenistic historians, some of whom have been mentioned in the survey above. Since Plutarch was not a historian, chronological precision is not a high priority for him (see Preface). Not only is he naive about the Spartan's reinvention of their own history, but he is also an active participant in the creation and perpetuation of the Spartan legend. The Sparta of Plutarch's day was a living museum, a theme park, in which some features of life in Sparta before Roman domination were revived or reenacted perhaps to the point of exaggeration or charicature. For example, Roman tourists accustomed to gladiatorial contests came to witness the spectacle of the boys enduring whipping until they met death. Whether such contests had ever been conducted with so much cruelty before the Hellenistic and Roman periods is questionable.[53]

Pausanias wrote a guide to Greece in the second century C.E. Women are not prominent among his interests, though he gives some tantalizing bits of information. Thus he reports that the length of the stadion is shortened for girls who race at the Heraea, but does not say why or how this alteration is done. He does give some useful information on women, particularly on religious practices, on commemorative statues erected by or in honor of women, and historical and mythological anecdotes in which women are the protagonists.[54] Thus he mentions that there is an island off the Peloponnese where Helen and Paris first had intercourse (3.22.1). Some women are remarkable for deeds usually performed by men. At Sparta, a statue of Artemisia stood along with images of Mardonius and other Persians in a stoa built with spoils from the Persian War (3.11.3).[55]

Athenaeus of Naucratis (second–third century C.E.) wrote a lengthy work, the *Sophists at Dinner*, a pastiche of valuable earlier sources including Sosibius and Polycrates.

52. Plut. *Cleom.* 38, and see chap. 4.

53. See further Kennell, *The Gymnasium of Virtue*, passim, and Pomeroy, *Families*, 62–66. Contra Kennell, Jean Ducat, "Perspectives on Spartan Education," in *Sparta: New Perspectives*, ed. S. Hodkinson and A. Powell (London, 1999), 43–66, esp. 44–46, argues that Plutarch does give some credible information on the classical period.

54. See further Darice Birge, "Women and the Greek Past in Pausanias' Descriptive Geography," paper delivered at the Annual Meeting of the American Philological Association, Dec. 29, 1998; abstract published in *American Philological Association 130th Annual Meeting: Abstracts*, 131.

55. Vitruvius (1.1.6) reports that the statues of the Persians, attired in barbaric costume, supported the roof like Caryatids.

Latin Authors

For the history of women, the most significant aspect of the Spartan tradition or mirage in authors who wrote in Latin is the emphasis on patriotic, self-sacrificing mothers. This focus derives from the Roman interest in motherhood. Intellectuals and politicians were particularly concerned with the declining birthrate among the Roman elite. They blamed the "new-style" Roman matron for abandoning the traditional role of mother.[56] Barbarian and non-Roman women were cited as exemplars. Thus the patriotic Spartan mothers of the past are mentioned in Ovid (43 B.C.E.–17? C.E.);[57] Valerius Maximus (first century C.E.);[58] Aelian (ca. 170–235 C.E.);[59] Sextus Empiricus, a Sceptic (end of the second century C.E.);[60] Himerius of Prusa (fourth century C.E.);[61] Palladas, a schoolteacher in Egypt (fifth century C.E.);[62] and Julianus (sixth century C.E.),[63] who writes of the armed Aphrodite who prompts Spartan mothers to bear brave warriors.[64] There is little that is new in these anecdotes and quotations from Spartan mothers; for the most part they echo one another and Plutarch as well. Cicero (106–43 B.C.E.) also writes of the Spartan mother who nobly sent her son to his death for his country, but he is unique among these Latin authors in observing that the Spartan women of his own day were no longer so willing to bear children as their foremothers had been.[65]

Byzantine Dictionaries

Much esoteric information about Spartan customs can be gleaned from explanations of unusual words in encyclopedic works by authors such as Pollux of Naucratis (second century C.E.), Hesychius of Alexandria (fifth century C.E.), and the collection called the *Suda* (tenth century). These compilations, though valuable, pose special problems for the historian for there is generally only one

---

56. See E. Fantham, Helene Peet Foley, Natalie Boymel Kampen, Sarah B. Pomeroy, and H. Alan Shapiro, *Women in the Classical World* (New York, 1994), 299–301, and Suzanne Dixon, *The Roman Mother* (Norman, Okla., 1989), passim.

57. *Ibis* 615, for the mother of Pausanias the traitor, cf. R. Ellis, *P. Ovidii Nasonis Ibis: ex novis codicibus edidit, scholia vetera commentarium cum prolegomenis appendice* (Oxford 1881), 165.

58. Val. Max. 2.7, ext.2.

59. *VH* 12.21.

60. *PH* 3.216.

61. *Orat.* 24 p. 118.63–66 (Colonna).

62. *Anth. Pal.* 9.397.

63. *Anth. Pal.* 9.447.

64. See also the Anonymous Epigram *Anth. Pal.* 9.61 for a mother who slew her cowardly son. For the Spartan tradition in post-classical times, see Rawson, *The Spartan Tradition in European Thought.* See also Conclusion, above.

65. *Tusc.* 1.42.102, 2.15.36, and see further chap. 3.

citation for each word and it is given out of context. (See, e.g., Hesychius on *Brudalicha* in chap. 6 n. 16).

Prosopographical Problems

Compared with the names of Greek men, relatively few women's names are known. A reluctance to name respectable women, at least while they were alive, was a feature of Athenian etiquette.[66] In Athens, however, women were named on their tombstones. In contrast, there are few inscriptions concerning family matters in pre-Hellenistic Sparta, for, in addition to the kings, only men who had died in battle or women who had died in childbirth were permitted to have inscribed epitaphs.[67]

In Sparta, there was no stigma attached to giving women's names in public. Considering how few words are extant in all of Alcman's poetry combined, the oeuvre includes many names. One of the names in the *Partheneia* appears in the work of an archaic poet outside Sparta. Mimnermus of Colophon and Smyrna had written a collection of elegies titled *Nanno*, after his beloved (Hermesianax in Athen. XIII.597f, Strabo 14.1.28 [643]). For Damareta, compare Damatria in Plutarch, *Sayings of Spartan Women*, 241.1, and in an epigram by Tymnes, who worked in the third century B.C.E.[68] Astaphis was a name used also by a man ca. 428–421.[69] Arete, the name also of the Phaeacian queen in Homer's *Odyssey*, reappears much later in the name of Pomponia Callistonice Arete.[70] Some of the names indicate that the girls were members of the royal houses. The prefix "Ag" that appears in the names of Agido and Hagesichora is common in royal nomenclature,[71] and suggests that they were Agiads, related to one line of Spartan kings. Timasimbrota (5 fr. 2 col. ii, line 16) is perhaps descended from the Spartan king Leotychidas (ca. 625–600).[72]

The names of twelve women are inscribed on a rooftile from the second half of the third century B.C.E., perhaps in connection with the cult of Apollo and

---

66. See further David Schaps, "The Woman Least Mentioned: Etiquette and Women's Names," *CQ* n.s. 27 (1977), 323–30.

67. See chap. 3 n. 3, Latte's emendation.

68. *Anth. Pal.* 7.433 = Gow and Page, *The Greek Anthology: Hellenistic Epigrams*, vol. 2, 556, Tymnes 6.

69. *IG* V.i, n. 1, for the date of 428–421: see further Poralla², no.160.

70. Alfred S. Bradford, *A Prosopography of Lacedaemonians from the Death of Alexander the Great, 323 B.C., to the Sack of Sparta by Alaric, A.D. 296* (Munich, 1977), 227, s.v. Kallistoneike (4), and see chap. 5 nn. 53, 90, above.

71. See Poralla², pp. 5–13, 173.

72. D. A. Campbell, *Greek Lyric*, vol. 2 (Cambridge, Mass., 1988), 391, understands her to be the daughter of the Eurypontid Eurycrates (ca. 665–640) and sister of Leotychidas.

Hyacinthus at Amyclae.[73] Nevertheless, we still have very few names of Spartan women, for most of the literary sources are non-Spartan. For example, Herodotus (5.39–41) speaks of the wives of Anaxandridas, but does not name them. Though Agesilaus was an old friend, Xenophon does not give the names of his wife and daughters.[74] Xenophon's etiquette was that of an Athenian gentleman in the classical period: he was too polite to ask Agesilaus, or if he knew the names he was reluctant to publicize them. Plutarch (*Ages.* 19.10) discovered the names. Xenophon does name Agesilaus' sister Cynisca (*Ages.* 9.6), but she was notorious because of her horseracing (see chap. 1). Though he refers to them, Plutarch does not give the names of Lysander's daughters (*Lys.* 2.5, 30.5).

The problem is exacerbated by the neglect of women by modern scholars. For example, before the publication of vol. 3A of *A Lexicon of Greek Personal Names*, on *The Peloponnese, Western Greece, Sicily, and Magna Graecia*,[75] the standard Spartan prosopographies[76] omitted some women, for example, Thylacis and Astumeloisa (Alcman, *Partheneia* 1.72, 2.64), Argeia, wife of King Aristodemus, and Euonyma, Eirana, Callicrateia (dedicators to Athena), or listed them under the name of their father, although the primary source for the woman's name may not have given the patronymic.

A related problem is the tendency of some scholars to interpret evidence in a narrow manner so as to eliminate any connection with women. A case in point is the Gymnopaideia ("Festival of Nude Youths"). The Greek word *paides* can mean "boys," or "slaves," but it can also refer to children of both sexes.[77] Those who understand the meaning of Gymnopaideia in the limited sense believe that only boys attended the festival; in contrast, those who take the word in an inclusive sense would have nude girls and boys at the festival together.

---

73. C. N. Edmonson, "A Graffito from Amyklai," *Hesperia* 28 (1959), 162–64.

74. *Ages.* 8, 7, 19.10, nor could Dicaearchus discover their names: fr. 65 Wehrli[2]. See further Jan Bremmer, "Plutarch and the Naming of Greek Women," *AJPh* 102 (1981), 425–26.

75. Ed. Peter M. Fraser and Elaine Matthews (Oxford, 1997). In the present volume, the citation to *LGPN* 3 is usually given in preference to earlier publications. *LGPN* gives brief succinct identifications, often referring back to the earlier publications which provide fuller documentation, including genealogical charts. In addition, S. Hodkinson, *Property and Wealth in Classical Sparta* (London, 2000), 414, suggests that Deinicha, who married Archidamus III, was descended from Deinis, whose name is inscribed on a sixthth-century aryballus, and that Euryleonis, the Olympic victor (see chap. 1, above), was descended from Euryleon companion of Dorieus in the late sixth century.

76. Poralla[2], and Bradford, *A Prosopography of Lacedaemonians from the Death of Alexander the Great*.

77. See Sarah B. Pomeroy, "*Technikai kai Mousikai*: The Education of Women in the Fourth Century and in the Hellenistic Period," *AJAH* 2 (1977), 51–68, esp. 52. Michael Pettersson, *Cults of Apollo at Sparta: The Hyakinthia, the Gymnopaidiai and the Karneia* (Stockholm, 1992), 120, finds no evidence for girls participating in the Gymnopaideia, nor (125) for their being part of the age class system connected to the agoge. See above, chap. 2 n. 2.

Secondary Sources

A book that continues to exert a tremendous influence on Spartanologists is F. Ollier, *Le mirage spartiate*, volume 1, *Étude sur l'idéalisation de Sparte dans l'antiquité grecque de l'origine jusqu'aux cyniques*, and volume 2, *Étude sur l'idéalisation de Sparte dans l'antiquité grecque du début de l'école cynique jusqu'à la fin de la cité* (Paris, 1933–43).

Despite their size and inclusiveness, however, the volumes offer little comment on women. Neverthless, it is illuminating to review the few categories in which Ollier distributes some ancient testimonia about women. Under "la vraie Sparte," Ollier (vol. 1, 34–35) includes women's gymnastic program, their pride, and their influence in the public sphere. Under "les forces adverses" to the idealization, he (vol. 1, 64–67) mentions the scandalous sexual practices of men and women alike. In his analysis of Aristotle's views of Sparta's faults Ollier (vol. 1, 302–3) draws attention to an absence of governmental controls on women and to economic problems resulting from women's ownership of property. In volume 2, Ollier (50–51) detects Cynic influence in some of the quotations attributed to Spartan women. He argues (194–97, 210–15) that Plutarch does not idealize Sparta in all his works, but that he certainly does so in the *Life of Lycurgus*. Ollier points out (212) that in his idealization of Lycurgus and the simple, austere way life he designed for Sparta, Plutarch accepts features such as breaches in sexual monogamy that he does not sanction elsewhere in his writings. Ollier, however, unlike some more recent scholars,[78] does not argue that such practices never existed or that reforms attributed to Lycurgus were actually innovations of the fourth century and Hellenistic period.

In 1979, Paul Cartledge published a solid historical survey of what were then regarded as facts: *Sparta and Lakonia*.[79] Cartledge, writing much later with A. J. S. Spawforth, described the gradual degeneration of the Lycurgan polity and dated the "normalization" to the later fifth century.[80] More recently, perhaps influenced by deconstruction and French literary theory, he has examined Sparta as a utopia, stating that "practically all our detailed evidence for what they were 'really' like comes from within the mirage."[81] The influence of Marxism and of M. I. Finley, who taught many ancient historians at Cambridge, has been in large part responsible for the popularity of the study of Spartan history through the lens of the mirage. Finley ignored women in his analyses of Greek economy,

---

78. E.g., recently Ellen Greenstein Millender, "Athenian Ideology and the Empowered Spartan Female," in *Sparta: New Perspectives*, ed. S. Hodgkinson and A. Powell (London, 1999), 365–66.

79. *Sparta and Lakonia: A Regional History, 1300–362 B.C.* (London, 1979).

80. Cartledge and Spawforth, *Hellenistic and Roman Sparta*, 110.

81. Paul Cartledge, "The Socratics' Sparta and Rousseau's," in *Sparta: New Perspectives*, ed. S. Hodkinson and A. Powell (London, 1999), 311–37, esp. 312.

slavery, and citizenship.[82] Thus it is no surprise that, as was customary among mainstream ancient historians until the end of the twentieth century, Cartledge did not devote much space to women in his books.

The most frequently cited and admired article on this subject, however, was published by Paul Cartledge in 1981.[83] In this article, which is now referred to as a "classic study,"[84] Cartledge gives priority to the testimony of Aristotle over that of Xenophon and Plutarch.[85] Despite (what seems to the modern reader) his misogynistic perspective, Aristotle does emphasize Spartan women's control over property and over their husbands, and labels Sparta a "gynaecocracy." Xenophon and Plutarch, in contrast, approve many features of the lives of Spartan women in comparison with the lives of women in other Greek states, but in this article Cartledge disdains the testimony of Xenophon and relegates Plutarch to the never-never land of utopia. Despite starting with Aristotle, Cartledge pictures Spartan women as "passive" victims who were exploited for purposes of reproduction. He does not fully recognize that Xenophon's report that the wives actively sought husband-doubling arrangements runs counter to his argument, for it indicates that wives employed their own childbearing strategies.[86] He argues away women's ownership of property by stating that only a few elite women enjoyed this economic power,[87] without making it clear that their brothers would be in similar straits. Cartledge also adopts a Victorian stance in questioning whether Spartan girls enjoyed homosexual relationships with older women.[88] Cartledge concludes (105) that he hopes his readers "hesitate before seeking to enlist the women of ancient Sparta as allies in the just cause of feminism." It is anachronistic to discuss Spartan women in terms of contemporary feminist criteria and goals, and these criteria and goals have been and are now multiple and diverse. Nevertheless, I venture to suggest that if Cartledge had compared Spartan women to other Greek women, and compared both to the men of their poleis, his conclusions concerning Spartan women would have been less pessimistic (see Conclusion, above).

82. M. I. Finley, "Sparta," in *The Use and Abuse of History* (London, 1975), 161–77, esp. 171 (orig. pub. in *Problèmes de la guerre en Grèce ancienne*, ed. J.-P. Vernant [Paris, 1968], 143–60): "For the sake of completeness, I record without discussion two further sources of tension: (a) the women, if Plato and Aristotle are to be believed." See further Pomeroy, *Xenophon. Oeconomicus*, 43, no.14.

83. "Spartan Wives: Liberation or Licence?" *CQ* 31 (1981), 84–105.

84. See most recently Michael Whitby, review of *Sparta: New Perspectives*, ed. S. Hodkinson and A. Powell, *Scholia Reviews* n.s. 9 (2000), 36.

85. "Spartan Wives," esp. 86 and 89.

86. "Spartan Wives," 103, and see chap. 3.

87. "Spartan Wives," 105, followed by Millender, "Athenian Ideology and the Empowered Spartan Female," 371.

88. "Even if we should prefer not to believe that Spartan maidens enjoyed tutelary homosexual relations with older women" (101). He was, of course, writing for a classical (presumably not feminist) audience.

Stephen Hodkinson generally retains the perspectives on the study of Sparta that were established by Finley and Cartledge. Whereas Cartledge treated Xenophon's works on Sparta with contempt, he was willing to accept some of Plutarch's reports.[89] In contrast, Hodkinson regards Plutarch's information about archaic and classical Sparta with suspicion. He often blames Ephorus as the original source for what he regards as Plutarch's misrepresentations about the Spartan economy, and argues that the land tenure system that Plutarch attributes to archaic Sparta was actually a Hellenistic invention designed to promote the reforms of Agis and Cleomenes.[90] Hodkinson does not explain why, if his hypothesis is true, the reformer kings (who had many opponents) were able to convince the Spartans themselves about the antiquity of their institutions.[91] Although Hodkinson discusses women in much of his book, *Property and Wealth in Classical Sparta*,[92] he has not fully integrated them into his picture of Spartan society. For example, in the Introduction he writes of "a political system ... which gave the mass of citizens in assembly a formal role in decision-making" (3); "Rich citizens were able to employ their surplus wealth with potentially significant socio-political consequences: through horse-rearing and engagement in equestrian contests" (5); and "The perioikoi ... were excluded from political decision-making which was reserved to the Spartiates alone" (7 n. 5). Since Spartan women did engage in equestrian contests, but did not have a formal role in making political decisions Hodkinson's generalizations appear inconsistent and demonstrate that he tends to consider only male citizens, except in the parts of the book where he specifically talks about women.

ARCHAEOLOGICAL SOURCES

Archaeological evidence has certainly been less influenced by the "mirage" and by interpretations from the perspective of the "mirage" than literary evidence, but it is not completely free of this bias. In any case, Sparta has not received the attention lavished on Athens and other sites that are generously endowed with

89. See, e.g., P. A. Cartledge, *Agesilaos and the Crisis of Sparta* (London, 1987), 70, where he points out that Plutarch did original research.

90. *Property and Wealth in Classical Sparta*, e.g., 26–28, 68, 166, and see chap. 4 n. 16, above. In defense of Ephorus, Aristotle, and Plutarch, see E. David, "Aristotle and Sparta," *Anc. Soc.* 13/14 (1982–83), 67–103, esp. 82–83, and chap. 4 n. 38, above. The debate over the use of Plutarch for the history of archaic and classical Sparta is not new. W. den Boer aptly writes in *Laconian Studies* (Amsterdam, 1954), 221: "Modern historians, though possessing no more material for interpretation than Plutarch, have all too often disposed of the customs related by him as ridiculous concoctions offered by him or his sources, and in so doing they have shown less modesty and historical discernment than Plutarch commanded."

91. See also chap. 4 nn. 61, 62, above.

92. London, 2000.

artistic monuments. Not only does Sparta boast few temples and public buildings predating the Roman period (cf. Thuc. 1.10), but owing in part to the much-vaunted Spartan austerity, archaeological evidence for private life is sparse.[93] Spartans may have owned some valuables, but the ethic prevailing at least to the end of fifth century discouraged and even forbade display.[94] Athenaeus (14.633a) actually uses the word *austeria* to describe life at Sparta. Because death was not commemorated by monuments before the Hellenistic period, there are no counterparts to the funerary reliefs that portray women in other parts of the Greek world. Only in the second century B.C.E., following the defeat at Sellasia (222) and the reforms of Nabis (207–192), do the Spartans begin to use the same reliefs as those found in the rest of the Greek world.[95] Building projects in the Hellenistic and Roman period also contributed to the disturbance and destruction of earlier remains. Numismatics also provides insights into the symbolic qualities and status of queens, goddesses, and female allegorical and mythical figures in Greece. The Spartans, however, did not mint their own currency until 280 B.C.E. Furthermore, since the modern city of Sparta not only sits on top of the ancient city but also is not located in a densely populated area of Greece, archaeological finds have not come to the surface serendipitously as the result of excavations for subways or the laying of foundations of buildings.

In terms of women's history, the most important finds have been at the sanctuary of Artemis Orthia, where the British School at Athens conducted extensive excavations for five years beginning in 1906.[96] Thousands of lead figurines, including many depicting adult women wearing nicely woven dresses, as well as pendants with a variety of incised patterns representing weaving, have been found. Interesting material, in some cases related to the finds at the Orthia sanctuary, has also been discovered at the sanctuary of Helen and Menelaus called the

93. Nevertheless, the concept of austerity at Sparta is currently being questioned by Stephen Hodkinson, "Bronze Dedications at Spartan Sanctuaries," in *Sparta in Laconia: Proceedings of the 19th British Museum Classical Colloquium*, ed. W. G. Cavanagh and S. E. C. Walker, British School at Athens Studies, vol. 4 (London, 1998), 55–63, and several other contributors to the same volume, including Förtsch (see n. 99). The concept of austerity is, of course, relative (one person's necessities are extravagances to another), but it must be admitted that Sparta simply has not yielded the precious metals, jewelry, fine tableware, and other personal luxury items that one might expect to find in the remains of such a powerful city. Domestic life was far more comfortable in Roman Sparta: see Stella Raftopoulou, "New Finds from Sparta," in *Sparta in Laconia: Proceedings of the 19th British Museum Classical Colloquium*, ed. W. G. Cavanagh and S. E. C. Walker, British School at Athens Studies, vol. 4 (London, 1998), 125–40, esp. 127–33.

94. See Xen. *Hell.* 6.4.27, 30, for searching Spartan houses for sequestered valuables.

95. See further M. N. Tod and A. J. B. Wace, *A Catalogue of the Sparta Museum* (Oxford, 1906), 127.

96. For the history of excavations at Sparta, see H. W. Catling, "The Work of the British School at Athens at Sparta and in Laconia," in *Sparta in Laconia: Proceedings of the 19th British Museum Classical Colloquium*, ed. W. G. Cavanagh and S. E. C. Walker, British School at Athens Studies, vol. 4 (London, 1998), 19–27.

"Menelaion" (see chap. 6). The finds have been published gradually but systematically in the *Annual of the British School at Athens*. The final synthetic report on the Orthia sanctuary was published by R. M. Dawkins and others in a single volume: *The Sanctuary of Artemis Orthia at Sparta*.[97] Since this major excavation nearly a century ago, little new archaeological evidence directly relevant to women's history has been published. Brief mentions of some dedications by women at the Menelaion constitute a minor exception.[98] Field surveys may produce some evidence for the lives of perioecic and helot women, but these women are doubly silenced in history as members of subordinate groups and as women.

Secondary scholarship in the field of archaeology has been devoted principally to the pottery, bronzes, and inscriptions from Laconia.[99] While there are several catalogues of the pottery, the rest of the material has usually been treated in articles; see, for example, the bibliographies to the articles on "Sparta", "Spartan Cults," and the "Menelaion," in the third edition of the *Oxford Classical Dictionary*. Some of the material remains, notably the bronze mirrors, support the evidence of the written sources. In contrast, a few depictions of women on pottery give evidence not supplied from the written sources, while others clarify the texts (see chap. 6, fig. 6). It must be admitted that the iconographical evidence alone is more difficult for the modern scholar to decipher than the written evidence (which is not without problems: see above). The figures depicted in Laconian sculpture and vase painting are not labelled: rather scholars must deduce their identity.[100] Representations of nudity and sexual activity pose problems of interpretation. In archaic and classical Athenian art, a woman playing a flute or reclining with men at a symposium would not be judged to be a respectable citizen. A scene of an orgy that includes satyr-like creatures and phalloi would be assumed to be connected to the cult of Dionysus, certainly not that of Artemis. The same scenes need not have the same implications in Laconian art. Furthermore the women or men who beheld or used these objects in

97. Society for the Promotion of Hellenic Studies Supplementary Papers, no. 5 (London, 1929), v–vi, and R. M. Dawkins, "Artemis Orthia: Some Additions and a Correction," *JHS* 50 (1930), 298–99.

98. See chap. 6, and Catling, "The Work of the British School at Athens at Sparta and in Laconia," 25.

99. For a survey of the number of various artifacts and their dates of manufacture, see R. Förtsch, "Spartan Art: Its Many Different Deaths," in *Sparta in Laconia: Proceedings of the 19th British Museum Classical Colloquium*, ed. W. G. Cavanagh and S. E. C. Walker, British School at Athens Studies, vol. 4 (London, 1998), 48–54. Förtsch, however, fails to take into account the falling population figures, and the concentration of wealth (see chaps. 3 and 4), both of which factors created a smaller market for the luxury items he surveys. W. G. Cavanagh, J. Crouwel, R. W. V. Catling, and G. Shipley, *Continuity and Change in a Greek Rural Landscape: The Laconia Survey*, vol. 2, *Archaeological Data*, *ABSA* suppl. vol. 27 (London, 1996), give laconic descriptions of material remains not yet synthesized so that they would be of much use for the writing of women's history.

100. E.g., Paul A. Clement, "The Recovery of Helen," *Hesperia* 27 (1958), 47–73. For criticism of the interpretations of Lilly B. Ghali-Kahil, *Les enlèvements et le retour d'Hélène dans les textes et les documents figurés* (Paris, 1955), see n. 111, below.

antiquity may have reacted to them intellectually and emotionally in ways totally different from our own. Ancient sentiments doubtless changed as the objects were reused over time. Places of manufacture and find spots varied as well: the reactions of the craftsmen and of the users in different localities varied accordingly. There is no point in speculating about women artists in Sparta. By the classical period no Spartiate engaged in manual labor.[101] Whether any lower-class women living in Sparta participated in manufacturing the objects depicting women is not known. Finally, it must be acknowledged that we are dealing with a very small oeuvre of recovered and published works that shed light on the history of mortal women. Scholars differ not only in interpreting the depictions, but on the place of manufacture of many of the objects, and on whether objects such as the Vix crater (see fig. 4) found outside the borders of Laconia (but resembling those found within) should be considered as Spartan art.[102]

Mirrors and Bronze Statuettes

Seven archaic bronzes showing naked girls have been found in Sparta and Messenia.[103] The majority of these were mirror handles, intended for use by women. Other examples have been found outside Spartan territory. Some of the girls are shown wearing a chiton that does not reach the knee and that covers only the left breast. The modern viewer may find the nudity most startling; in antiquity (though perhaps not in archaic Sparta), the bare female breast was an extremely potent image.[104] The unabashed nudity of the figures seems to reflect the athletic nudity of Spartan women. Therefore it is likely that this type of statuette was manufactured in Sparta, but was exported and imitated elsewhere in Greece.[105] Some of the girls hold musical instruments or other objects that may have been used for religious purposes.[106] Their date is ca. 570 to ca. 470.

101. Herod. 2.167, Xen. *Lac. Pol.* 7.1–2, and see R. M. Cook, "Spartan History and Archaeology," *CQ* 12 (1962), 156–58, and Paul Cartledge, "Did Spartan Citizens Ever Practice a Manual *Techne?*" *LCM* 1 (1976), 115–19.

102. On the Vix crater, see chap. 2, caption to fig. 4, and Marlene Herfort-Koch, *Archaische Bronzeplastik Lakoniens, Boreas,* suppl. 4 (Münster, 1986), 70–73, who argues for a Laconian origin.

103. See most recently Andrew Stewart, *Art, Desire, and the Body in Ancient Greece* (Cambridge, 1997), esp. 29–34, 108–19, and Appendix, 232–34, for a complete catalogue. See also Thomas Scanlon, "*Virgineum Gymnasium*: Spartan Females and Early Greek Athletics," in *The Archaeology of the Olympics*, ed. W. Raschke (Madison, Wis., 1988), 185–216, esp. 191–99, 203–4.

104. See Larissa Bonfante, "Nudity as a Costume in Classical Art," *AJA* 93 (1989), 558–68, and see most recently Beth Cohen, "Divesting the Female Breast of Clothes in Classical Sculpture," in *Naked Truths: Women, Sexuality and Gender in Classical Art and Archaeology*, ed. Ann Olga Koloski-Ostrow and Claire L. Lyons (London, 1997), 66–92.

105. Stewart, *Art, Desire, and the Body*, 108, estimates that at least 4,000 of these statuettes were manufactured.

106. Claude Rolley, "Le problème de l'art Laconien," *Ktèma* 2 (1977), 125–40, esp. 130, sees the girls as very young, and postulates a connection between the figurines and the cult of Artemis

These mirrors did not stand up on their own when women used them: a woman had to hold such a mirror in her hand. As in many ancient mirrors, the disk was convex.[107] The mirror reflected not only the face, as would a flat mirror, but hair, neck, and cleavage. The owner of the mirror would gaze at her own face and chest, reflected smaller than actual size, over the figure on the mirror handle. Grasping a mirror in one's hand is more intimate than merely looking at a vase. We may speculate about the esthetic and tactile pleasure a woman would feel while she was partially dressed herself and held the image of a nude slender female body. We may also suggest that this experience might be related to the fact that female children spent their time with each other and with adult women and engaged in homosexual erotic activities (see chap. 1).

Though works of art depicting nonmortal females are beyond the scope of this survey, it is relevant to the discussion of nudity in sculpture to point out that an archaic figure of Eileithyia is one of the earliest sculptures in the round of the nude female in the Greek world (see chap. 6, fig. 7).

Vase Painting

Sparta offers very little to compare with the huge number of vases from Athens that have been excavated and studied. Two ceramic cups that are significant for women's history which show women with men, one at a symposium, another at an orgy, are discussed in chap. 6. It is necessary to point out, however, that though the vase with the symposium scene was manufactured in Laconia, it was excavated in Samos. It has been argued that it may represent the artist's view of a feast in Samos, rather than a local Spartan scene.[108] It has also been argued that the women depicted in the orgy or komos scenes are hetairai and flute girls with no historical Spartan counterparts, and that the iconography is simply borrowed from Corinthian vases.[109] The closest parallels for this symposium scene, with women wearing Lydian mitres and reclining outdoors alongside men on the

Orthia. See further Uta Kron, "Sickles in Greek Sanctuaries: Votives and Cultic Instruments," in *Ancient Greek Cult Practice from the Archaeological Evidence (Proceedings of the Fourth International Seminar on Ancient Greek Cult, Organized by the Swedish Institute at Athens, 22–24 October 1993*, ed. R. Hägg (Stockholm, 1998), 187–215, esp. 206–7. See also Scanlon, "*Virgineum Gymnasium*," 194, 196.

107. G. Richter, "An Archaic Greek Mirror," *AJA* 42 (1938), 337–44, esp. 343–44, argues that such mirrors are not Spartan, but probably Corinthian, and that they portray hetairae, not naked athletes.

108. Maria Pipili, "Archaic Laconian Vase Painting," in *Sparta in Laconia: Proceedings of the 19th British Museum Classical Colloquium*, ed. W. G. Cavanagh and S. E. C. Walker, British School at Athens Studies, vol. 4 (London, 1998), 82–96, esp. 90, and J. Carter, review of *Laconian Iconography of the Sixth Century B.C.*, by Maria Pipili, *AJA* 93 (1989), 473–6, esp. 475.

109. E. A. Lane, "Lakonian Vase-Painting," *ABSA* 34 (1933–34), 99–189, esp 158, but see now Tyler Jo Smith, "Dances, Drinks, and Dedications: The Archaic *Komos* in Laconia," in *Sparta in Laconia: Proceedings of the 19th British Museum Classical Colloquium*, ed. W. G. Cavanagh and S. E. C. Walker, British School at Athens Studies, vol. 4 (London, 1998), 75–81, esp. 77–78.

(a)

Fig. 10. Athlete. Bronze mirror handle, front and back views.

Athlete as Mirror Caryatid. Bronze, ca. 550. Unknown provenance. Maiden wears an athlete's cap to hold her hair. She also wears flowers over her ears, a necklace with a pendant, and diagonally across her chest a strap holding amulets and a sickle that was awarded as a prize for

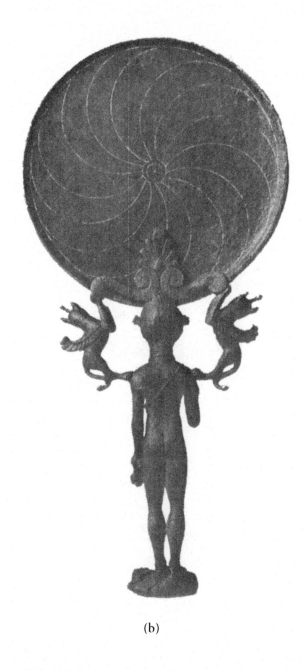

(b)

victors. She holds an oil flask or pomegranate in her left hand and probably held a flower in her right. Griffins flank the disk of the mirror. The maiden stands on a lion. New York, Metropolitan Museum of Art inv. 38.11.3. Fletcher Fund, 1938. Photos courtesy of Joan R. Mertens.

Fig. 11. Musician. Bronze mirror handle.

From the Sanctuary of Apollo at Amyclae. Bronze, ca. 550–530. Girl wears diadem with flowers above her ears, necklace with pendant, strap with sickle, and holds cymbals. Athens, National Museum, X 7548 = Maria Pipili, *Laconian Iconography of the Sixth Century* B.C., Oxford University Committee for Archaeology Monograph, no. 12 (Oxford, 1987),cat. no. 216 d, fig. 110. Photo courtesy Deutsches Archäologisches Institut, Athens.

ground are actually in Etruscan painting. In the Etruscan context there is no doubt that the women represented are wives, not hetairai.[110]

Sculpture

Helen is frequently depicted on Athenian vases as being threatened by Menelaus and running away from him. These scenes, however, were created outside Sparta for a non-Spartan clientele, and fall outside the limits of this study.[111] Spartan maidens raced in honor of Helen, but in Laconian art Helen herself is not shown fleeing. Helen appears on an archaic stele depicting Menelaus wooing Helen on one side, and their initial encounter after the fall of Troy on the other (see chap. 6, fig. 8).[112] Although Menelaus is taller than she is and armed with a sword, Helen meets him without cowering and faces him boldly, looking directly into his eyes. All who looked at this stele would know that although he had intended to kill her, when he saw her he changed his mind. Her beauty was a more potent weapon than Menelaus' sword. The recovery of Helen is also depicted on a few smaller works of Peloponnesian art from the end of the seventh to the mid-sixth century.[113] In these Helen is shown carrying a wreath. Her husband looks back at her and holds his sword aloft vertically. In contrast, on Athenian vases of ca. 550–470 which show the same recovery theme, Menelaus threateningly points his sword at her.

Conclusion

The wealth of Greek vase painting and sculpture depicting women has enabled some scholars of gender and women's history to interpret the visual arts in a

110. See H. A. Shapiro, "Modest Athletes and Liberated Women," in *Not the Classical Ideal*, ed. Beth Cohen (Leiden, 2000), 315–37, esp. 332.

111. See further Ghali-Kahil, *Les enlèvements et le retour d'Hélène*, 71, no. 24, and "Hélène," *LIMC* 4.1 (Zurich, 1988), 498–563, with an addendum on 951, and plates in 4.2 (Zurich, 1988), 291–358, s.v. Hélène; Guy Hedreen, "Image, Text, and Story in the Recovery of Helen," *CA* 15 (1996), 152–84, and figs. 1–12. On the political background of the depiction of Helen on Attic vases, see H. A. Shapiro, "Cult Warfare: The Dioskouroi between Sparta and Athens, in *Ancient Greek Hero Cult: Proceedings of the Fifth International Seminar on Ancient Greek Cult, Organized by the Department of Classical Archaeology and Ancient History, Göteborg University, 21–23 April 1995*, ed. R. Hägg (Stockholm, 1999), 99–107, esp. 105–6.

112. Ghali-Kahil, *Les enlèvements et le retour d'Hélène*, 18, 320–21, suggests that the judgment of Paris is depicted on an ivory comb from Sparta (= Dawkins, *AO* 223, pl. 127), and that an ivory relief (= Dawkins, *AO*, 214, pls. 109–10) shows Helen and Paris on a ship. On these identifications, see Evangelia-Lila Marangou, *Lakonische Elfenbein- und Beinschnitzereien* (Tübingen, 1969), 85–90, 107–9, 248–49 n. 510, and pls. 68, 78.

113. For these depictions on shield bands, see further Maria Pipili, "A Laconian Ivory Reconsidered," in *Philolakon: Lakonian Studies in Honour of Hector Catling*, ed. Jan Motyka Sanders (London, 1992), 179–84, esp. 183.

multiplicity of ways including as propaganda. Images of rape are common in Athenian vase painting,[114] as are scenes of women confined in the house or in the women's quarters, often weaving.[115] The message is generally designed to foster male sexual dominance and female subordination. Iconography oppressive to women is not confined to Athens. In a discussion of decorations on bronze mirrors of the fourth century from Elis and Corinth, Andrew Stewart comments:

> none of these case-mirrors offers an unequivocal vision of an independent, mature female sexuality. All of them may be made to conform to the peculiarly Greek dogma that unmarried girls are more like animals than human beings; that they are sexually voracious ... helping to ensure that these women remained exactly where their menfolk wanted them.[116]

How different was the iconography at Sparta? We have mentioned a statue of Artemisia who commanded her fleet admirably at the battle of Salamis (Herod. 8.88, 93); lead figurines showing women dressed in fine fabrics and pendants representing the textiles; statuettes and mirror handles in the form of female athletes; a vase showing luxuriously attired women playing musical instruments at a co-ed symposium; another vase showing men and women revelers; and a relief of Helen facing down Menelaus. As Thucydides indicated, there was not much material culture to attract the attention of a viewer in Sparta. Nevertheless, judging from the visual propaganda directed at women in the rest of the Greek world, a modern feminist might consider the absence of art as a positive and creative force for Spartan women.

114. E.g., Eva Keuls, *The Reign of the Phallus* (Berkeley, 1985).

115. See the archaic and classical images in Fantham, Foley, Kampen, Pomeroy, and Shapiro, *Women in the Classical World*, 5–135, passim.

116. "Reflections," in *Sexuality in Ancient Art*, ed. Natalie Boymel Kampen (Cambridge, 1996), 136–54, at 144–45.

WORKS CITED

Where necessary, specific editions of Greek and Latin works are cited within the text.

Africa, T. W. *Phylarchus and the Spartan Revolution*. Berkeley, 1961; repr. Millwood, N.Y., 1980.

Anderson, J. K. *Ancient Greek Horsemanship*. Berkeley, 1961.

Anger, Natalie. "Chemical Tied to Fat Control Could Help Trigger Puberty." *New York Times*, January 7, 1997, sec. C, pp. 1, 3.

Antonaccio, Carla M. *An Archaeology of Ancestors: Tomb Cult and Hero Cult in Early Greece*. Boston, 1995.

Arrigoni, Giampiera. "Donne e sport nel mondo greco: Religione e società." In *Le donne in Grecia*. ed. Giampiera Arrigoni., 55–201. Bari, 1985.

Asheri, David. "Sulla legge di Epitadeo." *Athenaeum* n.s. 39 (1961), fasc. i–ii, 45–68.

———. "Laws of Inheritance, Distribution of Land, and Political Constitutions in Ancient Greece." *Historia* 12 (1963), 1–21.

Aymard, André. *Les premiers rapports de Rome et de la Confédération Achaienne (198–189 avant J.-C.)*. Bordeaux, 1938.

Badian, E.. "Xenophon the Athenian." Paper delivered at The World of Xenophon conference, University of Liverpool, July 10, 1999.

Barber, Godfrey Louis, and Nigel Guy Wilson. "Sosibius." In *Oxford Classical Dictionary*, 3d edn. Oxford, 1996.

Beauvoir, Simone de. *The Second Sex*. New York, 1952. Originally published as *Le deuxième sexe*. Paris, 1949.

Beckerman, S., R. Lizarralde, et. al. "The Bari Partible Paternity Project: Preliminary Results." *Current Anthropology* 39.1 (1998), 164–67.

Bengtson, H. *Die Strategie in der hellenistischen Zeit*. 3 vols. Münchener Beiträge zur Papyrusforschung und antike Rechtgeschichte 32. Munich, 1964–67.

Birge, Darice. "Women and the Greek Past in Pausanias' Descriptive Geography." Paper delivered at the Annual Meeting of the American Philological Association, December 29, 1998. *Abstract published in American Philological Association 130th Annual Meeting: Abstracts*, 131.

Blackman, David. "Archaeology in Greece, 1999–2000: Lakonia." *AR* 46 (2000), 38–43.

Boedeker, Deborah D. *Aphrodite's Entrance into Greek Epic*. Leiden, 1974.

Boer, W. den. *Laconian Studies*. Amsterdam, 1954.

Bogino, Liana. "Note sul matrimonio a Sparta." *Sileno* 17 (1991), 221–33.

Bölte, F. "Platanistas." *RE* 20.2, cols. 2333–34. Stuttgart, 1950.

Bommelaer, J. F., *Lysandre de Sparte: Histoire et traditions*. Athens, 1981.

Bonfante, Larissa. "Nudity as a Costume in Classical Art." *AJA* 93 (1989), 558–68.

Boring, T. *Literacy in Ancient Sparta*. Leiden, 1979.

Bosanquet, R. C. "The Cult of Orthia as Illustrated by the Finds." *ABSA* 12 (1905–6), 331–43.

Bowie, E. L. "Greek Poetry in the Antonine Age." In *Antonine Literature*, ed. D. A. Russell, 53–90. Oxford, 1990.

Bradford, Alfred S. *A Prosopography of Lacedaemonians from the Death of Alexander the Great, 323 B.C., to the Sack of Sparta by Alaric, A.D. 296*. Munich, 1977.

———. "Gynaikokratoumenoi: Did Spartan Women Rule Spartan Men?" *AncW* 14 (1986), 13–18.

Brelich, A. *Paides e Parthenoi*. Vol. 1. Rome, 1969.

Bremen, Riet van. *The Limits of Participation: Women and Civic Life in the Hellenistic and Roman Periods*. Amsterdam, 1996.

Bremmer, Jan. "An Enigmatic Indo-European Rite: Paederasty." *Arethusa* 13 (1980), 279–98.

———. "Greek Maenadism Reconsidered." *ZPE* 55 (1984), 267–86.

———. "Plutarch and the Naming of Greek Women." *AJPh* 102 (1981), 425–26.

Brennan, T. C. "The Poets Julia Balbilla and Damo at the Colossus of Memnon." *CW* 91 (1998), 215–34.

Briscoe, John. *A Commentary on Livy, Books XXXIV–XXVII*. Oxford, 1991.

Brosius, Maria. *Women in Ancient Persia, 559–331 B.C.* Oxford, 1996.

Burkert, W. *Structure and History in Greek Mythology and Ritual*. Sather Classical Lectrues, 47. Berkeley, 1979.

Burstein, Stanley M. "Cleitarchus in Jerusalem." In *The Eye Expanded*, ed. F. B. Titchener and R. F. Moorton, Jr., 105–12. Berkeley, 1999.

Calame, Claude. *Alcman: Fragmenta edidit, veterum testimonia collegit*. Rome, 1983.

———. *Les chœurs de jeunes filles en Grèce archaïque*. Vol. 1, *Morphologie, fonction religieuse et sociale*. Vol. 2, *Alcman*. Rome, 1977.

———. "Iniziazioni femminili spartane: Stupro, danza, ratto, metamorfosi e morte iniziatica." In *Le donne in Grecia*, ed. G. Arrigoni, 33–54. Bari, 1985.

Campbell, D. A. *Greek Lyric*. Vol. 2. Cambridge, Mass., 1988.

Carney, Elizabeth. "'What's in a Name?' The Emergence of a Title for Royal Women in the Hellenistic Period." In *Women's History and Ancient History*, ed. Sarah. B. Pomeroy, 154–72. Chapel Hill, N.C., 1991.

Carter, Jane B. Review of *Laconian Iconography of the Sixth Century B.C.*, by Maria Pipili. *AJA* 93 (1989), 473–76.

———. "Masks and Poetry in Early Sparta." In *Early Greek Cult Practice: Proceedings of the Fifth International Symposium at the Swedish Institute at Athens, 26–29 June, 1986*, ed. R. Hägg, N. Marinatos, and G.C. Nordquist, 89–98. Stockholm, 1988.

———. "The Masks of Ortheia." *AJA* 91 (1987), 355–83.

Cartledge, P. A. *Agesilaos and the Crisis of Sparta*. London, 1987.

———. "Did Spartan Citizens Ever Practice a Manual *Techne*?" *LCM* 1 (1976), 115–19.

———. "Early Lacedaimon: The Making of a Conquest-State." In *Philolakon: Lakonian Studies in Honour of Hector Catling*, ed. J. M. Sanders, 49–55. London, 1992.

———. "Literacy in the Spartan Oligarchy." *JHS* 98 (1978), 25–37.

————. "The Politics of Spartan Pederasty." *PCPS* n.s. 27 (1981), 17–36.

————. "The Socratics' Sparta and Rousseau's." In *Sparta: New Perspectives*, ed. S. Hodkinson and A. Powell, 311–37. London, 1999.

————. *Sparta and Lakonia: A Regional History, 1300–362 B.C.* London, 1979.

————. "Spartan Wives: Liberation or Licence?" *CQ* 31 (1981), 84–105.

Cartledge, P. A., and A. J. S. Spawforth. *Hellenistic and Roman Sparta: A Tale of Two Cities.* London, 1989.

Catling, H. W. "Archaeology in Greece, 1975–76." *AR* 22 (1975–76), 3–33.

————. "Excavations at the Menelaion, Sparta, 1973–76." *AR* 23 (1976–77), 24–42.

————. "Excavations at the Menelaion, 1985." *Lak. Spoud.* 8 (1986), 205–16.

————. "A Sanctuary of Zeus Messapeus: Excavations at Aphyssou, Tsakona, 1989." *ABSA* 85 (1990), 15–35.

————. "Tsakona." In "Archaeology in Greece, 1999–2000: Lakonia," by David Blackman. *AR* 46 (2000), 38–43.

————. "The Work of the British School at Athens at Sparta and in Laconia." In *Sparta in Laconia: Proceedings of the 19th British Museum Classical Colloquium*, ed. W. G. Cavanagh and S. E. C. Walker. British School at Athens Studies, vol. 4, 19–27. London, 1998.

Catling, R. W. V. "The Archaic and Classical Pottery." In *Continuity and Change in a Greek Rural Landscape: The Laconia Survey*, ed. W. G. Cavanagh, J. Crouwel, R. W. V. Catling, and G. Shipley. Vol. 2, *Archaeological Data. ABSA* suppl. vol. 27, 33–89. London, 1996.

Cavanagh, W. G., and R. R. Laxton. "Lead Figurines from the Menelaion and Seriation." *ABSA* 79 (1984), 23–36.

Cavanagh, W. G., J. Crouwel, R. W. V. Catling, and G. Shipley. *Continuity and Change in a Greek Rural Landscape: The Laconia Survey.* Vol. 2, *Archaeological Data. ABSA* suppl. vol. 27. London, 1996.

Cawkwell, G. L. "The Decline of Sparta." *CQ* 33 (1983), 385–400.

Chrimes, K. *Ancient Sparta.* Manchester, 1949.

Christien, J. "La loi d'Épitadeus: Un aspect de l'histoire économique et sociale à Sparte." *RD* 52 (1974), 197–221.

Clader, Linda Lee. *Helen: The Evolution from Divine to Heroic in Greek Epic Tradition.* Leiden, 1976.

Clark, Christina A. "The Gendering of the Body in Alcman's Partheneion 1: Narrative, Sex, and Social Order in Archaic Sparta." *Helios* 23 (1996), 143–72.

Clement, Paul A. "The Recovery of Helen." *Hesperia* 27 (1958), 47–73.

Cohen, Beth. "Divesting the Female Breast of Clothes in Classical Sculpture." In *Naked Truths: Women, Sexuality and Gender in Classical Art and Archaeology*, ed. Ann Olga Koloski-Ostrow and Claire L. Lyons, 66–92. London, 1997.

Cole, Susan Guettel. "*Gynaiki ou Themis:* Gender Difference in the Greek *Leges Sacrae.*" *Helios* 19 (1992), 104–22.

————. "Landscapes of Artemis." *CW* 93 (2000), 471–81.

Constantinidou, S. "Spartan Cult Dances." *Phoenix* 52 (1998), 15–30.

Cook, J. M. "Laconia: Kalyvia Sokhas." *ABSA* 45 (1950), 261–81.

Cook, R. M. "Spartan History and Archaeology." *CQ* 12 (1962), 156–58.

Darwin, Charles. *The Descent of Man.* London, 1871. Repr. Princeton, 1974.

David, Ephraim. "Aristotle and Sparta." *Anc. Soc.* 13/14 (1982–83), 67–103.

————. "Dress in Spartan Society." *AncW* 19 (1989), 3–13.

———. "The Influx of Money into Sparta at the End of the Fifth Century B.C." *SCI* 5 (1979–80), 30–45.

———. "Sparta's Social Hair." *Eranos* 90 (1992), 11–21.

Davies, M. Review of *Alcman: Fragmenta,* by Claude Calame. *Gnomon,* 58 (1986), 385–89.

———. *Poetarum Melicorum Graecorum Fragmenta,* I (Oxford, 1991).

Davies, Martin. *The French School.* London, 1957.

Davis, Ellen N. "Youth and Age in the Thera Frescoes." *AJA* 90 (1986), 399–406.

Dawkins, R. M. "Artemis Orthia: Some Additions and a Correction." *JHS* 50 (1930), 298–99 and pl. XI.1.

———. "Excavations at Sparta, 1909." *ABSA* 15 (1909), 1–22

———. "Excavations at Sparta, 1910. Artemis Orthia: The History of the Sanctuary." *ABSA* 16 (1910), 18–53.

Dawkins, R. M., J. P. Droop, W. S. George, A. M. Woodward, G. Dickens, and A. J. B. Wace. *The Sanctuary of Artemis Orthia at Sparta.* Society for the Promotion of Hellenic Studies Supplementary Papers, no. 5. London, 1929.

Delcourt, M. *Stérilités mystérieuses et naissances maléfiques dans l'antiquité classique.* Liège, 1938.

Dettenhofer, Maria H. "Die Frauen von Sparta." *Klio* 75 (1993), 61–75.

Devereux, G. "Greek Pseudo-Homosexuality and the 'Greek Miracle.'" *SO* 42 (1968), 69–92.

Dewald, Carolyn. "Women and Culture in Herodotus' Histories." in *Reflections of Women in Antiquity,* ed. Helene Peet Foley, 91–125. New York, 1981.

Dickens, G. "Terracotta masks." In *The Sanctuary of Artemis Orthia at Sparta,* by R. M. Dawkins et al., 163–86. Society for the Promotion of Hellenic Studies Supplementary Papers, no. 5. London, 1929.

Dillon, Matthew P. J. "Did *Parthenoi* Attend the Olympic Games? Girls and Women Competing, Spectating, and Carrying Out Cult Roles at Greek Religious Festivals." *Hermes* 128 (2000), 457–80.

Dixon, Suzanne. *The Roman Mother.* Norman, Okla., 1988.

Dörig, José. "Eleuthia." In *Sculpture from Arcadia and Laconia,* ed. Olga Palagia and William Coulson, 145–51. Oxford, 1993.

Dover, K. J. *Greek Homosexuality.* London, 1978.

Drape, Joe. "Krone Adds Another First to Her Accomplishments." *New York Times,* August 8, 2000, sec. D, pp. 1, 5.

Droop, J. P. "The Bronzes." In *The Sanctuary of Artemis Orthia at Sparta,* by R. M. Dawkins et al., 196–202. Society for the Promotion of Hellenic Studies Supplementary Papers, no. 5. London, 1929.

Ducat, Jean. "La femme de Sparte et la cité." *Ktèma* 23 (1998), 385–406.

———. *Les hilotes. BCH* suppl. 20. Athens, 1990.

———. "Perspectives on Spartan Education in the Classical Period." in *Sparta: New Perspectives,* ed. S. Hodkinson and A. Powell, 43–66. London, 1999.

Edelstein, E. J., and L. Edelstein. *Asclepius: A Collection and Interpretation of the Testimonies.* Vol. 1. Baltimore, Md., 1945.

Edmonson, C. N. "A Graffito from Amyklai." *Hesperia* 28 (1959), 162–64.

Egger, Émile. "Un fragment inédit du poëte Alcman." In Émile Egger, *Memoires d'histoire ancienne et de philologie.* Paris, 1863.

Ellis, R. P. *Ovidii Nasonis Ibis: ex novis codicibus edidit, scholia vetera commentarium cum prolegomenis appendice.* Oxford, 1881.

Engels, F. *The Origin of the Family, Private Property, and the State.* 1884. With introduction by Eleanor Burke Leacock. New York, 1972.

Evans-Grubbs, Judith. "Abduction Marriage in Antiquity: A Law of Constantine (*CTh* IX.24.1) and Its Social Context." *JRS* 79 (1989), 59–83.

Fantham, E., Helene Peet Foley, Natalie Boymel Kampen, Sarah B. Pomeroy, and H. Alan Shapiro. *Women in the Classical World.* New York, 1994.

Farrell, J. "Excavations at Sparta, 1908: Archaic Terracottas from the Sanctuary of Orthia." *ABSA* 14 (1908), 48–73.

Farnell, L. R. *Cults of the Greek States.* 5 vols. Oxford, 1896–1909.

Faust, Page Gilpin. *Mothers of Invention.* Chapel Hill, N.C., 1996.

Figueira, Thomas J. "The Evolution of the Messenian Identity." In *Sparta: New Perspectives,* ed. S. Hodkinson and A. Powell, 221–44. London, 1999.

———. "Herodotus on the Early Hostilities Between Aegina and Athens." *AJP* 106 (1985), 49–74; repr. in Thomas J. Figueira, *Excursions in Epichoric History: Aeginetan Essays,* 35–60. Lanham, Md., 1999.

———. "Mess Contributions and Subsistence at Sparta." *TAPA* 114 (1984), 87–109.

———. "Population Patterns in Late Archaic and Classical Sparta." *TAPA* 116 (1968), 165–213.

Finley, M. I. "Sparta." In M. I. Finley, *The Use and Abuse of History,* 161–77. London, 1975. Originally published in *Problèmes de la guerre en Grèce ancienne,* ed. J.-P. Vernant, 143–60. Paris, 1968.

Fisher, N. R. E. "Drink, Hybris and the Promotion of Harmony in Sparta." In *Classical Sparta: Techniques behind Her Success,* ed. A. Powell, 26–50. Norman, Okla., 1989.

Flacelière, R. *Les aitoliens à Delphes.* Paris, 1937.

Flower, Michael. "The Invention of Tradition in Classical and Hellenistic Sparta." Paper delivered at the Celtic Conference in Classics, National University of Ireland, Maynooth, September 7, 2000.

Foley, Helene P. *Female Acts in Greek Tragedy.* Princeton, 2001.

Förtsch, R. "Spartan Art: Its Many Different Deaths." In *Sparta in Laconia: Proceedings of the 19th British Museum Classical Colloquium,* ed. W. G. Cavanagh and S. E. C. Walker, 48–54. British School at Athens Studies, vol. 4. London, 1998.

Foxhall, Lin. "Foreign Powers: Plutarch and Discourses of Domination in Roman Greece." In *Plutarch's Advice to the Bride and Groom and A Consolation to His Wife,* ed. Sarah B. Pomeroy, 138–50. New York, 1999.

———. "The Women of Artemis Orthia, Sparta." Paper delivered at the Annual Meeting of the American Philological Association, December 28, 1998. Abstract published in *American Philological Association 130th Annual Meeting: Abstracts,* 83.

Foxhall, Lin, and H. A. Forbes. "*Sitometreia:* The Role of Grain as a Staple Food in Classical Antiquity." *Chiron* 12 (1982), 41–90.

Frazer, J. G. *Pausanias's Description of Greece.* 6 vols. 2d edn. London, 1913.

Fraser, Peter M., and Elaine Matthews, eds. *A Lexicon of Greek Personal Names.* Vol. 3A. *The Peloponnese, Western Greece, and Magna Graecia.* Oxford, 1997.

Freeman, Kathleen. *The Pre-Socratic Philosophers.* Oxford, 1946.

French, Valerie. "The Spartan Family and the Spartan Decline." In *Polis and Polemos: Essays on Politics, War, and History in Ancient Greece in Honor of Donald Kagan,* ed. C. D. Hamilton and P. Krentz, 241–74. Cleremont, Calif., 1997.

Gardner, Jane. *Women in Roman Law and Society.* London, 1986.

Gera, Deborah. *Warrior Women: The Anonymous Tractatus de Mulieribus.* Leiden, 1997.

Ghali-Kahil, Lilly B. *Les enlèvements et le retour d'Hélène dans les textes et les documents figurés*. Paris, 1955.

————. "Hélène." In *Lexicon Iconographicum Mythologiae Classicae*. Vol. 4.1, pp. 498–563, with an addendum on 951. Zurich, 1988. Plates in vol. 4.2, pp. 291–358. Zurich, 1988.

Glotz, G. "L'exposition des enfants." *Études sociales et juridiqies sur l' antiquité grecque*, 187–227. Paris, 1906.

Goessler, L. "Plutarchs Gedanken über die Ehe." Diss. Zurich, 1962. Trans. by David and Hazel Harvey as "Advice to the Bride and Groom: Plutarch Gives a Detailed Account of His Views on Marriage," in *Plutarch's Advice to the Bride and Groom and A Consolation to His Wife*, ed. Sarah B. Pomeroy, 97–115. New York, 1999.

Golden, Mark. "Demography and the Exposure of Girls at Athens." *Phoenix* 35 (1981), 316–31.

Gow, A. S. F. *Theocritus*, 2 vols. Cambridge, 1952.

Gow, A. S. F., and D. L. Page. *The Greek Anthology: Hellenistic Epigrams*. 2 vols. Cambridge, 1965.

Graf, Fritz. "Women, War, and Warlike Divinities." *ZPE* 55 (1984), 245–59.

Guarducci, Margherita. *Epigrafia greca*. Vol. 3. Rome, 1967–68.

Hall, Edith. *Inventing the Barbarian*. Oxford, 1989.

Hall, Jonathan. *Ethnic Identity in Greek Antiquity*. Cambridge, 1997.

Hallock, R. T. *The Persepolis Fortification Tablets*. Chicago, 1969.

Hanson, Ann Ellis. "The Eight-Months' Child and the Etiquette of Birth." *Bulletin of the History of Medicine* 61 (1987), 589–602.

Harris, William V. *Ancient Literacy*. Cambridge, 1989.

Harvey, F. D. "Laconica: Aristophanes and the Spartans" In *The Shadow of Sparta*, ed. A. Powell and S. Hodkinson, 35–58. London, 1994.

————. "Literacy in the Athenian Democracy." *REG* 79 (1966), 585–635.

————. "Oxyrhynchus Papyrus 2390 and Early Spartan History." *JHS* 87 (1967), 62–73.

Hedreen, Guy. "Image, Text, and Story in the Recovery of Helen." *CA* 15 (1996), 152–84 and figs. 1–12.

Henderson, Jeffrey, ed. *Aristophanes' Lysistrata*. With introduction and commentary. Oxford, 1987.

Herfort-Koch, Marlene. *Archaïsche Bronzeplastik lakoniens*. *Boreas* suppl. 4. Münster, 1986.

Herington, J. *Poetry and Drama: Early Tragedy and the Greek Poetic Tradition*. Berkeley, 1985.

Hodkinson, S. "'Blind Ploutos?' Contemporary Images of the Role of Wealth in Classical Sparta." In *The Shadow of Sparta*, ed. A. Powell and S. Hodkinson, 183–222. London, 1994.

————. "Bronze Dedications at Spartan Sanctuaries." In *Sparta in Laconia: Proceedings of the 19th British Museum Classical Colloquium*, ed. W. G. Cavanagh and S. E. C. Walker. British School at Athens Studies, vol. 4, 55–63. London, 1998.

————. "Epitadeus." In *Oxford Classical Dictionary*, 3d edn. Oxford, 1996.

————. "Inheritance, Marriage and Demography: Perspectives upon the Success and Decline of Classical Sparta." In *Classical Sparta: Techniques Behind Her Success*, ed. A. Powell, 79–121. Norman, Okla., 1989.

————. *Property and Wealth in Classical Sparta*. London, 2000.

————. "Warfare, Wealth, and the Crisis of Spartiate Society." In *War and Society in the Greek World*, ed. J. Rich and G. Shipley, 146–76. London, 1993.

Höfer, O. "Orthia and Orthosia." In *Ausführlicher Lexikon der greichischen und römischen Mythologie*. 6 vols. Leipzig, 1884–1937; suppl. 4 vols., 1893–1921. Vol. 3.1, 1210–13.

Hondius, J., and A. Woodward. "Laconia, Inscriptions: Votive Inscriptions from Sparta." *ABSA* 24 (1919), 88–117.

Hrdy, Sarah Blaffer. *Mother Nature*. New York, 1999.

———. "The Optimal Number of Fathers: Evolution, Demography, and History in the Shaping of Female Mate Preferences." *Annals of the New York Academy of Sciences* 907 (2000), 75–96.

———. "Raising Darwin's Consciousness." *Human Nature* 8.1 (1997), 1–49.

Hume, D. "Of the Populousness of Ancient Nations" [1752]. In David Hume, *Essays, Moral, Political and Literary*, 381–451. Oxford, 1963.

Jenkins, I. "Dressed to Kill." *Omnibus* 5 (1983), 29–32.

Karabélias, Evangelos. "L'épiclerat à Sparte." *Studi in onore di Arnaldo Biscardi*. Vol. 2, 469–80. Milan, 1982.

Karouzou, S. "He Helene tes Spartes." *AE* 1985 (1987), 33–44.

Kelly, D. H. "Thucydides and Herodotus on the Pitanate Lochos." *GRBS* 22 (1981), 31–38.

Kennell, Nigel M. "The Elite Women of Sparta." Paper delivered at the Annual Meeting of the American Philological Association, December 28, 1998. Abstract published in *American Philological Association 130th Annual Meeting: Abstracts*, 84.

———. *The Gymnasium of Virtue: Education and Culture in Ancient Sparta*. Chapel Hill, N.C., 1995.

———. "Where Was Sparta's Prytaneion?" *AJA* 91 (1987), 421–22.

Keuls, Eva. *The Reign of the Phallus*. Berkeley, 1985.

Kilian, I. "Weihumgen an Eleithyia und Artemis Orthia." *ZPE* 31 (1978), 219–22.

Kleiner, Diana. *The Monument of Philopappos in Athens*. Rome, 1983.

Kron, Uta. "Kultmahle im Heraeon von Samos archaischer Zeit." In *Early Greek Cult Practice: Proceedings of the Fifth International Symposium at the Swedish Institute at Athens, 26–29 June, 1986*, ed. R. Hägg, N. Marinatos, and G. C. Nordquist, 136–48. Stockholm, 1988.

———. "Sickles in Greek Sanctuaries: Votives and Cultic Instruments." In *Ancient Greek Cult Practice from the Archaeological Evidence: Proceedings of the Fourth International Seminar on Ancient Greek Cult, Organized by the Swedish Institute at Athens, 22–24 October 1993*, ed. R. Hägg, 187–215. Stockholm, 1998.

Kunstler, Barton Lee. "Family dynamics and Female Power in Ancient Sparta." In *Rescuing Creusa*, ed. M. Skinner. Helios 13 (1986), 31–48.

———. "Women and the Development of the Spartan Polis: A Study of Sex Roles in Classical Antiquity." Ph.D. diss., Boston University, 1983.

Lacey, P. *The Family in Classical Greece*. Ithaca, N.Y., 1968.

Lane, E. A. "Lakonian Vase-Painting." *ABSA* 34 (1933–34), 99–189.

Larson, Deborah. *Greek Heroine Cults*. Madison, Wis., 1995.

Lazzarini, M. L. *Le formule delle dediche votive nella Grecia arcaica*. Atti dell' Accademia Nazionale dei Lincei. Memorie. Classe di Scienze Mor., Stor., e Filol., ser. 8.19. Rome, 1976.

Leitao, David. "The Exclusion of Agamoi from the Gymnopaidiai and the Politics of Viewing in Sparta." Paper delivered at the Annual Meeting of the American Philological Association, December 29, 1997. Abstract published in *American Philological Association 129th Annual Meeting: Abstracts*, 171.

Le Roy, C. "Lakonika." *BCH* 85 (1961), 228–32.

Lippold, A. "Sparta (die Ethnika)." *RE* 3A, cols. 1280–92. Stuttgart, 1929.

Lonsdale, Steven H. *Ritual Play in Greek Religion.* Baltimore, Md., 1993.

Luraghi, Nino. "Helotic Slavery Reconsidered." Paper delivered at the Celtic Conference in Classics, National University of Ireland, Maynooth, September 7, 2000.

MacDowell, Douglas M., ed. *Aristophanes: Wasps.* With introduction and commentary. Oxford, 1971.

Malkin, Irad. *Myth and Territory in the Spartan Mediterranean.* Cambridge, 1994.

Manfredini, Mario, and Luigi Piccirilli. *Plutarco: Le vite di Licurgo e di Numa.* 2d edn. Milan, 1990.

Mansfield, John Magruder. "The Robe of Athena and the Panathenaic Peplos." Ph.D. diss., University of California, Berkeley, 1985.

Marangou, Evangelia-Lila. *Lakonische Elfenbein- und Beinschnitzereien.* Tübingen, 1969.

Marasco, G. *Commento alle biografie Plutarchee di Agide e di Cleomene.* 2 vols. Rome, 1981.

Marchant, E. C. *Xenophon.* Vol. 7, *Scripta Minora.* Loeb Classical Library. Cambridge, Mass., 1925.

May, Elaine Tyler. *Barren in the Promised Land: Childless Americans and the Pursuit of Happiness.* New York, 1995.

McClure, Laura. *Spoken Like a Woman.* Princeton, 1999.

McInnis, R. M. "Childbearing and Land Availability: Some Evidence from Individual Household Data." In *Population Patterns in the Past,* ed. R. D. Lee, 201–27. New York, 1977.

Meillier, C. "Une coutume hiérogamique à Sparte?" *REG* 97 (1984), 381–402.

Ménage, Gilles. *Historia mulierum philosophorum.* 1690–92. Trans. B. H. Zedler as *The History of Women Philosophers.* Lanham, Md., 1984.

Millender, Ellen Greenstein. "Athenian Ideology and the Empowered Spartan Female." In *Sparta: New Perspectives,* ed. S. Hodkinson and A. Powell, 355–91. London, 1999.

———. "Exercise, Nudity and Spartan Female Sexual License: A Reconsideration." Paper delivered at the Annual Meeting of the American Philological Association, December 28, 1998. Abstract published in *American Philological Association 130th Annual Meeting: Abstracts,* 82.

Miller, Margaret C. "Reexamining Transvestism in Archaic and Classical Athens." *AJA* 103 (1999), 223–53.

Modrzejewski, J. "Régime foncier et statut social dans l' Égypte ptolémaïque." In *Terre et paysans dépendants dans les sociétés antiques: Colloque international, Besançon, 2–3 mai 1974,* 163–96. Paris, 1979.

Mossé, Claude. "Women in the Spartan Revolutions." In *Women's History and Ancient History,* ed. Sarah. B. Pomeroy, 138–53. Chapel Hill, N.C., 1991.

Murray, Julia Sargent. *The Gleaner.* 1798. Repr. Schenectady, N.Y., 1992.

Musti, D., and M. Torelli. *Pausania: Guida della Grecia.* Vol. 3, *La Laconia.* Milan, 1997.

Nagy, Blaise. "The Naming of Athenian Girls: A Case in Point." *CJ* 74 (1979), 60–64.

Nagy, G. *Pindar's Homer: The Lyric Possession of an Epic Past.* Baltimore, Md., 1990.

Napolitano, Maria Luisa. "Le donne spartane e la guerra: Problemi di tradizione." *AION (archeol.)* 9 (Naples, 1987), 127–44.

———. "Donne spartane e teknopoiia." *AION (archeol.)* 7 (1985), 19–50.

Nilsson, M. P. *Griechische Feste von religiöser Bedeutung.* Leipzig, 1906.

Nisbet, R. G. M., and M. Hubbard. *A Commentary on Horace, Odes, Book II.* Oxford, 1978, pbk. 1991.

North, Helen. *Sophrosyne: Self-Knowledge and Self-Restraint in Greek Literature.* Ithaca, N.Y., 1966.

Oakley, John H., and Rebecca H. Sinos. *The Wedding in Ancient Athens.* Madison, Wis., 1993.

Ogden, Daniel. "Crooked Speech: The Genesis of the Spartan Rhetra." *JHS* 14 (1994), 85–102.

————. *Greek Bastardy.* Oxford, 1996.

Ollier, F. *Le mirage spartiate.* Vol. 1, *Étude sur l'idéalisation de Sparte dans l'antiquité grecque de l'origine jusqu'aux cyniques.* Vol. 2, *Étude sur l'idéalisation de Sparte dans l'antiquité grecque du début de l'école cynique jusqu'à la fin de la cité.* Paris, 1933–43; repr. 1973.

————. *Xénophon: La république des Lacédémoniens.* Lyons, 1934.

O'Neil, Edward N., ed. *Teles, the Cynic Teacher.* Missoula, Mont., 1977.

Overbeek, M. "The Small Finds." In *Continuity and Change in a Greek Rural Landscape: The Laconia Survey,* by W. G. Cavanagh, J. Crouwel, R. W. V. Catling, and G. Shipley. Vol. 2, *Archaeological Data.* ABSA suppl. vol. 27, 183–98. London, 1996.

Page, Denys L. *Alcman: The Partheneion.* Oxford, 1951.

Paludetti, Giovanni. *Giovanni de Min.* Udine, 1959.

Paradiso, Annalisa. "Gorgo, la Spartana." In *Grecia al femminile,* ed. Nicole Loraux, 107–22. Bari, 1993.

Parke, H. W., and D. E. W. Wormell. *The Delphic Oracle.* 2 vols. 2d edn. Oxford, 1956.

Palmer, Robert. "Roman Shrines of Female Chastity from the Caste Struggle to the Papacy of Innocent I." *RSA* 4 (1974), 113–59.

Parker, Robert. "Demeter, Dionysus, and the Spartan Pantheon." In *Early Greek Cult Practice: Proceedings of the Fifth International Symposium at the Swedish Institute at Athens, 26–29 June, 1986,* ed. R. Hägg, N. Marinatos, and G. C. Nordquist, 99–103. Stockholm, 1988.

————. "Spartan Religion." In *Classical Sparta: Techniques Behind Her Success,* ed. A. Powell, 142–72. Norman, Okla., 1989.

Patterson, Cynthia B. *The Family in Greek History.* Cambridge, Mass., 1998.

————. "Plutarch's Advice to the Bride and Groom: Traditional Wisdom through a Philosophic Lens." in *Plutarch's Advice to the Bride and Groom and A Consolation to His Wife,* ed. Sarah B. Pomeroy, 128–37. New York, 1999.

Perentidis, S. "Réflexions sur la polyandrie à Sparte dans l'Antiquité." *RHD* 75 (1997), 7–31.

Pettersson, Michael. *Cults of Apollo at Sparta: The Hyakinthia, the Gymnopaidiai, and the Karneia.* Stockholm, 1992.

Piccirilli, Luigi. "Chronologia relativa e fonti delle *Vitae Lycurgi et Numae* di Plutarco." In *Philias Charin: Miscellanea di studi classici in onore di Eugenio Manni,* ed. M. J. Fontana, M. T. Piraino and F. P. Rizzo, 1751–64. 6 vols. Rome, 1980.

Pickard-Cambridge, A. W. *Dithyramb, Tragedy, and Comedy.* 2d edn. revised by T. B. L. Webster. Oxford, 1927.

Pingiatoglou, Semeli. *Eileithyia.* Würtzburg, 1981.

Piper, Linda J. "Spartan Helots in the Hellenistic Age." *Anc. Soc.* 15–17 (1984–86), 75–88.

————. *Spartan Twilight.* New Rochelle, N.Y., 1986.

Pipili, Maria. *Laconian Iconography of the Sixth Century B.C.* Oxford University Committee for Archaeology Monograph, no. 12. Oxford, 1987.

————. "A Laconian Ivory Reconsidered." In *Philolakon: Lakonian Studies in Honour of Hector Catling,* ed. Jan Motyka Sanders, 179–84. London, 1992.

————. "Archaic Laconian Vase Painting." In *Sparta in Laconia: Proceedings of the 19th British Museum Classical Colloquium*, ed. W. G. Cavanagh and S. E. C. Walker. British School at Athens Studies, vol. 4, 82–96. London, 1998.

Pirenne-Delforge, Vinciane, and Andre Motte. "Aphrodite." In *Oxford Classical Dictionary*, 3d edn. Oxford, 1996.

Pohlenz, M. *Ciceronis tusculanorum disputationum: Libri V.* Stuttgart, 1957.

Pomeroy, Sarah B. *Families in Classical and Hellenistic Greece.* Oxford, 1997.

————. *Goddesses, Whores, Wives, and Slaves: Women in Classical Antiquity.* New York, 1975. Repr. with a new preface, New York, 1995.

————. "Infanticide in Hellenistic Greece." In *Images of Women in Antiquity*, ed. A. Cameron and A. Kuhrt, 207–22. London, 1983.

————. "Reflections on Plutarch's *Advice to the Bride and Groom*: Something Old, Something New, Something Borrowed." In *Plutarch's Advice to the Bride and Groom and A Consolation to His Wife*, ed. Sarah B. Pomeroy, 33–42. New York, 1999.

————. "The Spartan Family." Paper delivered at the University of Cambridge, October 13, 1998.

————. "Spartan Wives and Their Strategies." Paper delivered at the Celtic Conference in Classics, National University of Ireland, Maynooth, September 7, 2000.

————. "Spartan Womanpower." Paper delivered at the Annual Meeting of the American Philological Association, December 28, 1998. Abstract published in *American Philological Association 130th Annual Meeting: Abstracts*, 81.

————. "*Technikai kai Mousikai*: The Education of Women in the Fourth Century and in the Hellenistic Period." *AJAH* 2 (1977), 51–68.

————. *Women in Hellenistic Egypt: From Alexander to Cleopatra.* New York, 1984. Pbk. with a new foreword and addenda, Detroit, 1990.

————. *Xenophon, Oeconomicus: A Social and Historical Commentary.* Oxford, 1994.

————. "Xenophon's Spartan Women." Paper delivered at The World of Xenophon conference, University of Liverpool, July 8, 1999.

————, ed. *Plutarch's Advice to the Bride and Groom and A Consolation to His Wife.* New York, 1999.

————, ed. *Women's History and Ancient History.* Chapel Hill, N.C., 1991.

Pomeroy, Sarah B., Stanley M. Burstein, Walter Donlan, and Jennifer Tolbert Roberts. *Ancient Greece.* New York, 1998.

Pool, Phoebe. "The History Pictures of Edgar Degas and Their Background." *Apollo* 80 (1964), 306–11.

Poralla, Paul. *A Prosopography of Lacedaemonians from the Earliest Times to the Death of Alexander the Great (X–323 B.C.).* 2d edn. with an introduction, addenda, and corrigenda by A. S. Bradford. Chicago, 1985.

Powell, A. "Spartan Women Assertive in Politics? Plutarch's Lives of Agis and Kleomenes." In *Sparta: New Perspectives*, ed. S. Hodkinson and A. Powell, 393–419. London, 1999.

Préaux, C. *L'économie royale des Lagides.* Brussels, 1939.

Preller, L. *Polemonis Periegetae Fragmenta.* Leipzig, 1838.

Pritchett, W. K. *The Greek State at War.* 4 vols. Berkeley, 1971–85.

Raftopoulou, Stella. "New Finds from Sparta." In *Sparta in Laconia: Proceedings of the 19th British Museum Classical Colloquium*, ed. W. G. Cavanagh and S. E. C. Walker. British School at Athens Studies, vol. 4, 125–40. London, 1998.

Rawson, Elizabeth. *The Spartan Tradition in European Thought.* Oxford, 1969.

Redfield, James. "The Women of Sparta." *CJ* 73 (1977–78), 146–61.

Richer, N. "Aspects des funerailles à Sparte." *Cahiers du Centre G. Glotz* 5 (1994), 51–96.

———. *Les éphores: Études sur l'histoire et sur l'image de Sparte (VIIIe–IIIe siècle avant Jésus-Christ)*. Paris, 1998.

Richter, G. "An Archaic Greek Mirror." *AJA* 42 (1938), 337–44.

Robert, L. "Les femmes théores à Éphèse." *CRAI* (1974), 176–81.

———. "Laodicée du Lycos: Les inscriptions." In *Laodicée du Lycos: Le Nymphée, campagnes 1961–1963*, ed. J. des Gagniers et al., 247–387. Paris, 1969.

Rolley, Claude. "Le problème de l'art laconien." *Ktèma* 2 (1977), 125–40.

Romano, David G. "The Ancient Stadium: Athletics and Arete." *AncW* 7 (1983), 9–15.

Romano, Irene Bald. "Early Greek Cult Images." Ph.D. diss., University of Pennsylvania, 1980.

———. "Early Greek Cult Images and Cult Practices." In *Early Greek Cult Practice: Proceedings of the Fifth International Symposium at the Swedish Institute at Athens, 26–29 June, 1986*, ed. R. Hägg, N. Marinatos, and G. C. Nordquist, 127–34. Stockholm, 1988.

Rose, H. J. "The Cult of Artemis Orthia." In *The Sanctuary of Artemis Orthia at Sparta*, by R. M. Dawkins et al., 399–407. Society for the Promotion of Hellenic Studies Supplementary Papers, no. 5. London, 1929.

Roussel, Pierre. "L'exposition des enfants à Sparte." *REA* 45 (1943), 5–17.

Salus, Carol. "Degas' Young Spartans Exercising." *Art Bulletin* 67 (1985), 501–6.

Saunders, Trevor J. *Aristotle, Politics: Books I and II*. Translation with commentary. Clarendon Aristotle Series. Oxford, 1995.

Scanlon, Thomas. "The Footrace of the Heraia at Olympia." *AncW* 9 (1984), 77–90.

———. "*Virgineum Gymnasium*: Spartan Females and Early Greek Athletics." In *The Archaeology of the Olympics*, ed. W. Raschke, 185–216. Madison, Wis., 1988.

Schaps, David M. *The Economic Rights of Women in Ancient Greece*. Edinburgh, 1979.

———. "The Woman Least Mentioned: Etiquette and Women's Names." *CQ* n.s. 27 (1977), 323–30.

———. "The Women of Greece in Wartime." *CPh* 77 (1982), 193–213.

Schütrumpf, E. "The Rhetra of Epitadeus: A Platonist's Fiction." *GRBS* 28 (1987), 441–57.

Serwint, N. "The Female Athletic Costume at the Heraia and Prenuptial Initiation Rites." *AJA* 97 (1993), 403–22.

Shapiro, H. A. "Cult Warfare: The Dioskouroi Between Sparta and Athens." In *Ancient Greek Hero Cult: Proceedings of the Fifth International Seminar on Ancient Greek Cult, Organized by the Department of Classical Archaeology and Ancient History, Göteborg University, 21–23 April 1995*, ed. R. Hägg, 99–107. Stockholm, 1999.

———. "Modest Athletes and Liberated Women." In *Not the Classical Ideal*, ed. Beth Cohen, 315–337. Leiden, 2000.

Shefton, B. B. "Three Laconian Vase Painters." *ABSA* 49 (1954), 299–310.

Shimron, B. *Late Sparta*. Buffalo, N.Y., 1972.

Shipley, D. R. *A Commentary on Plutarch's "Life Of Agesilaos"*. Oxford, 1997.

Shipley, Graham. "The Extent of Spartan Territory in the Late Classical and Hellenistic Periods." *ABSA* 95 (2000), 367–90.

———. *The Greek World After Alexander, 323–30 B.C.* London, 2000.

Skutsch, Otto. "Helen: Her Name and Nature." *JHS* 107 (1987), 188–93.

Smith, Tyler Jo. "Dances, Drinks, and Dedications: The Archaic *Komos* in Laconia." In *Sparta in Laconia: Proceedings of the 19th British Museum Classical Colloquium*, ed.

W. G. Cavanagh and S. E. C. Walker. British School at Athens Studies, vol. 4, 75–81. London, 1998.

Sourvinou-Inwood, Christiane. "Erotic Pursuits: Images and Meanings." *JHS* 107 (1987), 131–45.

———. *Studies in Girls' Transitions: Aspects of the Arkteia and Age Representation in Attic Iconography.* Athens, 1988.

Spawforth, A. J. S. "Balbilla: The Euryclids, and Memorials for a Greek Magnate." *ABSA* 73 (1978), 249–60.

———. "Families at Roman Sparta and Epidaurus: Some Prosopographical Notes." *ABSA* 80 (1985), 191–258.

———. "Notes on the Third Century A.D. in Spartan Epigraphy." *ABSA* 79 (1984), 263–88.

———. "Spartan Cults Under the Roman Empire." In *Philolakon: Lakonian Studies in Honour of Hector Catling,* ed. Jan Motyka Sanders, 227–38. London, 1992.

Sprague, Rosamond Kent. *The Older Sophists.* Columbia, S.C., 1972.

Ste Croix, G. E. M. de. "Some Observations on the Property Rights of Athenian Women." *CR* n.s. 20 (1970), 273–78.

Stehle, Eva. *Performance in Ancient Greece.* Princeton, 1997.

Stewart, Andrew. *Art, Desire, and the Body in Ancient Greece.* Cambridge, 1997.

———. "Reflections." In *Sexuality in Ancient Art,* ed. Natalie Boymel Kampen, 136–54. Cambridge, 1996.

Stibbe, Conrad M. *Das andere Sparta.* Mainz, 1996.

———. *Lakonische Vasenmaler des sechsten Jahrhunderts v. Chr.* Amsterdam, 1972.

Sturtz, F. W. *Lexicon Xenophonteum.* 4 vols. 1801–4. Repr. Hildesheim, 1964.

Sykes, M. H. "Two Degas Historical Paintings: *Les jeunes spartiates s'exercent à la lutte* and *Les malheurs de la ville d'Orléans.*" Master's thesis, Columbia University, New York, 1964.

Texier, J.-G. *Nabis.* Paris, 1975.

———. "Nabis and the Helots." *DHA* 1 (1979), 189–205.

Thesleff, Holger. *An Introduction to the Pythagorean Writings of the Hellenistic Period.* Åbo, 1961.

Tigerstedt, E. N. *The Legend of Sparta in Classical Antiquity.* 2 vols. Stockholm, 1965–74.

Tod, M. N., and A. J. B. Wace. *A Catalogue of the Sparta Museum.* Oxford, 1906.

Toher, M. "On the *Eidolon* of a Spartan King." *RhM* n.s. 142 (1999), 113–27.

Torelli, M. "Il santuario greco di Gravisca." *PP* 32 (1977), 398–458.

Tracy, Stephen V., and C. Habicht. "New and Old Panathenaic Victor Lists." *Hesperia* 60 (1991), 187–236.

Tregaro, Christien J. "Les bâtards spartiates." In *Mélanges Pierre Lévêque,* ed. M.-M. Mactoux and E. Geny, 33–40. Paris, 1993.

Tuplin, C. "Xenophon, Sparta, and the Cyropaedia." In *The Shadow of Sparta.* ed. A. Powell and S. Hodkinson, 127–81. London, 1994.

Turner, E. G. *Greek Manuscripts of the Ancient World.* Princeton, 1971.

Vérilhac, Anne-Marie, and Claude Vial. *Le mariage grec du VIe siècle av. J.-C. à l'époque d'Auguste. BCH* suppl. 32. Paris, 1998.

Vernant, J.-P. "Entre la honte et la gloire: L'identité du jeune spartiate." *Métis* 2 (1987), 269–99. Repr. in J.-P. Verant, *L'individu, la mort, l'amour: Soi-même et l'autre en Grèce ancienne,* 173–209. Paris, 1989.

Voyatzis, Mary. "Votive Riders Seated Side-Saddle at Early Greek Sanctuaries." *ABSA* 87 (1992), 259–79.

Wace, A. J. B., M. S. Thompson, and J. P. Droop, "The Menelaion." *ABSA* 15 (1908), 108–57.

Walbank, F. W. *A Historical Commentary on Polybius.* 3 vols. Oxford, 1957–79.

Walker, Susan. "Two Spartan Women and the Eleusinion." In *The Greek Renaissance in the Roman Empire*, ed. S. Walker and A. Cameron. *ICS Bull.* suppl. 55 (19889), 130–41.

Wehrli, F. *Die Schule des Aristoteles*, suppl. 1. Basel, 1974.

West, M. L. "Alcmanica." *CQ* 15 (1965), 188–202.

———. *Immortal Helen.* London, 1975.

Whitby, Michael. "Two Shadows: Images of Spartans and Helots." in *The Shadow of Sparta*, ed. A. Powell and S. J. Hodkinson, 87–125. London, 1994.

———. Review of *Sparta: New Perspectives*, ed. S. Hodkinson and A. Powell. *Scholia Reviews* n.s. 9 (2000), 36.

Willetts, R. F. *The Law Code of Gortyn. Kadmos* suppl. 1. Berlin, 1967.

Woodward, A. M. "Excavations at Sparta, 1908: Inscriptions from the Sanctuary of Orthia." *ABSA* 14 (1908), 74–141.

Ziehen, L. "Das spartanische Bevölkerungsproblem." *Hermes* 68 (1933), 218–37.

Ziehen, P. "Sparta." *RE* 18.3, col. 1466. Stuttgart, 1949.

Zuckerman, L. "Spartan Women, Liberated." *New York Times*, Jan. 1, 2000, sec. F, pp. 1, 3.

Zweig, Bella. "The Only Women Who Give Birth to Men: A Gynocentric, Cross-Cultural View of Women in Ancient Sparta." In *Woman's Power, Man's Game: Essays on Classical Antiquity in Honor of Joy K. King*, ed. Mary DeForest, 32–53. Wauconda, Ill., 1993.

INDEX

Lightning Source UK Ltd.
Milton Keynes UK
UKOW01f2243230817
307839UK00001B/63/P